"Trauma is no respecter of persons—not of age, gender, status, or position." Heather Gingrich's new edition of *Restoring the Shattered Self* continues to be on the cutting edge in this emerging field. For counselors new to trauma work, the therapeutic examples and approaches based on Dr. Gingrich's extensive counseling experience provide thoughtful, professionally sound, and spiritually sensitive ways to work with complex trauma. This is a 'must read' for new counselors as well as seasoned counselors who can benefit from her seamless spiritual integration."

Kathie Erwin, associate professor, Regent University

"Save yourself a decade of frustration, pain, and hard work through the wisdom in *Restoring the Shattered Self.* I constantly meet counselors, pastors, prayer ministers, and leaders of healing programs who have no idea of the established and verified models for treating complex trauma. Caring people continue to 're-invent the wheel' and prolong the recovery process for trauma, suffer as counselors, and fall short of the recovery that is possible because they do not know the solid body of knowledge that Dr. Gingrich organizes and teaches in *Restoring the Shattered Self.* Even experienced counselors should read this revised book. Let us be clear about what we know and know what we are doing."

Jim Wilder, neurotheologian and theoretician at Life Model Works (formerly Shepherd's House), author and international speaker on relational Christianity, trauma recovery, and character development in community

"In *Restoring the Shattered Self,* Heather Gingrich distills years of wisdom gleaned from counseling victims through the three phases of establishing safety, processing traumatic memories, and consolidating selves shattered through complex trauma. Her compassionate presence as a counselor and supervisor is conveyed through many poignant illustrations. Now helpfully updated in its second edition, this invaluable textbook needs to be read by every Christian counselor."

Carrie Doehring, associate professor of pastoral care, Iliff School of Theology, Denver

"Heather Davediuk Gingrich, a trauma specialist, has invested her professional lifetime searching out productive pathways for restoration following dense identity upheavals. Extraordinary brokenness finds its way into the ordinary practice of Christian mental health professionals. Thankfully, these pages offer wisdom from a clinical authority to guide us on the frontlines as we lead others back from the abyss."

Stephen P. Greggo, professor of counseling at Trinity Evangelical Divinity School, author of *Assessment for Counseling in Christian Perspective*

"*Restoring the Shattered Self* is an excellent resource for both Christian and non-Christian counselors. It contains many useful techniques, wise cautions, and useful resources and provides a thoughtful overview of the literature. Non-Christian counselors can benefit from the author's clinical wisdom without having to adopt the explicitly Christian treatment techniques included in the book."

Colin A. Ross, founder and president of the Colin A. Ross Institute for Psychological Trauma

"Caring effectively for complex trauma survivors—those whose lives have been deeply shattered—requires a distinct set of resources and skills. Christian counselors need wise, competent guidance to bring their faith to bear on this issue. In *Restoring the Shattered Self*, anchored by years of experience, Heather Davediuk Gingrich provides a well-researched, accessible, and practical book that is honest about the challenges yet full of hope in the healing power of God and of well-informed Christian communities."

Tim Clinton, president of the American Association of Christian Counselors

"The effects of trauma are surprisingly complex and often counterintuitive. This is particularly true with the most extreme results of trauma—complex traumatic stress disorder. Until very recently there has been little literature on this subject, particularly from a Christian perspective. Thus, Heather Davediuk Gingrich has provided a most valuable resource in *Restoring the Shattered Self*. This is an excellent, sensitive work guiding clinicians and pastors in caring for those suffering from complex trauma. Whether or not one agrees with all her therapeutic techniques (which is not to be expected with this complex issue), this book fills a glaring gap in the literature and will be a welcome resource to clinicians, pastors, and mentors. Few authors are able to give such a readable overview of such a complex subject. I am grateful for this new resource to help the body of Christ care for the deeply wounded in its midst."

Steven Tracy, professor of theology and ethics at Phoenix Seminary, founder and president of Mending the Soul ministries

RESTORING THE SHATTERED SELF

A Christian Counselor's Guide to Complex Trauma

SECOND EDITION

Heather Davediuk Gingrich

IVP
Academic
An imprint of InterVarsity Press
Downers Grove, Illinois

InterVarsity Press
P.O. Box 1400, Downers Grove, IL 60515-1426
ivpress.com
email@ivpress.com

InterVarsity Press® is the book-publishing division of InterVarsity Christian Fellowship/USA®, a movement of
students and faculty active on campus at hundreds of universities, colleges, and schools of nursing in the United
States of America, and a member movement of the International Fellowship of Evangelical Students. For
information about local and regional activities, visit intervarsity.org.

All Scripture quotations, unless otherwise indicated, are taken from The Holy Bible, New International Version®,
NIV®. Copyright © 1973, 1978, 1984, 2011 by Biblica, Inc.™ Used by permission of Zondervan. All rights reserved
worldwide. www.zondervan.com. The "NIV" and "New International Version" are trademarks registered in the
United States Patent and Trademark Office by Biblica, Inc.™

While any stories in this book are true, some names and identifying information may have been changed to protect
the privacy of individuals.

Cover design and image montage: Autumn Short
Interior design: Daniel van Loon
Images: marble photo: © Wesley Tingey / unsplash.com/photos
        blue glazed ceramic surface: © Zen Rial / Moment Collection / Getty Images
        gold background: © studiocasper / E+ / Getty Images

ISBN 978-0-8308-2866-1 (print)
ISBN 978-0-8308-3189-0 (digital)

Printed in the United States of America ♾

InterVarsity Press is committed to ecological stewardship and to the conservation of natural resources in all our
operations. This book was printed using sustainably sourced paper.

Library of Congress Cataloging-in-Publication Data
Names: Gingrich, Heather Davediuk, 1958- author.
Title: Restoring the shattered self : a Christian counselor's guide to
complex trauma / Heather Davediuk Gingrich.
Description: Second edition. | Downers Grove, Illinois : IVP Academic, an imprint of InterVarsity Press, [2020] |
        Series: Christian association for psychological studies books | Includes bibliographical references and index.
Identifiers: LCCN 2019052310 (print) | LCCN 2019052311 (ebook) | ISBN 9780830828661 (paperback) | ISBN
        9780830831890 (ebook)
Subjects: LCSH: Psychic trauma in children. | Psychic trauma in children—Treatment—Religious aspects. |
        Dissociative disorders in children—Treatment—Religious aspects. | Child development—Psychological aspects.
        | Child psychotherapy.
Classification: LCC RJ506.P66 D38 2020 (print) | LCC RJ506.P66 (ebook) | DDC 618. 92/8521—dc23
LC record available at https://lccn.loc.gov/2019052310
LC ebook record available at https://lccn.loc.gov/2019052311

| P | 25 | 24 | 23 | 22 | 21 | 20 | 19 | 18 | 17 | 16 | 15 | 14 | 13 | 12 | 11 | 10 | 9 | 8 | 7 | 6 | 5 | 4 |
| Y | 41 | 40 | 39 | 38 | 37 | 36 | 35 | 34 | 33 | 32 | 31 | 30 | 29 | 28 | 27 | 26 | 25 | 24 | 23 | 22 |

CONTENTS

LIST OF TABLES AND FIGURES

TABLES

FIGURES

This book is dedicated to my husband,
Fred Gingrich, who has been my biggest fan for
over thirty-five years; to five-year-old Rico, who
made me a "Grandma-mother" and who was only
a thought in God's mind when I wrote the
first edition of this book; and to "Haley," who
is living proof of the resiliency of the
human spirit and God's power to heal.

ACKNOWLEDGMENTS

THEY SAY IT TAKES A VILLAGE to raise a child. I feel as though it has taken a village to write this book. Without the encouragement of my husband, Dr. Fred Gingrich, I would not even have contemplated beginning this project, let alone completing it. I appreciate both his emotional support and his practical suggestions with regard to content and format.

To my good friend Dr. Lynette Roth I owe a debt of gratitude for her feedback on multiple drafts of each chapter. The countless hours she spent reading and critiquing were truly a labor of love.

Many other people offered encouragement along the way. Becky Harling has been a prayerful cheerleader, and Dr. Ruth Blizard patiently listened to me talk about this project years before I actually began to write. Dr. Kristy Eldredge offered helpful feedback on some of the initial chapters.

Attendees at conference presentations where I presented on complex trauma spurred me on by their requests for more information, as have my students at Denver Seminary.

Without my former and current clients who struggled with complex post-traumatic stress disorder this book would not have been possible. I am thankful for the privilege of walking with them, and for all they have taught me.

Finally, I am grateful to the team at InterVarsity Press for believing that both editions of this book were worth publishing. Gary Deddo and David Congdon, the editors who worked with me on the first edition, were wonderful to work with. Rebecca Carhart and Jon Boyd, both of whom were involved in making the second edition a reality, have been great encouragers.

1

SHATTERED

"HALEY, WHAT HAPPENED TO YOU?!" In shock I looked at the young woman I had seen for only a couple of counseling sessions. The exposed parts of her face, neck, and arms were covered in cuts and scrapes, with bandages hiding what appeared to be more serious wounds. Gradually Haley's horrific story unfolded. A new Christian, Haley had succumbed to the wishes of a group of women from her new church who, knowing that Haley had recently attempted suicide and was plagued with nightmares and overwhelming flashbacks of childhood torture, wanted to pray for her healing. In the midst of the prayer time one of the women "discerned" demonic activity and proceeded with deliverance prayer, attempting to cast out the offending evil spirits. Without any warning, Haley, not aware of what she was doing but desperate to get away, jumped up and blindly started to run, not realizing that she was heading toward a plate-glass window until her body hurtled through it, shattering the glass with the impact.

I wanted to just sit there in the session and cry as I saw with my own eyes the damage caused by these well-intentioned but ignorant women. I managed to hold my tears in check at the time, but now, twenty years later, I am letting them flow as I write about this incident. I recognize that these women had sincerely been doing their best to help Haley. They saw her pain and did not want her to continue to suffer. I did not know this client very well yet, but her flashbacks were a good indicator that she was a trauma survivor. Unfortunately, the prayer group's lack of understanding about the process of healing for complex trauma survivors not only prevented them from helping her but resulted in further trauma.

Physical wounds usually heal in time, but emotional ones often take longer. The saddest part of this particular incident is not that Haley had to be rushed to the ER for medical treatment, but that the women who had prayed for her subsequently abandoned her emotionally. Understandably they were freaked out. But rather than acknowledge that they had made a tactical error in their attempts to be helpful, they did what people often do—they blamed Haley, the victim. Haley stayed connected to the church for a short while, but without anyone else coming alongside her, and finding it difficult to deal with the constant rejection she faced from the women who had vowed to support her in her journey toward healing, she eventually stopped attending. The shattered glass of the window that broke due to the impact of Haley's body crashing through it somehow seemed symbolic to me not only of those broken relationships but also of Haley's fragmented sense of self and personal history.

Fortunately, there is a happy ending to Haley's larger life story. Although she gave up on church, Haley did not give up on her fledgling relationship with God. Throughout seven years of therapy with me, and several with another therapist after I moved from the area, I watched Haley's faith grow as God used the counseling process to heal the deep wounds of the sadistic physical, sexual, emotional, and spiritual torment she somehow endured as a child.

I marvel as I talk to Haley these days. She is moving up in the company that employs her, doing work that she loves with colleagues she enjoys. Haley's extensive social circle includes several very close friends. Although she shies away from church involvement, fearing that no church community will be able to accept her as she is, she loves God with all her heart and has good Christian friends. This is not to say that scars do not remain. Abuse-related health problems only increase as she ages, and she will probably never be nightmare-free. But she is full of joy, evidence of God's miraculous restorative power.

THE NEED FOR COUNSELOR TRAINING

The women in the prayer group were concerned laypeople, not counselors, so perhaps they can be excused for not understanding that Haley's healing process would be excruciatingly painful, complicated, and long-term—that a couple of prayer sessions would not cure her. Unfortunately, Christian counselors also run the risk of unintentionally retraumatizing such clients. While professional counselors are not likely to be as simplistic about the process of change, most have not been adequately trained to work with a client like Haley. While graduate programs in counseling and psychology are beginning to recognize the need to add a class on treating trauma to their course offerings, the focus tends to be on disaster relief or the treatment of posttraumatic stress disorder. Therefore students often are not adequately prepared to work with survivors of chronic relational trauma— such as child abuse—a category of trauma that has come to be known as complex trauma. This is disturbing, as many clients are likely to have had this kind of complex trauma history, even if they have never revealed that information or perhaps do not even know it themselves. This book is intended to help fill the gap between the reality of what counselors face in their clinical work and the deficits in their counselor training programs, particularly regarding the treatment of complex posttraumatic stress disorder in adults.

WHAT IS COMPLEX POSTTRAUMATIC STRESS DISORDER?

Perhaps the best way to gain an understanding of complex posttraumatic stress disorder (C-PTSD) is to briefly examine the history of the psychological trauma field, including posttraumatic stress disorder (PTSD), the early child sexual abuse literature, and the more recent publications on C-PTSD. I will also use case examples to illustrate the differences between PTSD and C-PTSD.

Posttraumatic Stress Disorder (PTSD). The literature on PTSD has its base primarily in research studies on United States war veterans who served in the two World Wars, Vietnam, the Gulf War, and more recently Iraq and Afghanistan. Studies on Vietnam veterans were particularly influential in identifying specific clusters of symptoms that were associated with exposure to psychological trauma. This lead to the first inclusion of PTSD in the third edition of the *Diagnostic and Statistical Manual of Mental Disorders* (*DSM*), which was released in 1980.[1]

---

[1]The *DSM* is the system used to diagnose mental disorders by mental health professionals and researchers in the United States, Canada, and many other countries (American Psychiatric Association, 2013).

The symptom clusters that currently make up part of the diagnostic criteria for PTSD in the fifth edition of the *DSM* (*DSM-5*) are intrusive, avoidance, alterations in cognitions and mood, and alterations in arousal and reactivity. This represents some changes in terminology from the fourth edition of the manual (*DSM-IV*) as well as the addition of new clusters.

SYMPTOM CLUSTERS OF PTSD

- intrusive symptoms
- avoidance symptoms
- negative alterations in cognitions and mood
- marked alterations in arousal and reactivity

Intrusive symptoms occur when aspects of the traumatic event are relived in some way. This is the equivalent of the *DSM-IV* category labeled *reexperiencing*. I think that a combination of these terms—that is, *intrusive reexperiencing*—provides the best description of this symptom cluster because it makes clear that these symptoms intrude into the lives of traumatized individuals, and that the intrusion takes the form of reexperiencing, or reliving, aspects of a traumatic experience. Although not an official term, the word *flashback* is commonly used by both professionals and laypeople to indicate a type of intrusive symptom in which the survivor relives the trauma as though it is happening here and now. Other intrusive symptoms include nightmares, visual images, intense emotions associated with the traumatic event (e.g., terror or shame), intrusive thoughts, and physical reactions.

The PTSD symptom cluster of *avoidance* includes attempts to stay away from anything that could trigger an intrusive symptom. Individuals with PTSD tend to alternate between intrusive and avoidance symptoms as they try desperately, but often unsuccessfully, to not be at the mercy of the traumatic event they experienced at some earlier point in their lives.

Falling under the symptom cluster of *negative alterations in cognitions and mood* are increased frequency of negative emotional states, diminished interest in significant activities, social withdrawal, and reduction in expression of positive emotions. This category was not included in earlier versions of the *DSM*, but these symptoms were found to be so common that they were added to the diagnostic criteria for PTSD.

While *hyperarousal* was the term used for a symptom cluster in the *DSM-IV*, in the *DSM-5* it was changed to *marked alterations in arousal and reactivity*. Use of the word *alteration* could imply that the change in arousal involves either heightened arousal (i.e., hyperarousal) or the opposite, lessened arousal (i.e., hypoarousal). However, this posttraumatic symptom cluster only includes hyperarousal. High anxiety, anger outbursts, irritability, lack of concentration, and sleep disturbance are some examples of increased reactivity as a result of a nervous system that is in a highly excited or aroused state. I had one client, for example, whose pulse never went below 120 because his nervous system was always highly activated. New to this symptom category in the *DSM-5* is inclusion of increased reckless or dangerous behavior.

At times hyperarousal takes the form of hypervigilance, when individuals are on high alert for danger in specific situations. This prepares them to either fight the perceived source of the danger or to run away from it. Such a "fight-or-flight" response is common not only in humans but also in other mammals and will be discussed in more detail later.

Irene's story. The following vignette illustrates a straightforward case of PTSD that was easily resolved.

"Would anyone be willing to volunteer to be the 'counselee' so that I can demonstrate this technique?" I was teaching a counseling theories course in a seminary graduate counseling program in the Philippines and wanted to demonstrate the behavioral technique of systematic desensitization. A middle-aged woman, Irene, raised her hand, explaining that she was terrified of the sound of airplanes flying overhead. Upon investigation I found out that she was a recent trauma survivor. Just over a month before, Irene had barely escaped with her life when the entire hillside subdivision in which she lived was swept away by a raging river of mud produced by torrential rains. The sound of jet engines reminded Irene of sliding mud and triggered flashbacks of this traumatic event.

Irene showed evidence of typical PTSD symptoms. The terror she felt when she heard airplanes flying overhead was actually an intrusive re-experiencing of her previous trauma-related fear, the panic she felt as she ran for her life from the mud she could hear gaining on her. Nightmares that replayed scenes from the night of the mudslide were also evidence of intrusive posttraumatic symptoms. Irene showed evidence of avoidance because she actively pushed away intrusive thoughts and was reluctant to talk to anyone about the mudslide. Also, despite missing her former neighbors, Irene's desire to avoid reminders of the tragedy kept her from seeking them out. Finally, Irene's alertness to a sound that resembled moving mud and her impulse to run upon hearing such a sound were examples of hyperarousal. Many people who live close to an airport will not even notice a plane's presence, yet Irene's instinctive response was to flee before even identifying the source of the sound.

If Irene had volunteered for the class demonstration within the first four weeks after the mudslide, her diagnosis would have been acute stress disorder (ASD) rather than PTSD because PTSD can only be diagnosed if symptoms persist for over a month. The posttraumatic symptoms that are listed as part of ASD criteria are very similar to those of PTSD but are stated in slightly different ways, with less specific criteria. For example, a diagnosis of ASD requires nine posttraumatic symptoms regardless of specific symptom cluster while a diagnosis of PTSD requires a specific number of symptoms within each cluster. Given that the mudslide happened more than a month prior to the class demonstration, PTSD was the correct diagnosis for Irene.

IRENE'S PTSD

- one traumatic event
- natural disaster
- good ego strength
- supportive relationships

If I had been teaching in North America, I likely would have referred Irene to a trauma counselor and asked for a different volunteer upon recognizing that she suffered from PTSD. In Irene's case, I thought the class demonstration might alleviate her posttraumatic symptoms to some extent in the absence of an appropriate referral source. So I began walking her through the process of systematic desensitization, which involves relaxation paired with visualization of the feared situation. To my amazement, the forty-minute demonstration effectively eliminated Irene's adverse reaction to planes flying overhead, even many weeks after the class. Of course, Irene still had to grieve the loss of friends and readjust to a whole new community, but specific PTSD symptoms appeared to no longer be a major problem. She was able to continue working on her graduate degree and function productively.

There were factors that made Irene more resilient than another individual might have been under the same circumstances. Before the tragic mudslide that profoundly altered her life, Irene was a healthy, highly functional adult. Irene grew up in a poor but loving family. Despite considerable hardship, she had found effective ways of coping. The result was a relatively well-adjusted individual who was able to form and maintain healthy relationships with God and others, attain a high level of education, become a productive employee, and find fulfillment in Christian ministry.

When tragedy struck, Irene was able to draw on the strong foundation of her internal psychological and spiritual resources, as well as the external support systems that still surrounded her. This is likely the reason that the very limited therapeutic intervention in the form of a classroom demonstration was so effective.

Current status of PTSD diagnosis and treatment. While war trauma is still an important focus of investigation, in recent years research efforts on PTSD have expanded to include natural disasters, like the mudslide that Irene experienced. Victims of terrorism, kidnapping, prostitution, rape, and sex trafficking have also recently been included as possible susceptible populations. Basically, the literature addresses whether victims of certain traumatic events meet diagnostic criteria for PTSD and evaluates their prognosis. The literature also compares the effectiveness of various treatment approaches, with components of behavior and cognitive-behavioral therapy (CBT) coming out on top. Exposure therapy and trauma-focused CBT are two such approaches.[2] The International Society for Traumatic Stress Studies (ISTSS) is one of the main organizations involved in research on PTSD and its treatment.

Irene's posttraumatic symptoms were more quickly resolved than those of many individuals with PTSD. War veterans with PTSD symptoms associated with watching a friend get blown up or being injured themselves may require weeks or months of exposure therapy or CBT interventions. However, in all cases of PTSD the focus of treatment is a specific event(s) that is subjectively experienced as traumatic by an individual. Left untreated, PTSD symptoms can last for decades or appear for the first time even many years

---

[2]See various chapters in *Treating Trauma in Christian Counseling,* a book edited by myself and my husband, for specific interventions that are best used with particular types of trauma; a brief description of evidence-based trauma treatments can be found in chapter one of that volume (H. D. Gingrich & F. C. Gingrich, 2017, pp. 319-38).

after the traumatic event (what the *DSM-5* calls "delayed expression" of post-traumatic symptoms). With focused intervention, however, posttraumatic symptoms can be either totally eliminated or made more manageable.

Child sexual abuse and complex trauma. While C-PTSD is not restricted to survivors of child sexual abuse (SA), the abuse literature has informed the current understanding of complex trauma. The early SA literature is replete with descriptions of "flashbacks," "body memories," nightmares, and intrusive thoughts and feelings, all of which could be viewed as PTSD intrusive symptoms. Frequent reference is made to "memory blocks" or "repressed memories" when discussing abuse memories that have been forgotten but which could be triggered at some later time. Amnesia for such traumatic events would fall under the category of PTSD avoidance symptoms. Similarly, symptoms fitting PTSD changes in arousal and reactivity are described in the SA literature. However, few if any of these early SA authors used the term *PTSD,* perhaps because the early literature on SA preceded the inclusion of PTSD as a diagnostic category. Differing terminology between SA literature and PTSD literature could also be partially explained by the segregated nature of each clinical population in that counselors working with SA survivors would not necessarily see clients who were war veterans and vice versa. Whatever the reasons, the literatures tended to develop along relatively independent pathways until more recently.

PTSD symptoms are, therefore, described quite clearly in the SA literature even if not explicitly labeled as such. Many other symptoms, however, are also described in the SA literature but are *not* mentioned in the PTSD literature. These include distorted views of self, such as low self-esteem to the point of self-hatred. In addition, SA survivors tend to blame themselves for their abuse, experiencing high degrees of guilt and shame. Identity formation is often impaired, leading to identity confusion. Trust levels are described as severely impaired, which interferes with the development of healthy relationships of any kind. This is just a sample of the kinds of issues described in the SA literature, and it is clear that a diagnosis of PTSD does not adequately prepare a counselor to treat an individual with such a complex presentation.

Current status of complex posttraumatic stress disorder diagnosis and treatment. Much to my dismay and that of my colleagues who specialize in work with survivors of complex trauma, the *DSM-5* does not include a separate diagnostic category for complex PTSD. It does include a new *dissociative subtype* of PTSD which helps to identify some complex trauma survivors, but in our view, it does not go far enough in that it does not encompass all of the additional symptoms discussed in the child abuse literature.

Lack of inclusion in the *DSM* has made it difficult to come up with common language around complex trauma. Over the past couple of decades various diagnostic labels have been suggested in attempts to remedy this situation. Some of these include: disorders of extreme stress, Type II trauma, betrayal trauma, complex traumatic stress disorder, complex posttraumatic stress disorder, and, for children, developmental trauma disorder. In the first edition of this book I used the term *complex traumatic stress disorder* or *CTSD* because that was the terminology in greatest use at that time. Currently the term *complex posttraumatic stress disorder* or *C-PTSD* is more commonly used, which is why I have chosen to use it in the second edition of this book.

SYMPTOMS OF C-PTSD

Difficulties with:

- affect regulation
- dissociation
- self-perception
- perception of perpetrator
- relationships
- physical problems
- systems of meaning

Another consequence of the lack of consistency in terminology and the *DSM* not including complex trauma as a separate diagnostic category is that pertinent research findings and treatment guidelines have been scattered in various places throughout the broader trauma and child abuse literatures. The International Society for the Study of Trauma and Dissociation (ISSTD, not to be confused with the ISTSS mentioned previously) is an organization that has focused on complex trauma, including dissociative disorders, for several decades.

The publication of the book *Treating Complex Traumatic Stress Disorders* (Courtois & Ford, 2009) represented a significant contribution toward understanding posttraumatic symptoms that were not outlined in the *DSM*. The formation of Division 56 of the American Psychological Association, which focuses on trauma, is also noteworthy. Members are attempting to bridge the gap between the two trauma worlds by addressing both types of trauma.

While there is consensus in the literature that child abuse and neglect are sources of complex trauma, there are some differences of opinion as to whether other types of trauma can also result in C-PTSD. For example, Judith Herman, a pioneer in this field, writes that the prerequisite condition of C-PTSD is the experience of being totally controlled over a period of months or years. While those who have been abused as children fit this criterion, Herman also includes hostages, prisoners of war, concentration camp survivors, survivors of religious cults, and those who have been victims of intimate partner violence (Herman, 1992/2015). I prefer Herman's wider inclusion of traumatized individuals, as treatment principles can be more broadly, yet still appropriately, generalized.

Despite varying views with respect to the types of trauma that can result in C-PTSD, there is agreement as to the kinds of symptoms that are the focus of treatment. They include *difficulties with affect regulation* (anger, self-injury), *dissociation* (amnesia, depersonalization), *problems with self-perception* (shame, self-hatred), *distorted perception of the perpetrator* (taking on perpetrator's views, feeling sympathy toward perpetrator), *relational difficulties* (distrust, lack of intimacy), *physical problems* (related to abuse, medical problems), and *alterations in systems of meaning* (hopelessness about recovery) (Herman, 1992/2015).

Haley's story as compared to Irene's. Haley, the client discussed at the beginning of this chapter, is a good example of an individual with C-PTSD. Flagrant PTSD symptoms were the primary motivating factor for Haley to seek counseling. Intrusive symptoms in the form of frequent, vivid flashbacks were the most distressing as she had difficulty knowing whether she was remembering past horrors or whether she was in current danger. Haley's sleep was also severely disturbed due to intrusive symptoms in the form of nightmares. Even a slight noise startled her awake, her nervous system fully aroused and ready to respond to danger. This illustrates severe hyperarousal in the form of hypervigilance. In one instance Haley's hypervigilance resulted in assault charges. In what she thought was self-defense, Haley spun

HALEY'S EXPERIENCE

- child sexual, physical, spiritual, and emotional abuse; severe neglect
- chronic abuse
- PTSD symptoms
- a multitude of other symptoms
- minimal social support

around and punched a colleague in the face after being approached from behind and touched on the shoulder.

Avoidance symptoms were also present. Haley could not handle learning how to drive because of a traumatic memory associated with a car. She avoided contact with family members associated with abuse, and only gradually accessed some particularly sadistic abuse memories that she had buried for years.

Despite the prevalence of Haley's PTSD symptoms, there were significant differences between Haley's presentation and that of Irene. Haley had not experienced one isolated traumatic event, but hundreds. In addition, she was a child when she was traumatized, which had a profound impact on the development of basic trust, identity formation, and her ability to develop intimate relationships. The relational nature of the chronic physical, sexual, emotional, and spiritual abuse, as well as the severe physical and emotional neglect she suffered, were particularly destructive, leading to severe dissociative symptoms.

Haley had neither the internal cohesiveness nor the well-established network of relationships that Irene had available to her. The secure attachment relationship to a parent, prerequisite to forming a core sense of self, did not exist. After all, the very people who were supposed to nurture, protect, and help Haley overcome developmental milestones were the very ones who sadistically abused and neglected her. Therefore, the standard PTSD treatment of exposure therapy and CBT interventions would have been inadequate in treating Haley. Instead of the brief intervention that was sufficient for the alleviation of Irene's posttraumatic symptoms, Haley required over a decade of counseling. Table 1.1 makes some comparisons between PTSD and C-PTSD.

SPECIAL CONSIDERATIONS FOR CHRISTIAN COUNSELORS

The wounds of complex trauma survivors are often so deep that their ability to live out of who God created them to be is severely hampered. Some have been damaged to the extent that they are not able to function at school or work and are forced to rely on disability income for basic needs. Others may be able to provide for themselves. However, day-to-day survival comes at great psychological and emotional cost as they battle depression, anxiety, insomnia, nightmares, flashbacks, and other posttraumatic and dissociative symptoms. Self-blame, shame, guilt, fear, and rage are not uncommon. Many wrestle spiritually, not understanding why God did not protect them from the horrors of the violence perpetrated against them. Loneliness and social isolation are often the norm. Any relationships that do exist tend to be unhealthy if not abusive.

Table 1.1. Posttraumatic stress disorder compared to complex posttraumatic stress disorder

POSTTRAUMATIC STRESS DISORDER	COMPLEX POSTTRAUMATIC STRESS DISORDER
Literature on war-related trauma	Literature on child sexual abuse
Isolated traumatic events	Multiple traumatic events; chronic trauma
Trauma source not usually an intimate relationship	Trauma source includes intimate relationships
Examples: war-related trauma, natural disasters, single rape (adult), physical injury	Examples: child abuse and/or neglect (physical, sexual, emotional, spiritual, or combinations), domestic violence
Relatively short-term therapy	Long-term therapy

Living this way does not seem to fit with the abundant life promised in Scripture (Jn 10:10). Recognizing that God created all of us for something more, Christian counselors are in a unique position to not focus solely on alleviating their clients' symptoms, but to envision the potential inherent in their clients as men or women whom God has created for his purposes.

Working with such brokenness can test the courage, skills, and patience of even the best therapist. However, Christian counselors have resources not available to secular therapists: We can rely on the wisdom and discernment of the Holy Spirit to guide the therapeutic process, whether or not our complex trauma clients acknowledge Christ. We can also depend on God to take care of us, the counselors, in the midst of some very taxing therapeutic work. With proper training, and the active recognition of God's healing power, we potentially have a lot to offer counselees with C-PTSD.

Increased responsibility. Luke 12:48 states, "From everyone who has been given much, much will be demanded; and from the one who has been entrusted with much, much more will be asked." While all counselors have a responsibility to continually upgrade their knowledge and skills, the onus on Christian counselors is even greater. The Bible spurs us on to excellence. "Whatever you do, work at it with all your heart, as working for the Lord, not for human masters" (Col 3:23). But we are not doing just any work! As Christian counselors we are entrusted with the hearts and souls of individuals who are created in the very image of God, marred though it may be (Gen 1:26).

Specific areas in which Christian counselors can be of particular help. Some excellent secular books have been published on complex trauma, as well as other valuable resources available to mental health professionals (see chapter eight). However, there are gaps in the literature that could best be addressed by a book written specifically for evangelical Christian counselors that deals with the treatment of complex trauma.

For example, with secular therapists, Christian C-PTSD clients may have a particularly difficult time satisfactorily addressing issues related to their faith and church involvement. While good secular counselors will give their counselees the freedom to work through these concerns, it may be more difficult for counselors who have no personal faith of their own to recognize the difference between healthy and unhealthy spirituality. Therefore, Christian C-PTSD clients could benefit from having a counselor who understands their faith background. Similarly, non-Christian clients sometimes choose Christian counselors expressly because they want the freedom to tackle issues of faith as part of the counseling process.

Spiritual and existential concerns. Whether or not complex trauma survivors identify themselves as Christians, they will inevitably present with spiritual issues and existential concerns. Christian counselors need to be prepared to wrestle through these complicated questions alongside their clients. Telling a Christian client who has been gang-raped that "in all things God works for the good of those who love him" (Rom 8:28) could be very damaging. A counselor's simplistic prayer begging God to take care of a Christian counselee in the coming week, a prayer that could easily originate out of an overwhelmed counselor's feelings of helplessness rather than the client's felt need, may seem trite to the counselee. How meaningful can such a prayer be to a complex trauma survivor whose cries are more likely to be in the vein of, "God, why did you allow me to be tortured even after I pleaded with you for protection? How could a loving God let a little child suffer so much?" Of course I am not suggesting that we do not pray for our clients. But what we pray for and when we pray for them—whether in the session or outside of the session—are the relevant therapeutic questions. A trained Christian counselor will be better able to make good decisions about the appropriate use of Scripture and prayer with complex trauma clients who are Christians.

The demonic. Unfortunately Haley's story of deliverance prayer gone awry is not uncommon for survivors of complex trauma, both those purporting to be Christians as well as those who do not hold to a religious faith. Christian counselors need to be apprised of the complexities involved in helping their clients heal from such events, and they must circumvent potential future damage by Christians and churches that may misinterpret posttraumatic symptoms and assume a spiritual cause. Of course there is also the dilemma for Christian counselors of trying to determine whether their clients are being spiritually attacked or are just psychologically disturbed.

Toxic churches. As illustrated by Haley's story, some churches can create further damage to complex trauma survivors. One of my clients referred to these churches as "Kool-Aid" churches (in reference to the Jimmy Jones cult where church members committed suicide with poisoned Kool-Aid). Christian counselors can teach their clients to avoid or get out of such spiritually abusive churches. Of course a good secular therapist will also help a Christian client recognize the "Kool-Aid," but if not familiar with the spectrum of evangelicalism, they may characterize all evangelical churches as dysfunctional.

The Bible, however, talks about the church as the body of Christ. A properly educated church can be a powerful healing resource for complex trauma survivors, particularly if church members are willing to partner with Christian counselors in a common endeavor to help such individuals.

MY PERSONAL THERAPEUTIC JOURNEY: WHY I AM PASSIONATE ABOUT WORK WITH COMPLEX PTSD

My vision is that more clients like Haley will find abundant life in Christ with the aid of Christian counselors who are knowledgeable about good C-PTSD treatment. My desire to help these clients compelled me to begin working in this field in the first place. Trauma survivors, carrying horrible stories of child abuse and rape, started finding their way into my counseling office in the early 1980s, and I scrambled to try to understand and help them. However, there were very few resources available to me at that time. The literature on child sexual abuse was in its infancy, and very little was known about dissociative disorders. I struggled to find anyone who could give me feedback about how to help these clients.

Despite the lack of readily available information, I can see now that the Lord was guiding me into the field, giving me the support and training that I needed. Unlike many of my peers, I was familiar with the concept of dissociation because I had written a research paper on multiple personality disorder (MPD, now called dissociative identity disorder or DID) during my graduate training. Furthermore, one of my graduate school professors had a client with DID, and watching him navigate this mainly uncharted territory helped me, years later, to recognize the signs of dissociation in a client, Maggie.

Maggie revealed that she had started to hear threatening voices. I suggested that she listen to the voices in order to find out more about them rather than attempt to push them away out of fear. I will never forget the following session, my initiation into this kind of work. Maggie announced that two of her voices had been arguing all week about who got to talk to me first! According to Maggie the voices had informed her that their names were Sandra and Cindy, and they were five years old. So I pulled out crayons and paper, sat on the floor with my adult client, and began conversing with what sounded like a young child.

I was desperate for supervision but had not been successful at finding any, until an opportunity arose that was better than anything I had hoped for. At a time when such an MPD diagnosis was considered extremely rare, I was fortunate to have the opportunity to be trained and supervised by one of North America's experts in the field. By what I consider divine intervention, this psychiatrist offered to do live supervision and training, inviting the client and me to meet with him once a week for almost a year.

When my husband and I moved to another city, I was forced to refer this client to my supervisor. While I was in agreement with our move, I could not understand God's timing. Why, I wondered, had God pulled me away from this client who was making remarkable progress and this incredible training opportunity, when I would likely never again have the chance to use what I had been learning about working with dissociative clients?

God, of course, did know what he was doing! I had been working at a part-time counseling job in our new city only a few weeks when a counselee walked into my office, said, "I've been diagnosed with MPD and would like a second opinion," and I began to work with my second highly dissociative client. Within the next few years several people with previously undiagnosed MPD ended up becoming my clients, as well as others who had histories of child abuse.

Another amazing training opportunity presented itself in the form of once-weekly, three-hour training sessions over an eight-week period made available free of charge through a government grant. The instructor offered invaluable training from a slightly different perspective than that of my original supervisor. I also became a member of what is now called the International Society for the Study of Trauma and Dissociation, a secular organization with a membership full of compassionate people who are dedicated to conducting research, training clinicians, and educating the general public about dissociation and the impact of chronic relational trauma.

In the late 1990s I moved to the Philippines along with my husband and two young sons to teach in a graduate counseling program in a seminary in Manila. In my supervision of student interns, I saw evidence of severe dissociation among their Filipino and Filipino Chinese counselees. This was one of the motivating factors in my decision to study trauma and dissociation in a nonclinical population in the Philippines for my doctoral dissertation. From that time on my clinical specialization in the area of trauma and dissociation expanded to also become my teaching, research, and writing passion. All of this coalesces in a deep desire to share with others what God has taught me over the past three decades about working with this client population.

SHATTERING THE SELF

The Effects of Trauma on Childhood Development

PEOPLE OFTEN BELIEVE that young children are not greatly impacted by negative events, assuming that if children are too young to understand what is happening, they will not be harmed by the situation or their resilience will enable them to bounce back easily. In fact, the opposite is true. The younger the child, the greater the impact a potentially traumatic event often has, both in terms of neurobiology and psychology.

Think, for example, of Ben, a child going through the terrible twos. One afternoon Ben discovers that the soil in the potted plant in the living room is fun to play with. His father, who has been drinking, yells at Ben to stop.

AREAS OF CHILD DEVELOPMENT AFFECTED BY TRAUMA

- physical development
- emotional regulation
- attachment relationships
- identity development
- spiritual health

Ben ignores him and continues to throw handfuls of dirt onto the carpet. Screaming profanities, Ben's dad lunges at the child, pins him to the floor, and proceeds to lash his bare legs with a belt. As Ben shrieks in pain and terror, his father grows livid and hits harder until Ben's legs are covered in welts. His anger finally spent, Ben's father exits the room, leaving the sobbing child alone, huddled on the carpet.

An hour prior to this incident, Ben and his father were cuddled together on the couch, looking at a picture book. How does Ben make sense of what has just happened? Which one is the real Daddy: the gentle, loving man or the monster that hurt him so badly? At a deep level, a seed of belief could set in that "I must be a really, really bad boy for Daddy to hurt me this way." However, as Ben's language at this age is not very developed, he will not have the cognitive ability even to formulate this thought, let alone to sort out that his father was at fault for disciplining him in a totally inappropriate way. To add to the complexities, Ben is completely dependent on his parents for his very survival.

As the title suggests, this chapter will discuss how trauma impacts both neuropsychological and psychological processes. We will first look at how trauma impacts the physical body. The discussion will then focus on normal psychological development which will lay a foundation for understanding how trauma negatively impacts the formation of personality, sense of identity, and ability to form healthy relationships. Obtaining this knowledge about why relational trauma in childhood has such a devastating, long-term impact lays the theoretical foundation for the treatment-oriented chapters that follow. The techniques introduced in the treatment-focused chapters will make much more sense if you have first waded through the denser material of this chapter. So hang in there! The rest of the book will be a breeze!

HOW THE BODY RESPONDS TO TRAUMA

Research studies have used brain scans, blood work, and other medical technology to determine exactly what happens neurologically and physiologically when individuals are faced with a threatening situation. Entire volumes have been written on the neurobiological impact of trauma both at the time of the trauma and in the aftermath. This material is covered in broad strokes here, highlighting a few areas that will give you some sense of how the body is affected by trauma. If you wish to know more about this topic, I highly recommend Bessel van der Kolk's book *The Body Keeps the Score*. Van der Kolk has an amazing way of making complex neurobiological principles easy

HOW THE BODY RESPONDS TO TRAUMA

- subcortical brain systems, such as the limbic system, become hyperactive
- cerebral cortex is bypassed
- stress hormones flood the nervous system
- fight, flight, or freeze responses are repeatedly triggered
- negative long-term effects on physical and mental health result

to understand for those who have not made an in-depth study of this area (van der Kolk, 2014).[1]

The brain.[2] The brain consists of a multitude of systems and anatomical subsections. Yet it is frequently divided into *cortical* and *subcortical* regions. While every section of the brain is remarkably complex, the cortical regions contained within the cerebral cortex direct the most complex functions, while the subcortical regions tend to direct more basic neurological functions. The cerebral cortex, which is the outermost area of the brain, is the rational, thinking brain that regulates much of the conscious behavior and decision making unique to humans. One particularly important subcortical structure, the brainstem, is geared toward basic physical survival, controlling activities such as breathing, heart rate, and digestion. In close proximity lies the *limbic system*, another subcortical region, which, among other things, assesses what is pleasurable or scary, determines when the person is in danger, and is the emotional center of the brain.

Under normal circumstances these interconnected areas of the brain work together as an integrated whole. But if the *amygdala*, which is part of the limbic system, signals danger as a result of sensory input processed by the *thalamus*, the cerebral cortex, in effect, goes offline. Instead, two different hormonal stress response systems are activated, resulting in the instantaneous release of stress hormones, including *cortisol* and *adrenaline*. Stress hormones ultimately result in either *fight, flight,* or *freeze* responses,

---

[1]If you wish to geek out on the topic of complex trauma and neurobiology, the edited book *Neurobiology and Treatment of Traumatic Dissociation* by Lanius, Paulsen, and Corrigan (2014) will provide all the detail you would ever want. The chapter by Struthers, Ansell, and Wilson in *Treating Trauma in Christian Counseling* (2017) is also helpful.

[2]This section draws from Lanius, Paulsen, and Corrigan (2014); van der Kolk (2014).

all of which are activated without the involvement of the cerebral cortex. Without easy access to their conscious decision-making capacities, individuals in situations of perceived danger, therefore, are unable to make a conscious choice about what to do, at least initially. The response is instinctual; in a sense their body just takes over.

Fight, flight, or freeze responses: Which gets used?[3] The particular defensive response that is triggered at a given point in time depends both on the particulars of the specific situation and on the past history and personal characteristics of the individual. Two people can be faced with an identical threat but respond in opposite ways. For example, being trapped in a car after an accident may mobilize one person to attempt to get out (i.e., flee), while someone else in the same position may fight off the attempts of firefighters and paramedics to help them.

In a court case, the instinctual fight response could be argued to be self-defense. Physiologically, preplanned aggression toward someone, such as premeditated murder, looks quite different from aggression triggered by the need for basic survival. Just as a cornered animal, even your pet, will often lash out when wounded or frightened, so even normally mild-mannered people can become highly aggressive when their lives are on the line. Both fight and flight responses trigger high physiological arousal states. For example, the heart beats faster, neurologically the individual is on high alert, and muscles are poised for quick action. Adrenaline pumps through the system, making possible seemingly super-human feats (e.g., running faster or hitting harder than possible under normal circumstances). I have had counselees describe times where they were able to outrun their adult perpetrators as children or adolescents due to the instinct to flee. Unfortunately fight responses are not generally successful for children when adults have superior physical strength and the ability to psychologically intimidate.

If the brain determines that fight-or-flight responses are not viable options, as is often the case for children, the only alternative is one of a number of freeze responses, which physiologically vary greatly. One type of freeze response is similar to that of prey animals in the final moments before death, when the predator is upon them and their fate seems sealed. The animal

---

[3]I have drawn heavily from the following sources in this section: Corrigan (2014a), Corrigan (2014b), van der Kolk (2014); most of the practical applications are my own.

appears lifeless because the muscles become limp and the heart rate slows down. Morphine-like opioids are released in such circumstances that reduce the amount of pain experienced. This is the opposite of the hyperaroused state that is the hallmark of both flight and fight responses; it is a *hypo*aroused state, or a "low-activation" freeze. The technical term for this type of freeze state is a *dorsal-vagal response*.

Some of my clients have described experiencing dorsal-vagal responses when they realized, as children, that there was no hope of escape from their perpetrators. They may initially have attempted to flee and been caught, or been immobilized in a freeze response. But upon realizing that their attempts to protect themselves were futile, their nervous systems collapsed in a kind of inevitable submission. When such situations are reexperienced as part of trauma processing in Phase II of treatment, these clients can go into a dorsal-vagal freeze that can be very disconcerting to both counselor and counselee, particularly if the counselor does not recognize what is happening. In extreme cases the heart rate slows down to such an extent that the individual could actually die.

Another common freeze response is a paralyzed "frozen fear" one, which may be triggered if someone is trapped. Unlike the state of low arousal in the dorsal-vagal freeze, this is a "high-activation" freeze similar to that seen in fight-or-flight responses. Physiologically, two opposing forces are at play here, as both the *sympathetic* (responsible for arousal) and *parasympathetic* (which functions to conserve energy during rest) branches of the *autonomic nervous system* (ANS) are activated. This state could be considered "frozen flight" or "frozen fight." In both of these the nervous system is highly aroused, but the muscles are immobilized. This state of frozen fear can also be reenacted during a flashback or in a trauma-processing session.

There are two additional freeze states. One is an "attentional focus freeze," where the person's body is immobilized and their gaze cannot be torn away from the potential threat. This involves a narrowing of the field of attention with peripheral vision blurred. The other is a "vigilant freeze," where the senses are on hyperalert. For example, the individual may be straining their ears in an attempt to listen for danger. Again, counselors will sometimes see these states replaying themselves. Having an explanation as to what might be happening can be helpful.

Long-term effects. Every time individuals experience traumatic situations their bodies are impacted. Hormones and neurochemicals related to high activation of the nervous system (e.g., flight, fight, frozen flight/fight responses) or its opposite, low arousal (e.g., dorsal-vagal freeze state), course through their bodies. Respiration, heart rate, digestion, sexual function, and so on are also impacted. In complex trauma where abuse is chronic, the body is constantly going in and out of these states because trauma happens so frequently. But it is not just when the abuse is happening that the body responds in these ways. When flashbacks occur, the body does not know the difference between these intrusive posttraumatic symptoms and an actual traumatic event, and so reacts in an identical fashion.

I have known people who virtually live in hyperaroused states where their body is rarely in a state of relaxation. Ruby is one example. Ruby's childhood was fraught with danger. Even when she was not being physically or sexually abused, in which she was in a state of frozen fear, she was constantly targeted for emotional and verbal abuse. Ruby tried desperately to avoid doing anything that would elicit a detrimental reaction from her parents. This meant that she was continually in high alert, either in a vigilant freeze or a more active state of hypervigilance, as she attempted to perceive if she was in imminent danger. Now that she is an adult, it is almost as though Ruby's body does not know how to relax because it has been in a highly aroused state for so long. Her "resting" heart rate is more than double what it should be, and her breathing is rapid and shallow. She is also disengaged from her body, often not even able to feel someone touch her.

The research literature indicates that Ruby is not alone (Struthers, Ansell, & Wilson, 2017). While any traumatic event in adulthood can set off similar neurobiological cycles, when the trauma happens in infancy or childhood, the impact is particularly serious. The brain is especially vulnerable during critical neurological developmental windows. When trauma happens during these periods the resulting neurological dysregulation increases the sensitivity and duration of the stress response, which has ongoing implications. For example, trauma within the first five years of life has been shown to significantly reduce brain volume, increase cortisol levels (a hormone that at increased levels impacts the heart and weight among other things), and decrease the ability of the child to recover from an acute trauma.

Over time such dysregulated neurological systems can have devastating effects on both physical and mental health. The findings from the Adverse Childhood Experiences (ACE) Study provide support for this.[4] The ACE study was conducted jointly by Kaiser Permanente and the US government's Centers for Disease Control (CDC). It gathered data from 17,000 patients between the years of 1995 and 1997 with follow-ups continuing to the present day. The results showed that there is a positive correlation between the number of ACEs and a vast number of conditions, including pulmonary/ cardiovascular disease, depression, alcoholism, liver disease, and many more (Centers for Disease Control and Prevention, 2019). See figure 2.1 for a list of significant associations.

The researchers also recognized, however, that it is not ACEs alone that impact physical and psychological health. The two categories at the base of the pyramid in figure 2.2 indicate that generational factors, historical trauma, social conditions, and other contextual factors provide the foundation for

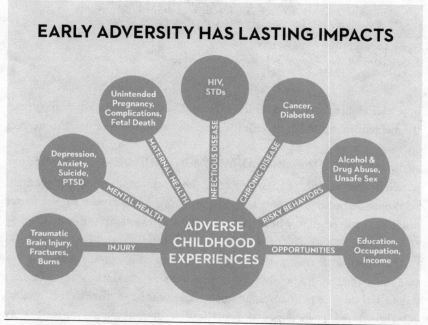

Figure 2.1. The impact of adverse childhood experiences on physical and emotional health
Source: Centers for Disease Control and Prevention, www.cdc.gov/violenceprevention/childabuseandneglect/ acestudy/ace-graphics.html

[4]See www.cdc.gov/violenceprevention/acestudy/about.html for more information on the ACE study.

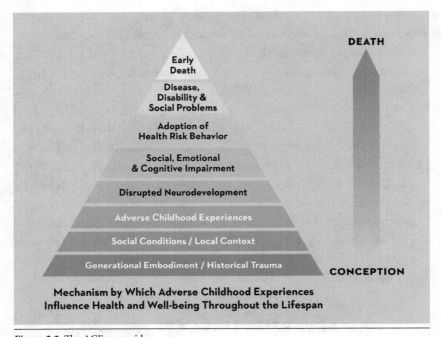

Figure 2.2. The ACE pyramid
Source: Centers for Disease Control and Prevention, www.cdc.gov/violenceprevention/childabuseandneglect/acestudy/ace-graphics.html

how ACEs will affect particular individuals. The diagram as a whole illustrates the mechanism by which ACEs impact health and well-being over the lifespan.

THE TIES THAT BIND: ATTACHMENT AND DEVELOPMENT

Research findings increasingly show that the formation of healthy attachment relationships between infants and primary caregivers is crucial for the future emotional and relational health of children (see, for example, Berlin, Cassidy, & Appleyard, 2008). The primary caregiver is often the mother, but it could be the father, a nanny, a grandmother, an older sibling, or anyone who emotionally invests in or spends a lot of time with the child. For convenience, I will talk about the primary attachment figure as the mother in this section. Attachment theory focuses mainly on how children develop a sense of safety and security with their primary caregivers and on how those relationships impact the child's ability to develop healthy relationships later in life, topics we will discuss in this section. Additionally, the same caregiving behaviors that are associated with the development of secure attachment can be viewed as more broadly impacting the formation of personality, the ability to regulate affect (emotion), and a unified sense of self.

> ## ATTACHMENT AND DEVELOPMENT
> - Safety and security
> - Personality development, affect regulation, and integration of self
> - Attachment, trauma, and the developing brain

Safety and security. The formation of healthy attachment bonds requires an attuned caregiver who senses what is happening with the baby and then appropriately responds. For example, a loving mother is likely to know the difference between the "I'm hungry," "I'm tired," "I hurt," and "I need changing" cries of her baby and to take the appropriate action to alleviate her child's distress.

My husband, Fred, and I are raising our grandson, Rico, whom we have adopted. When Rico was a toddler I volunteered in the church nursery one Sunday. Rico was playing contentedly when one of the babies began crying. I picked her up and tried, unsuccessfully, to settle her. I began to feel anxious and helpless when nothing seemed to work.

I would have known exactly what to do, or at least what to try, if that baby had been Rico, because I had cared for Rico since infancy and knew his idiosyncrasies. We had a connection that worked well because I was attuned to his needs, and I was able to quickly, and effectively, meet them. While it was obvious that this other baby was distressed, it took a lot of trial and error to figure out how to calm her down.

The development of secure, healthy attachment is not only reliant on the ability of the primary caregiver or attachment figure to help regulate the infant's emotion when upset, but it is also dependent on positive interactions when the infant is not dysregulated. For example, when her infant is smiling or cooing, an attuned mother looks into her baby's eyes, smiles, and talks to her infant.

The "still face" experiment. A great example of such reciprocal attachment behavior can be seen in a film clip recorded as part of the "still face" experiment

(Tronick, 2007).[5] The clip shows a mother and infant clearly engaged with each other. They are making eye contact, the infant makes excited sounds in response to the mother's voice, the baby points and the mother looks to where she is pointing. It is easy to see that mother and baby are emotionally connected in those moments, and how similar interactions repeated thousands of times over would result in a strong attachment bond.

The mother is then asked to turn her head away for a few seconds, and, on turning back, keep her face expressionless (i.e., still) and be otherwise unresponsive. The baby's response is disturbing. She tries various tactics to gain her mother's attention, such as smiling, gurgling, and pointing, which is what she was doing before with good results. But when unable to get a response the baby becomes obviously more distressed with every passing second, making high-pitched cries, turning her head away, crying harder, and ultimately losing control of her posture. At the end of two minutes the mother once again engages with the baby, who quickly returns to her happy, playful state.

Of course we cannot be fully attentive to our children one hundred percent of the time because life demands involvement in other tasks. Fortunately, this is not necessary. What is important for the development of secure attachment is that relational ruptures, even small ones, are repaired. The film clip demonstrated this well; while the unresponsiveness of the mother resulted in a temporary rupture of relationship, it was quickly and easily repaired once the mother reengaged. This means that I do not have to worry too much when I am at the stove cooking dinner and Rico demands my attention. While he may be frustrated that I cannot fully attend to him, when I turn to smile at him occasionally and continue to chat even if I cannot make eye contact, the little relational ruptures are continually being repaired.

Exploration behavior of toddlers and the "strange situation" experiment. When caregivers are appropriately responsive to them, children develop a sense of safety and security because their needs are being met and their environment is predictable. The attachment figure becomes a "safe haven," providing a "secure base" from which the child can begin to explore his or her world (Bowlby, 1988).

A good illustration of this is the exploration behavior of toddlers. When securely attached, they will wander out of sight of their mothers, running

---

[5]The video clip can be found at www.youtube.com/watch?v=apzXGEbZht0 or by searching "Still face experiment: Edward Tronick" on YouTube. Edward Tronick first conducted this research in the 1970s, but similar studies have been done since (see Adamson & Frick, 2003).

back to them every now and then to remind themselves that Mommy is still there and, consequently, that everything is okay. In this way the mother provides a secure base for the toddler to explore. If, however, toddlers are not securely attached to their mothers, their exploration behavior is diminished. They do not want to let Mommy out of their sight because they cannot trust that she will still be there for them when they return.

The strange situation research protocol has revealed the differences between children who are securely attached to their mothers and those exhibiting various styles of insecure attachment (Ainsworth, Blehar, Waters, & Wall, 1978). It has become the standard procedure by which attachment style at various ages is assessed (Weinfield, Sroufe, Egeland, & Carlson, 2008). In studies using the strange situation, mother and child are placed in a room and their interactions observed. The mother then leaves the room, and a stranger enters it while the child's behavior is monitored for signs of distress. When the mother returns, the child's response is again observed. Table 2.1 summarizes the findings of studies that have used the strange situation, as well as findings from studies that have looked at the association between attachment style and relational behavior in adulthood (Ainsworth et al., 1978; Cassidy & Shaver, 2016; Main, Hesse & Kaplan, 2005).

Table 2.1. Attachment styles

ATTACHMENT STYLE	BEHAVIOR OF CHILD AFTER ATTACHMENT FIGURE REENTERS THE ROOM	IMPACT ON ADULT BEHAVIOR
Secure	• Shows moderate distress • Actively seeks contact • Shows need for comfort and nurturance • When comforted returns to play/exploration	• Assumes others will be trustworthy and responsive • Believes oneself to be lovable and able to elicit caring
Anxious/Preoccupied	• Shows extreme distress • Seeks contact/clings • Does not return easily to exploration	• Deeply desires intimacy but expects to be let down
Avoidant/Dismissing	• Shows little apparent distress • Avoids attachment figure • Focuses on tasks (e.g., play)	• Denies need for intimate relationships • Avoids intimacy
Disorganized/Ambivalent	• Shows extreme distress • Approaches/clings and withdraws • Dissociates (appears dazed, frozen)	• Believes others are both the solution to and source of fear • Overly dependent and then withdraws

The impact of abuse. While other factors can influence the development of an insecure attachment style, imagine how child abuse wreaks havoc with the development of secure attachment, particularly if the perpetrator is the same person on whom the child is totally dependent for survival. If the caregiver is minimally tuned in to the baby, emotional and/or physical neglect result. Remember how distressed the baby in the still face experiment became after only two minutes of unresponsiveness in her mother? If instead of minutes there are hours or days in which the baby is not engaged emotionally, and there is no repair of such huge relational ruptures, the implications for formation of secure attachment are enormous, even if there is no physical neglect or explicit physical, sexual, or verbal abuse.

Perhaps, however, the caregiver is appropriately responsive some of the time but then unpredictably abuses the child. Insecure attachment, in particular a disorganized/ambivalent attachment style, is often the result, because the source of both safety and danger for the child resides in the same person.[6] The ambivalence the child experiences toward the caregiver can be seen in the child's behavior when the caregiver walks into the room. For example, the child may begin to run, arms outstretched, toward the caregiver, then suddenly stop, arms by the side of the body, with a confused facial expression, and abruptly turn and run in the opposite direction. This behavior indicates the simultaneous desire for, and fear of, the attachment figure.

In cases where the perpetrator is not a primary caregiver, attachment bonds with caregivers still can be adversely affected. Children tend to assume that somehow caregivers know what is happening, perhaps even throwing out hints that they are being harmed. They do not understand why caregivers are choosing to ignore their pain.

Similarly, even if only one parent perpetrates abuse, the child often blames the nonoffending parent for not stopping it. Whether or not the primary attachment figure knows that the child is being harmed, the reality is that the child remains unprotected, which shakes the very foundations of any sense of safety and security that the child has already built.

If, however, parents respond in supportive, constructive ways upon discovering that their child has been abused (e.g., comforting them, assuring them that it was not their fault, seeking justice, and protecting them from

---

[6]A more in-depth discussion of various attachment styles can be found in numerous sources, including *Handbook of Attachment* (Cassidy & Shaver, 2016), which is now in its third edition.

further harm), the attachment relationship can be salvaged or perhaps even strengthened. This is particularly true if there is little delay between the traumatic event and appropriate parental intervention.

Often, though, children are afraid to reveal what has been done to them, either because they have been explicitly warned by perpetrators not to tell, or because they inevitably blame themselves. This may inadvertently circumvent the help that they could otherwise receive from caregivers or others. Even if traumatized children do somehow work up the courage to take a caregiver into their confidence, caregivers all too often do not rescue them. Instead caregivers may accuse children of lying or tell them that they are to blame for what happened and punish them. In cases of incest, for example, it is all too common for the nonoffending parent, most often the mother, to either not believe the child or minimize the trauma. In effect the child is sacrificed so that the mother does not have to deal with the implications for herself and her marriage that acknowledging her spouse as a perpetrator would bring about. Of course this deepens the attachment wound for the abused child.

As early attachment relationships provide the foundation for intimacy in all future relationships, individuals who have experienced relational trauma in childhood are at great risk for dysfunctional relationships throughout life. Unless there is a redemptive relationship later on, or a positive intervention through therapy, this cycle will tend to perpetuate itself even into future generations through the inability of parents who were abused themselves to establish healthy bonds with their own children due to their own relational deficits. The good news is that the positive ripple effects of the healing of attachment wounds also can extend into future generations.

Personality development, affect regulation, and integration of self. Viewing child development through the lens of Putnam's Discrete Behavioral States model (DBS; Putnam, 1997) can be very helpful in understanding the impact of trauma on an individual's development (see Arnold & Fisch, 2011 and various chapters in Dell & O'Neil, 2009 for additional information on how trauma impacts various aspects of development).

Personality development. According to the DBS, discrete states, or ways of being, are the building blocks of personality. A one-month-old has a very limited number of states: a quiet and focused state, sometimes referred to as "bright and shining eyes"; a "fussy" state; full-fledged crying; and two sleep states. When babies are hungry they will scream at the top of their lungs, with their faces scrunched up and arms and legs flailing. Once offered the mother's breast or a bottle, the state change is instantaneous as the body relaxes and contented murmurs replace crying.

As children grow, new states appear, and the number of possible behavioral pathways from which a child can go from one state to another become more complex. According to Putnam, personality formation is related to how much time an individual spends in particular states, how the individual switches between states, and the specific pathways between states that are more or less predictable for a specific person.

For example, my son is not a morning person. I have learned that, on a regular basis, an irritable state immediately follows a sleeping state, and that I should wait until he switches to a more content, alert state before attempting to talk to him about anything significant. To use another example, I have discovered that when I am physically ill, I am prone to feelings of depression with which I do not usually struggle. Understanding that this is the result of the unique way my particular pathways have been formed helps me to gain perspective, knowing that once I feel better physically my mood will also improve.

The normal process of personality development, however, breaks down for children who have been traumatized, because the regular states do not adequately provide the means to deal with the horror, fear, guilt, shame, pain, and other intense emotions that are associated with abuse. Therefore, discrete trauma states are created to help cope with the situation. These states can then be reactivated following a triggering stimulus. If they are entered into regularly, such traumatic responses can become "hardwired" through neurobiological processes (Siegel, 2003) and can ultimately evolve into behavioral or personality traits.

Understanding that trauma states can be reactivated helps to explain some of the posttraumatic intrusive symptoms discussed in chapter one and sheds some light on why the attempts of adult survivors to protect themselves are often inadequate. Take Cindy, for example, a woman abused as a child who has a black belt in martial arts. One evening as Cindy is leaving the studio after teaching a class, she is assaulted and raped in the parking garage. Instead of using the skills she ably demonstrated only ten minutes previously, Cindy becomes paralyzed, having entered a trauma state that was created when her father sexually molested her decades before. Let's look a little more closely at the reasons behind Cindy's inability to make use of her skills.

In both chapter one and the beginning of this chapter we discussed how the posttraumatic symptom of hyperarousal prepares trauma survivors for a fight-or-flight response to perceived danger. In some trauma states survivors are hyperaroused, but when they enter other trauma states they may instead be in a "freeze" mode. Just as the deer that freezes in your car headlights is more likely to get hit, so too a freeze response does not generally protect complex trauma survivors from further harm. As children such individuals learned that there was nothing they could do to stop the abuse; that is, they learned that they were helpless,[7] and this, along with fear, became encapsulated in a trauma state. This explains why Cindy was not able to make use of her expertise in martial arts. Thirty-year-old Cindy would be more than capable of defending herself, but when in that trauma state she feels as though she is seven years old again, the age at which she first experienced sexual assault and was helpless to stop her perpetrator.

Affect regulation. Newborns have no ability to regulate their states on their own. They are totally dependent on someone else to fix whatever is wrong by picking them up when they are crying, changing their diapers, and so on. As children grow, they develop an increasing capacity to deal with distressing feelings. Sucking a thumb or pacifier or deriving comfort from a favorite toy or blanket are examples of a developing ability to self-soothe. Similarly, while caregivers may rock babies to quiet them, thus regulating their affect by helping them go from a state of distress to one of calmness or sleep, older children can be seen rocking themselves back and forth when they are upset.

Attuned caregivers, then, have the ability not only to calm children down, thereby helping them to develop a sense of safety and security, but also to help children learn how to manage their own emotions. We do not anticipate one-year-olds to be capable of calming themselves down, but we expect five-year-olds to be farther along in the process, and we assume that adults are fully able to control their emotions and associated behavior.

For example, if dinner will be ready in fifteen minutes, most parents would expect five-year-olds to be able to cope with the delay without

---

[7]The concept of learned helplessness was first discovered as a result of Seligman's research in the 1970s. See Maier & Seligman, 1976 and Seligman (1972).

throwing temper tantrums. The ability of young children to actually do so, however, is facilitated by caregivers who have helped their children develop the capacity to delay gratification. This can be done by many means, including distracting them from their hunger pangs, teaching them the beginnings of appropriate self-talk (e.g., "It's okay, Dolly. I know you're hungry, but if you eat something now you won't be hungry for dinner, and dinner will be ready soon!"), and disciplining them whenever they lose control of their anger. Over time, if caregivers consistently respond in appropriate ways, children continue to increase their capacities to control their emotions. The result is grown children who have developed enough inner resources to enable them to deal with a distressing state, such as hunger, over an extended period of time.

Early childhood trauma disrupts the process of learning to regulate affect both directly and indirectly. As mentioned earlier, if parents are the perpetrators, an insecure, disorganized attachment style often develops, because the source of both safety and danger reside in the same person. In addition to the impact of the abusive behavior itself, parents who maltreat their children are often deficient in other aspects of parenting even when they are attempting to parent well. For example, such parents tend to have difficulty helping children acquire control over their behavior, are not proficient at recognizing and tracking their children's states, lack the ability to intervene in ways that help disrupt inappropriate states in their children, and are poor role models of self-control (Putnam, 1997).

Difficulties with affect regulation are a symptom of many psychological problems. For example, anxiety disorders, depressive disorders, impulse control disorders, attention deficit disorder, obsessive-compulsive disorder, PTSD, psychotic disorders and personality disorders (to name a few) all have affect dysregulation as a component (Bradley, 2000). Attempts to compensate for deficits in state regulation can also lead to posttraumatic avoidance symptoms and/or addictive behaviors.

Integration of self. Integration of information, memory, affect, and behavior across states is essential to healthy functioning. In my attempts to teach our children to respect me and their father, I trust that in the process they are learning to respect teachers, employers, and people in general. Similarly, I hope that the etiquette around eating that is drilled into them at home is not forgotten when they eat at friends' houses. In other words, I expect the information they learned in one state and context to generalize so that their behavior is positively impacted in another state and context.

As children develop, integration is also evident as the states become less discrete. So rather than going from acute distress when hungry to pure contentment when presented with a good meal after being hungry, a healthy adult's mood will gradually and less obviously shift as hunger is satiated. When integration takes place as it should, adults will be aware of their various states, have the ability to seamlessly switch from one state to another, and have a sense of themselves as a unified, continuous whole.

Trauma disrupts the process of integrating functions across states. It is difficult for traumatized individuals to retrieve information learned in other states when they are in a traumatized state. The example cited previously of the woman who was unable to use her martial arts training because a trauma state was activated illustrates such interference. In addition, abused children are often threatened with worse consequences if they reveal their trauma. The maintenance of such secrets requires the separation of states because children are forced to keep aspects of their lives distinct. Therefore, in any particular state, adults who were traumatized as children may not be aware of all of their other states. They are also less likely to have developed a unified, integrated sense of identity. For the traumatized person the sense of "what is me," "what sort of seems like me," and "what is not me" is less certain.

In summary, healthy attachment bonds between primary caregivers and infants are essential for the formation of a sense of safety and security in relationships in adulthood. The same attuned and responsive caregiving behaviors that result in securely attached children and adults also help personality to form in healthy ways, making possible the ability to regulate affect and to develop an integrated sense of self. Conversely, adults who were abused as children are more likely to be insecurely attached, with negative relational consequences. They may also have created trauma states, which then impact overall personality development, resulting in less ability to regulate affect and a less integrated sense of self.

Attachment, trauma, and the developing brain. *Interpersonal neurobiology* is an interdisciplinary approach that links knowledge of the developing brain with that of the infant attachment process.[8] This is a very complex subject, but I will point out some of the general research findings

---

[8]In this section I have drawn on the following resources: Siegel (2003, 2009) and Schore (2003, 2009).

because they complement so well the above discussions on attachment theory and the DBS model.

There is a genetic basis for how the brain develops, but according to interpersonal neurobiology, stimulation from one's environment and interpersonal interactions are also important, particularly experiences related to the interaction of infants and their caregivers during the first two years of life. These years are the most crucial, both for how the basic circuitry of the brain is laid out and for the development of attachment relationships. As infants and caregivers interact, new neural connections are formed in the infant's brain and existing ones are strengthened in response to the relational experiences. Over the course of development, these neurons form differentiated yet interconnected pathways that ultimately allow the brain to carry on functions such as attention, perception, memory, and emotional regulation.

The infant-caregiver interaction has been found to most directly impact the development of the right side of the brain, which is involved in the regulation of emotions. When the caregiver is appropriately attuned and responsive to the distressed infant, the fear response is modulated, positively impacting the limbic system in the right side of the brain. However, if the caregiver is unresponsive or abusive, it sets off an alarm reaction in the right side of the brain. Initially this results in hypervigilance as the autonomic nervous system is activated. A later, second response is dissociation, where infants disengage from the external world and shut down physiologically.

Left-brain functions develop later. In contrast to the primal, emotionally based reactions of the right brain, the left brain is about "linear processing using linguistics in a logical fashion" (Siegel, 2003). It is the part of the brain that makes it possible to tell a story about one's experience. However, in order to come up with a coherent autobiographical narrative, the left brain needs to draw on the emotional memory stored in the right side of the brain. This requires neural integration between the two hemispheres. However, trauma interferes with neural integration. Brain studies of abused and neglected children, for example, have shown that trauma can impair the growth of the corpus callosum, the brain tissue that connects the left and right hemispheres. Therefore, early childhood relational trauma impedes the ability of children to properly integrate their experiences.

These neurobiological findings help to make sense of the psychological symptoms found in adults who were abused as young children. Difficulties with affect regulation, inability to tolerate stress well, memory impairment, psychosomatic difficulties, and dissociative disturbances are all consequences of alterations in how the right-brain limbic system matured due to trauma.

DISSOCIATION: GOD'S GIFT TO THE TRAUMATIZED CHILD

The word *dissociation* was only briefly mentioned in the above discussion on attachment and the DBS, so I will expand on it here. Dissociation is the psychological mechanism by which discrete states are kept separate and trauma states are formed (Lyons-Ruth, Dutra, Schuder, & Bianchi, 2006). The *DSM-5* definition of dissociation is "the disruption of and/or discontinuity in the normal integration of consciousness, memory, identity, emotion, perception, body representation, motor control, and behavior" (American Psychiatric Association, 2013, p. 38). The *DSM-IV* did not include the last three aspects, which refer to somatoform dissociation (i.e., dissociation that is specifically connected to the physical body) (Nijenhuis, 2009). I welcome the *DSM-5* addition of somatoform dissociation because acknowledging it has significant clinical relevance. Also, the *International Classification of Diseases*, the diagnostic system used by much of the world outside of North America, had long included the somatoform elements in its definition of dissociation (Escobar, 1995). Basically, dissociation can be conceptualized as compartmentalization or disconnection of aspects of self or experience. While I have already discussed how an abused child creates trauma states using the language of the DBS, I will now describe the same process using the concept and language of dissociation.

When the normal developmental, integrative process is disrupted through the effects of trauma, the person's inner states remain more discrete or dissociated. Also, if abuse is ongoing, not only are regular states not integrated, but trauma states can also continue to be created and expanded, resulting in even greater use of dissociation. Therefore, dissociation can be viewed as a psychological defense against the effects of trauma.

I believe that the physical pain and psychological torture that some of my counselees endured as children would have been so overwhelming that they would now be dead if it were not for their ability to dissociate. For this reason, many of my clients have come to see dissociation as God's gift to them in that it enabled them to survive.

Let me illustrate with an example. Six-year-old Mona is an incest victim. Her father regularly enters her bedroom in the early morning and rapes her, after which he sneaks back to his bed before the alarm goes off. The sound of the door opening is the trigger that puts Mona into a trauma state. Within that state is held the horrible realization that the very daddy who gives her nice toys and attends her soccer games is hurting her badly. The trauma state (or perhaps a combination of trauma states) also serves to compartmentalize the physical pain, terror, guilt, shame, and other devastating emotions associated with the abuse.

The ability to dissociate in this way serves Mona well. With the click of her bedroom door closing as her father leaves her bedroom, Mona immediately switches out of the trauma state. If this state is completely discrete, Mona will not even remember the horror that took place only minutes before. This means that when faced with the incongruous situation of having to sit down at the breakfast table with her family, including her perpetrator, Mona is able to act as though nothing is amiss. Furthermore, she can go to school, get good grades, and look as though she is a well-adjusted child. In time, however, the very mechanism that helped her navigate these atrocities will create social and emotional difficulties as a result of dissociative symptoms.

THE LEGACY OF CHILD DEVELOPMENT

This chapter has focused both on healthy child development and the negative impact of early childhood trauma on development. But what happens when these children become adults?

While a normal, healthy developmental process in childhood is not a guarantee of psychological health in adulthood, it serves to increase the chances that an individual will be relatively emotionally healthy. In Matthew 7:24-25, Christ tells the parable of a wise man who built his house on a rock so that it would stand firm in times of storm. While this passage refers to building a solid spiritual foundation, the principle also can be applied to the laying of a solid psychological foundation for life. Children who develop a secure attachment style are predisposed to successfully navigate intimate relationships as adults. Both the neural networks and psychological mechanisms that are in place will allow them to appropriately regulate emotion and integrate their experiences. As adults, these individuals do not generally dissociate to any great extent. While they play different roles at various times (e.g., spouse, parent, employee), they can navigate easily between these, resulting in a cohesive sense of self across different roles and relationships.

It is still possible for negative life experiences or trauma in adulthood to derail such individuals. However, the solid foundation built in childhood will help them be resilient in the face of life's challenges and losses so that they will be able to weather all but the most severe of storms. By contrast, adults who were traumatized as young children are at a disadvantage. It is as though their houses have been built on the sand (Mt 7:26-27). Without the development of secure attachment, they are less equipped to manage intimate relationships. The hardwiring of their brains is faulty, and they do not have the psychological mechanisms in place to regulate their emotions or integrate their experiences. Dissociation is used more frequently to compartmentalize cognitive knowledge, affect, or other aspects of traumatic experiences or negative events, resulting in a less cohesive sense of self. When the storms of life come their way, such individuals do not have the resources to cope. Their "houses" fall flat.

Fortunately, humans are amazingly resilient; adults, even those with traumatic backgrounds in childhood, can change. Neural networks continue to develop throughout life, and faulty psychological mechanisms can be unlearned and new ones developed. In other words, faulty foundations can be repaired, and a solid structure can be built. The rest of this book seeks to address how we can facilitate the process of helping victims of childhood trauma rebuild their foundations so that they can become integrated wholes, establish healthy relationships, and find a sense of spiritual well-being.

3

REBUILDING THE SHATTERED SELF

The Process of Counseling

BEFORE DEVELOPING THE DETAILS of specific therapeutic techniques, I think it is important to get a bird's-eye view of the overall process of treatment for clients with C-PTSD. To walk with someone from the beginning of their healing journey to the point when they no longer need intensive therapy is a long process, spanning not months but years. The reality is, though, that either the counselor or the client may not have the luxury of that amount of time; people move, they change jobs, they have babies, health insurance benefits run out, clients get discouraged, or therapists shy away from the emotional intensity inherent in trauma work. There are countless factors that could potentially interfere with a counselor and client completing the entire journey together.

Regardless of the length of time a counselor and C-PTSD client work together, understanding the whole process can make a considerable difference in how therapy proceeds. For example, it can impact whether or not a counselor will take on a client in the first place. Or if a therapeutic contract is entered into, it can affect what the counselor commits to, the immediate and longer-term goals, the appropriateness of specific techniques, the timing of interventions, the frequency of sessions, and decisions around termination and/or referral.

Parenting serves as an analogy—though an imperfect one—since raising a child is also a long-term process. When my sons were preschoolers, most of my energy was taken up with tending to their immediate needs while trying to keep myself sane in the process. (Sometimes that is what doing counseling feels like too!) Developmental milestones were worked toward and celebrated: sleeping through the night, learning to feed themselves, taking first steps, saying first words, using the toilet, tying shoelaces, beginning to share toys, learning to wait for food. Yet these goals were not ends in themselves. Each skill was developed in the overall context of their growth toward adulthood. I have had to substantially change the way I mother over time to adapt to my sons' changing needs. But what has remained constant all along, even now that two of them are young adults, is that I have worked toward the ultimate goal of helping them become mature, responsible men who love God, love others, and will hopefully make a difference in the world. I think God works with us in these ways too. His ultimate desire is that we become more like Christ, but what he uses to help get us there varies depending on where we are in our faith journeys at any given point in time.

As Christian counselors working with C-PTSD clients, we need to keep the overarching goal in mind, even as we are sensitive to the current needs and capabilities of our clients. That way, if we do stick with a particular counselee over the long haul, we know we are headed in a fruitful direction. However, even if God uses us for only a brief time in a client's life, we will be appropriately preparing our client for the next phase of the healing process, whether or not that involves further therapy.

In this chapter I will first discuss assessment of clients for complex PTSD, including an extensive discussion of dissociative symptoms. I will then give an overview of the three phases of treatment for C-PTSD.

ASSESSING FOR C-PTSD

Before counselors can appropriately treat complex trauma survivors, they need to determine if their clients are actually struggling with C-PTSD. Whether informal or formal procedures are used, assessment is important.

There are the occasional counselees who know that they have a trauma history and enter therapy with the express intention of working through the trauma. Often, however, C-PTSD clients come to counseling for apparently unrelated reasons such as marital conflict, difficulties at work, or difficulty sleeping. Also, many psychological disorders, such as major depressive disorder, various anxiety disorders, dissociative disorders, personality disorders,

ASSESSING FOR C-PTSD
- Listen for trauma history
- Conduct a formal assessment
  - SIDES or SIDES-SR
  - TEC
- Watch for dissociative symptoms

eating disorders, and substance abuse or dependence are comorbid (occurring together) with C-PTSD, further complicating the assessment process (Ross, 2000). What uninformed clinicians may miss is the possible association between these disorders and a history of complex trauma.

Listen for trauma history. Some clinicians routinely assess for trauma with all their clients, including administration of written trauma assessment tools. I discuss formal assessment below, but I prefer to do a less formal assessment initially. For example, when inquiring about family background, I will listen for hints of abuse or neglect and follow those up. Counselors must be careful to not be suggestive, but instead ask general questions about whether clients have ever been harmed as children or whether they have experienced other potentially traumatic events in either childhood or later on in life. Of course, clients may deny a history of trauma even if they have C-PTSD, because they have amnesia for the events, they do not recognize the difference between appropriate parental discipline and abuse, or they minimize the impact of their experiences. However, at least asking clients about trauma can give counselors some potentially valuable information.

Formal assessment for C-PTSD. There are many assessment instruments available for help in making a PTSD diagnosis, but fewer that assess specifically for C-PTSD. The Trauma Center at Justice Resource Institute offers a trauma assessment package that covers the spectrum of types of trauma. The cost for the package includes scoring software. The instruments specifically developed to assess C-PTSD are the Structured Interview for Disorders of Extreme Stress (SIDES) and the Self-Report Instrument for Disorders of Extreme Stress (SIDES-SR). More information can be found on the Trauma Center website (traumacenter.org).

The Traumatic Experiences Checklist (TEC) and its scoring template are available in eight languages for free download from the website of its

developer, Ellert Nijenhuis (enijenhuis.nl). The TEC is a self-report instrument that identifies potentially traumatic experiences as well as clients'
subjective sense of the impact of any of the items they endorsed.

Dissociation as an indicator of C-PTSD. Clients frequently initially deny
or minimize a trauma background. Dissociative symptoms, however, can be
viewed as indirect indicators of possible childhood trauma. For this reason,
it is important to be able to recognize indicators of dissociation even when
there is no reported trauma history.

ASSESSING FOR DISSOCIATION

In addition to dissociative symptoms potentially being signs of a previous
trauma history, in the chapters that follow I will discuss how counselors can
treat C-PTSD by making extensive use of their clients' abilities to dissociate.
Therefore, assessing for dissociation is crucial. In this section we will examine the concept of the dissociative continuum as a way of differentiating
normal versus pathological dissociation, what to look for with respect to
dissociative symptoms, and how identifying BASK components can indicate
use of dissociation. Formal and informal assessment procedures for dissociation and dissociative disorders will also be examined.

The dissociative continuum. Everyone dissociates to some extent, but
there are differences between these normal dissociative experiences and
more problematic, pathological dissociation. A counselor must recognize
the distinctions between the two. Dissociation can be conceptualized as a
continuum. Figure 3.1 indicates normal dissociation on the left-hand side,
some dissociative episodes in the middle, and dissociative disorders toward
the right-hand side. I will discuss normal dissociation first, followed by a
description of dissociative symptoms.

As illustrated by the DBS model, people have different states of being.
Therefore, everyone dissociates to some extent. A certain amount of dissociation is normal in that we are not fully aware of all aspects of our experience
at all times. When I ask students in a class, "How many of you have ever
gotten out of the shower only to wonder if you washed your hair?" the vast
majority sheepishly acknowledge that this has happened to them. With reference to figure 3.1, washing one's hair could be considered an automatism—
that is, a behavior that is repetitive so does not take undivided attention to
perform. If individuals do not remember whether or not their hair was

NORMAL CONSCIOUSNESS	DISSOCIATIVE EPISODE	ACUTE STRESS DISORDER (UP TO 4 WEEKS)	POSTTRAUMATIC STRESS DISORDER (4 WEEKS+)	DISSOCIATIVE DISORDER	OTHER SPECIFIED DISSOCIATIVE DISORDER (OSDD)	DISSOCIATIVE IDENTITY DISORDER
• highway hypnosis • ego states/self-states • automatisms • childhood imaginary play • absorption • daydreaming	• religious experiences (e.g., meditation, ecstatic experiences)	• flashbacks • numbness, detachment • absence of emotional response • reduced awareness of surroundings (dazed) • derealization • depersonalization • amnesia for aspects of the trauma		• Dissociative amnesia (with or without dissociative fugue) • Depersonalization/derealization disorder	• DID • Polyfragmented DID	• OSDD (with features of DID, dissociative trance, etc.) • Polyfragmented OSDD

Figure 3.1. Continuum of dissociation. *Source: Adapted from Braun (1988).*

washed, some aspect of the entire experience of having a shower was not integrated, and therefore was dissociated. Similarly, it is not uncommon to get so absorbed in a task, such as writing a school assignment or reading a novel, that minutes or even hours go by unnoticed.

Highway hypnosis is another example of normal dissociation. This term refers to the experience of driving a car on an uncrowded stretch of road, being startled back to reality, and realizing that while your body was driving the car, the rest of you was focused elsewhere! Daydreaming is also an example of not being fully aware of what's happening around you.

Religious experiences can be dissociative in nature, such as being caught up in worship so that you are not even aware of the other people around you. An intense time of prayer or meditation are likewise examples of times with God that are so intense, nothing else seems to matter.

None of these dissociative experiences would be considered dysfunctional unless taken to an extreme. If, for example, a mother gets so caught up in writing her school paper that she is oblivious to the needs of her toddler, the child could be in danger. A phrase I heard in my church circles growing up, "He's so heavenly minded he's no earthly good," also describes dissociation that is problematic. Similarly, if someone daydreams to the extent that they cannot fulfill their responsibilities, the situation is very different from one in which daydreaming is an occasional, even relaxing, occurrence.

It is normal for children to dissociate more than adolescents, and adolescents more than adults, with the degree of dissociation leveling off after early adulthood (Ogawa, Sroufe, Weinfield, Carlson, & Egeland, 1997). These research findings make sense given our previous discussion on how healthy attachment figures play an essential role in helping children to integrate information and behavior across states. When states are not integrated, they are, in effect, dissociated. I still remember my seven-year-old niece becoming distraught when I sat on her imaginary pet dinosaur! The dinosaur

ASSESSING FOR DISSOCIATION

- Dissociative continuum
- Symptom observation
- BASK model
- Formal assessment
- Informal assessment

was not real, but my niece could see it clearly. The ability to use fantasy in this way is normal for children. However, if my niece—now in her twenties—continued to treat this object of her imagination as real, it would be evidence of a potential psychological problem.

One of the exceptions to this general rule that adults dissociate less than children is in cases of creative individuals who retain an ability to dissociate because it helps them perform. So, for example, actors can sometimes use their dissociative abilities to help them better portray a character. Painters, musicians, athletes, and anyone who excels at a highly focused activity may sometimes enter a "zone" that is dissociative in nature. If not problematic, the increased use of dissociation by these adults would not be considered pathological.

Symptom observation. Watching out for dissociative symptoms in the midst of regular therapeutic work is one way to identify that a counselee may be exhibiting dissociation that is problematic or pathological. The *DSM-5* outlines four dissociative symptom areas: amnesia, depersonalization/derealization, identity confusion, and identity alteration. Depersonalization and derealization were categorized as separate symptoms in the *DSM-IV* but have been combined in the *DSM-5*. Anyone can experience mild forms of these symptoms, which are better described as normal dissociative experiences. However, moderate or severe dissociative symptom levels are more indicative of psychopathology.

Child abuse or neglect under the age of six is most highly linked to dissociative disorders, particularly DID, because, as has already been discussed, the younger the child, the less developed his or her ability to modulate between states. This does not mean that early childhood trauma will necessarily result in DID; rather, in order to develop DID, the trauma almost always needs to have occurred below the age of six. While not all individuals with trauma histories will necessarily meet diagnostic criteria for a dissociative disorder, they may still exhibit significant dissociative symptoms. Although dissociation is not always listed in the *DSM-5* criteria for other disorders, dissociative symptoms are actually common to many disorders, including psychotic disorders, anxiety disorders, depressive disorders, somatoform disorders, and personality disorders. Whichever diagnostic category may best fit a trauma survivor, identifying dissociative symptoms in such clients can be of immense help in the treatment process.

Following is a description of the four *DSM-5* symptom areas mentioned earlier. I will use the case study of Mel to illustrate how these dissociative symptoms manifested in her life. Mel is a freshman I interviewed for a research project. At the time of the interview, she was attending a prestigious university in the Philippines. Mel was a research participant, not a counselee, and despite considerable internal distress and struggles with managing her day-to-day activities, she managed to function well enough to continue with her studies. Mel's symptom profile (severe amnesia, severe depersonalization, severe derealization, severe identity confusion and severe identity alteration) fits that of DID. However, with the exception of identity alteration, the dissociative symptoms that Mel describes are similar to what many of my clients with C-PTSD experience, even those who do not fit diagnostic criteria for a dissociative disorder.

SYMPTOM OBSERVATION

- Amnesia
- Depersonalization/derealization
- Identity confusion
- Identity alteration

Amnesia. Clients experiencing this symptom have specific and significant memory blocks for time that has passed but cannot be accounted for. This is a very common symptom for survivors of all kinds of traumatic experiences, including single-episode events. For example, counselees may acknowledge that they have almost no childhood memories or that they do not remember much of anything from the ages of eight to ten. If counselors ask careful questions, they may discover that there are current memory gaps for hours or days at a time. Difficulties with memory may also take the form of frequently forgetting to do daily activities such as go to class or work. Some may have people approach them who call them by name, but whom they do not recognize. While anyone can experience these types of things from time to time, it is not a regular occurrence for individuals who are not highly dissociative. Amnesia is the main symptom of the disorder dissociative amnesia.

Mel persistently experiences difficulty with her memory. She cannot remember large periods of time from the past and the present, and describes these memory gaps as happening "almost all the time." She forgets her friends' and professors' names, and does not remember meeting her class-mates, which, in a group-oriented culture, is more unusual and problematic than it would be in a more individualistic, Western culture. Mel often forgets how old she is. She has a great deal of difficulty remembering what she has studied, but to her amazement, when she takes multiple-choice exams, she exclaims, "I'm very good at guessing the answers." Mel's exam-taking experience is an example of how information can seep through from one state to another. In this case, the state she was in when she studied was not totally discrete from the state she was in when she took the exam, even though there were obvious difficulties in integration between states.

Depersonalization/derealization. While depersonalization and derealization have been combined into one symptom area, they manifest in different ways. They will, therefore, be described separately.

Depersonalization involves a sense of detachment from self that can take many forms. For some, depersonalization involves going through the motions of life while feeling like a robot. Others may watch themselves as though from an outside stance. For example, if I were experiencing an episode of depersonalization, I would see myself typing on my computer as though I were another person in the room, looking on. The sense of alienation from self could also take the form of looking in the mirror and having no felt sense that the image looking back is actually me. It could also take the form of distortions in how I view my body. I could perceive my hands, for example, as either bigger or smaller than they actually are. Severe depersonalization is the primary symptom experienced by those with depersonalization disorder.

Mel sometimes experiences depersonalization when she draws or paints, saying that it is "like I was painting, but the strokes don't come from me." The finished product is also not typical of her usual style. Additionally, when Mel writes, she does not feel as though she is the one in control of the writing. She asks, "Okay, why did I write these things? The feeling was a different feeling—I felt different . . . It's like a continuous flow, and I keep on ranting about things, and I wasn't thinking, I don't know—it's like [my] hand moving and—I don't know." But the resulting poems have been good enough that her classmates have actually bought her poetry.

Mel also experiences emotional outbursts or rapid changes in mood that feel out of her control and seem unusual to her. At these times she feels disconnected from both her body and her behavior, as though she is watching someone else throw a temper tantrum. When Mel looks down at her body, she sometimes sees her hands and feet as though she is viewing them from a different perspective—as though "my neck should be higher [from my current position] in order to receive that kind of angle."

Unlike depersonalization, where the perceptual distortion has to do with how individuals experience themselves, when experiencing *derealization*, their surroundings or other people seem strange or unfamiliar. Sometimes dissociative clients have told me that they know I am their therapist, but that I seem different somehow. Others have told me that they got lost on their way home from the session because their neighborhood seemed unfamiliar and it took them a while to figure out which house was theirs. Daydreaming is an example of derealization if what is viewed in the daydream seems more real than what is actually there.

Mel has been told by her family that she slept through class during most of kindergarten and that her grandfather had to take down her class notes. But Mel says, "I know I wasn't asleep . . . I felt like I was awake . . . the classroom was different . . . it was like cloudy." At various times in her life Mel would experience other sensory abnormalities. She reports that sometimes "everything turns black," and "suddenly I can't hear things" for a few seconds until things return to normal.

Identity confusion. Highly dissociative individuals often struggle profoundly with their sense of self and identity. This makes sense given the lack of integration of states experienced by many dissociative individuals. With so much inconsistency, people can become very confused as they try to sort out who they really are.

Mel feels continually confused about who she is, and she struggles with what she really wants, to the extent that she experiences chest pains and headaches in the effort to sort it all out. Mel frequently imagines herself as another person in another world, as a way of trying to figure out if she would be happier as another person doing different things from what she does now.

Identity alteration. Those experiencing identity alteration assume different identities that are much more distinct than separate social or functional roles. Such individuals often feel as though they are a different person, get feedback from others that they seem like a different person, or give themselves different names. Their subjective experience of feeling as though they are different ages at various times is also a clue. Identity alteration is the distinguishing feature of DID. If there is a sense of internal separateness but those parts of self do not actually take executive control of the body, other specified dissociative disorder (OSDD)[1] may be a more accurate diagnosis.

Mel frequently gets feedback from others that she seems like a different person, and she sometimes feels as though she is a different person. She often finds things such as towels, pencils, and even underwear in her possession, as well as phone numbers in her list of contacts, that she neither recognizes nor remembers entering. While the latter could be an example of the symptom of amnesia, they all are indicators of identity alteration in that it is as though another person did those things. Mel often feels younger than her age. She says, "I act really childish sometimes . . . I play with toys for three-year-olds and still—I like video games a lot, going to arcades and stuff." Mel associates the name Mimi with feeling eight years old or younger, and reports that Mimi has tantrums. She associates the name Roland with feeling fourteen. Unlike Mimi, Roland is happy, carefree, and creative. When she feels like Roland, she says, "I'm a bit boyish." Rather than being interested in guys, wearing makeup or accessories, or reading the magazines other girls her age like to read, Mel states, "I'm more into comic books. I'm totally different." Seventeen-year-old Mel is composed, quiet, and responsible. Therefore, the contrasts in her behavior are quite marked.

Mel's counselor could be alerted to the need to conduct a more formal assessment with her by listening for how she describes her day-to-day life and by watching to see if there are any indications of her zoning out or of potential identity alteration. For example, while I learned of Mel's symptoms through asking specific questions about dissociative symptom areas, if she had been my counselee rather than a research study participant, Mel might have volunteered that she did not always like the things that other girls her age seemed to like, or that when she was journaling she did not feel connected to what she was writing. Few counselees are going to state outright that they are dissociative, because often they do not realize that they are dissociating, nor do they necessarily understand that not everyone experiences what they do.

---

[1]OSDD was known as dissociative disorder not otherwise specified (DDNOS) in the *DSM-IV.*

The BASK model. The BASK model is an alternative way to assess dissociation (Braun, 1988).[2] It does not rely on the *DSM-5* dissociative symptom
areas discussed above, but users look for other clues that an individual may
be dissociating. I believe that the two approaches are complementary.
Making use of both can be very helpful in identifying and understanding
individuals who are dissociative, whether or not they meet diagnostic criteria for a dissociative disorder. I will be referring to the BASK model
throughout this book. It is helpful not only in the assessment process but also
in conceptualizing the goals of therapy at each phase of the treatment process.

BASK is an acronym for Behavior, Affect, Sensation, and Knowledge, four
components of any experience. A child who, through the help of attuned
caregivers, develops the ability to integrate information and behavior across
states becomes an adult who appropriately integrates these components. For
example, a woman who is fully integrating her current experience as she
reads this book would be able to tell me later on that she was reading a
chapter on child development and trauma, but that she was distracted by her
eight-year-old coming home from school and wanting a snack. In other
words, she will have cognitive knowledge (K) of what has transpired. She
would also be able to describe her emotions of joy at seeing her daughter
again, alternating with her frustration at being interrupted (A). If her experience is fully integrated, upon being asked what physical sensations she was
experiencing at the time, she might mention that she was aware that her
lower back was aching from sitting in one position for too long and that
once her daughter asked for a snack she realized that she too was hungry (S).
She would also be aware that her daughter really did not deserve the edge
of impatience in her voice that was present as she reluctantly joined her child
in the kitchen. The following afternoon, she would be cognizant that she
chose not to begin reading a new chapter although her daughter was not
expected home for another fifteen minutes, because she did not want to be
interrupted again. Therefore, she was aware of her behavior (B). All BASK
components can be dissociated from each other, or just some of them.

Dissociative symptoms can help to make sense of some of the comorbidity referred to earlier in this chapter. The BASK model of dissociation can

---

[2]The concept of the BASK model and its components are Braun's. However, I have gone beyond
what Braun has written in terms of how the BASK model can be conceptualized and used
throughout the treatment process.

be of help in this regard. Take, for example, an undiagnosed male C-PTSD client who fits *DSM-5* diagnostic criteria for major depressive disorder and has no memory of trauma in his background. According to the BASK model, his depressive symptoms could be the result of affect (A) of which he is aware, that is dissociated from the cognitive knowledge (K) he has of the abuse of which he is unaware. Similarly, a client who has panic disorder may be unaware that her anxiety is actually an intrusive reexperiencing symptom that has been separated from its traumatic origins; once again the BASK "A" has been dissociated from "K." An example of comorbidity and a different BASK component could be a young woman with bulimia who has dissociated her binging behavior (B) from cognitive knowledge of her past child abuse (K). Similarly, a client with a somatoform disorder might have a presenting complaint of intermittent blindness, which could be interpreted as the physical sensation (S) component of the BASK model, and the cognitive knowledge of a traumatic event (K) being dissociated from the rest, perhaps as a result of a visual trauma trigger that the client unconsciously wants to avoid by becoming temporarily unable to see. All of these counselees have used dissociation as a means of protecting themselves from trauma that felt too overwhelming to deal with at the time it happened.

In cases like this, where there is amnesia for trauma, counselors may not know for sure whether their clients have C-PTSD or not, as traumatic memories may not become conscious until later in treatment. Under circumstances where it is clear that clients dissociate, I would proceed with initial stages of treatment, suspecting a trauma history but recognizing that if indeed there is such a history, it will be disclosed in time.

Again, care must be taken to not suggest to such clients that they have been abused. I have heard horror stories of therapists insisting to bewildered clients that they must have repressed memories of child abuse. This is unethical misuse of the implicit power present in the therapeutic relationship, as well as fertile ground for lawsuits. I educate my clients about dissociation, but when asked about why they dissociate I will say something like the following, provided my client professes Christianity: "There is likely some explanation for why you dissociate to the extent you do. But it looks as though you've been dissociating for many years, so I don't think there needs to be a big rush to figure it all out now. I believe that if you sincerely bring that question before God in prayer, he will reveal to you in his time anything that is important for you to know in order to be healed. Until that time, let's look at how you can get to the point of functioning better day to day."

Meanwhile, does the counselor treat for possible C-PTSD, or treat the symptoms of which the client is currently aware and for which they are seeking treatment? The immediate focus needs to be on the current symptoms and possible diagnosable disorder. For instance, it would be unethical not to utilize evidence-based interventions with a severely depressed client. Similarly, use of cognitive-behavioral approaches for the client with symptoms of panic disorder is imperative, as is behavioral management of food and eating disorder symptoms. If, as discussed above, these symptoms are actually dissociated affect or behavior, the processing of associated trauma memories would effectively deal with their root cause. However, as premature trauma processing is potentially dangerous, it is best to focus on stabilizing the symptoms, no matter how tempting it may be to get to the core issues. In the next chapter I will discuss some specific techniques for symptom stabilization that can be used in addition to standard cognitive-behavioral approaches by counselors who are tuned in to their clients' use of dissociation and the possibility of a C-PTSD diagnosis.

Formal assessment. There are some very simple tools for assessing dissociation. Fortunately, a number of the developers of these instruments have made them available free of charge for professional use.

Dissociative Experiences Scale-II (DES). The DES (Putnam, 1989) is one of the most commonly used instruments for assessing an individual's use of dissociation. It is a twenty-eight-item questionnaire that uses a ten-point Likert-type scale. It is not a diagnostic tool in that it measures both normal and pathological dissociation. It is scored by simply adding up the individual item scores and dividing by twenty-eight. This overall score can be helpful, but looking at responses to specific questions can also give the clinician a lot of information about the nature of a client's dissociative experiences. Best of all, the DES is public domain and is simple and quick to use. It is included in its entirety in appendix A.

Somatoform Dissociation Questionnaire (SDQ-5). The short form of the Somatoform Dissociation Questionnaire (Nijenhuis, Spinhoven, Van Dyke, van der Hart, & Vanderlinden, 1997) is another brief assessment tool that has only five items. Although it is focused on somatoform dissociation (i.e., the sensation (S) aspect of the BASK model), there has been a high correlation

FORMAL ASSESSMENT

- Dissociative Experiences Scale (DES)
- Somatoform Dissociation Questionnaire (SDQ-5)
- Structured Clinical Interview for *DSM-IV* Dissociative Disorders Revised (SCID-D)
- Dissociative Disorders Interview Schedule (DDIS)
- Multidimensional Inventory of Dissociation (MID)

between the SDQ-5 and psychological dissociation. If clients endorse several SDQ-5 items, follow-up assessment will be in order.

Structured Clinical Interview for DSM-IV Dissociative Disorders Revised (SCID-D). The SCID-D (Steinberg, 1993) is considered the gold standard for diagnosing dissociative disorders. Although it is based on *DSM-IV* diagnostic criteria, the changes to the *DSM-5* dissociative disorder criteria are not vastly different, so the SCID-D can still be very helpful. It differentially diagnoses dissociative disorders and PTSD (Welburn et al., 2003). It is a semi-structured interview from which an overall score is obtained as well as a specific diagnostic profile. The SCID-D is flexible enough to allow for follow-up questions. I have heard that a revision of the SCID-D updated to the *DSM-5* is being developed, but I have not been able find out any specific information. This instrument does have a cost involved.

Dissociative Disorders Interview Schedule (DDIS). The DDIS (Ross, 1997) has been updated to *DSM-5* criteria (rossinst.com/Downloads/DDIS-DSM-5. pdf). It has been used extensively to diagnose dissociative disorders as well as somatic symptom disorder, borderline personality disorder, and major depressive disorder. It takes less time to administer than the SCID-D as it is fully structured, with clients simply responding "yes" or "no" to a set of questions. Colin Ross, its developer, makes it available for use free of charge.

Multidimensional Inventory of Dissociation (MID). The MID (Dell, 2006) is a diagnostic tool differing from the other two in that it is a written questionnaire rather than an interview (although a follow-up clinical interview is required for a full diagnostic assessment). Adolescent and adult versions are available, and it has been translated into seven languages other than

English. The MID, along with an updated interpretive manual, is available without cost for professional use (mid-assessment.com/mid-and-manual).

Screening versus diagnostic instruments. With potential C-PTSD clients I would recommend use of the brief screening instruments at any point in the process of therapy, as counselors can use the results to educate clients about dissociation in general without pathologizing their use of dissociation. However, I would exercise caution before administering one of the diagnostic instruments early on in the therapy process. Sharing of a dissociative disorder diagnosis could unnecessarily precipitate a crisis in highly dissociative clients, who may feel extremely vulnerable when their dissociative disorder is revealed, thus offsetting any advantage to administering the instrument in the first place. These diagnostic instruments are most helpful if a therapist already suspects a dissociative disorder and is seeking a diagnosis, or when therapeutic work has sufficiently progressed to the point that clarifying whether or not a client has a dissociative disorder diagnosis might be helpful in planning further treatment.

Informal assessment. An alternative to using formal assessment tools is for counselors to become familiar enough with how dissociative symptoms tend to be experienced by individuals that they can watch for signs of them in their clients. One option is to verbally ask the types of questions that appear as items on the assessment instruments. For example, the SCID-D has an entire section devoted to assessing the dissociative symptom area of amnesia, with questions such as, "Have you ever experienced large gaps in your memory?" and "Do you ever have trouble remembering to do your day-to-day activities?" Similar questions can be asked informally in order to get a sense of whether a particular client is dissociating. Such informal methods can then be followed up with the screening tools or diagnostic instruments identified above.

THE THREE-PHASE TREATMENT PROCESS

Treatment for C-PTSD is conceptualized as occurring in three phases. The term *phase* is used instead of *stage* to imply an active rather than static process. The phases are overlapping, and clients may move back and forth between phases. However, each phase has a specific focus and particular goals, so it is helpful to identify which phase of treatment a particular client is in at a given time.

Why a phase-oriented model is necessary. The pioneers in work with
C-PTSD clients talked about ensuring client safety and the necessity of stabilizing symptoms. However, in the early years (the 1970s to the early 1990s),
counselors tended to quickly jump into encouraging their clients to process
the content of their flashbacks, nightmares, and memories. I confess to being
guilty of doing this very thing early on in my work with C-PTSD. In my
defense, that is what the experts taught me to do. This is small consolation
though when I look back at some of the detrimental effects of this approach
for some of my clients.

What I and other therapists discovered through experience is that the
processing of traumatic memories without adequate client preparation increased the risk of further destabilization. The thinking at the time was that
working through the memories would free clients from the power the traumatic events had over them. While this may have been an accurate as-
sumption for clients who stuck with the process long term, in the short term
such clients were sometimes so overwhelmed that they became totally inca-
pacitated, and at least for a period of time were not able to function at previous levels. Clients who formerly had been capable of employment sometimes were unable to function at their jobs. Others became suicidal for
extended periods of time and required hospitalization. Marriages sometimes fell apart as spouses were unable to cope with the exacerbated posttraumatic symptoms. Fortunately, the introduction of phase-oriented
treatment protocols has enabled C-PTSD clients to heal while minimizing
some of the previous risks.

Recently there has been pushback from some authors with respect to a
phase-oriented approach. De Joung et al. (2016), for example, argue that
evidence-based approaches to treating PTSD could be potentially helpful
without a stabilization phase. At this point, however, a phased approach
continues to be the accepted standard of care among mental health professionals who work with C-PTSD.

What the three phases involve. Judith Herman, in her classic book *Trauma
and Recovery* (1992/2015), first proposed a five-phase treatment model for
more complicated presentations of clients who had been traumatized in
various ways. Her original five phases since have been collapsed by others
into three. Therapeutic work within the structure of these three phases has
now become the current standard of care for C-PTSD clients, differing little

from what Herman first outlined. Various authors have labeled the phases differently and, depending on their theoretical orientation, have suggested differing techniques within each phase (Courtois & Ford, 2009). However, despite these variations, there has been consensus in the literature on the basic goals and tasks of each phase. I am going to refer to these phases by labels that describe their function: Phase I, safety and stabilization; Phase II, trauma processing; and Phase III, consolidation and resolution.

THREE-PHASE TREATMENT MODEL
- Safety and stabilization
- Trauma processing
- Consolidation and resolution

Phase I: Safety and stabilization. Intrusive posttraumatic symptoms are often what propel C-PTSD clients into therapy. It is hard to feel safe when flashbacks intrude upon waking hours, nightmares terrorize sleep, intense emotions arise out of the blue, and startled responses punctuate daily life. These clients have trouble trusting their own perceptions because everything seems chaotic. Highly dissociative clients can experience large memory gaps and other dissociative symptoms that only add to the overall confusion and sense that safety does not exist.

Counseling may be seen as a last resort. After all, developing a relationship with a therapist requires at least a minimal sense of trust in another person. When trauma has been inflicted at the hands of other people, trust, even in a counselor, is bound to be extremely fragile. If clients have been wounded by other counselors or religious leaders, however inadvertently, establishment and maintenance of the therapeutic relationship becomes even more problematic.

Nevertheless, for clients to take the risks that are inherent in the healing process, some sense of safety has to be present. As discussed in the previous chapter, individuals need a safe haven to which they can retreat and a secure base from which they can step out to explore their world. It is the counselor's role to help provide that sense of safety.

In many cases, posttraumatic symptoms are front and center, interfering drastically with daily life. The immediate goal, therefore, needs to be better functioning, which can be accomplished through stabilizing symptoms. To some extent, safety and stabilization go hand in hand. Without some level of trust, clients will be too fearful to step out in ways that will help make their symptoms more manageable. And as symptoms dissipate with the aid of good counseling, trust grows and with it comes an increased sense of safety.

Assessment happens during Phase I. If posttraumatic or dissociative symptoms are displayed, counselors need to determine whether their clients have PTSD or C-PTSD. Some clients may not exhibit symptoms until later on in Phase I. However, as all good counseling involves developing a sense of safety for clients, counselors may be doing Phase I work without knowing for sure if their clients have a trauma history.

Therapy with C-PTSD clients often does not progress beyond Phase I. Many factors determine how long this phase should last, but generally it will be months if not years for clients who are just beginning their journey of healing. If clients are partway through their healing process when they begin with a new therapist, the timeframe may be reduced.

Successful Phase I work is extremely important, whether or not clients ever go on to Phase II. Counselors should not feel badly if, for whatever reason, they do not have the opportunity to engage in Phase II work. However, how the Phase I work is done will be impacted by the counselor's knowledge of the overall healing process. Phase I work will be the focus of the next chapter.

Phase II: Trauma processing. Phase II is potentially quite dangerous as going too deep too soon can create a crisis situation. However, when an adequate foundation of safety has been laid in Phase I and symptoms have been stabilized, there is every reason to expect that Phase II will be navigated productively and with minimal risk.

Pacing is the crucial element of this phase. Processing of traumatic material needs to proceed at an intensity and speed that allows clients to function well between sessions. The techniques of symptom stabilization that have been the focus of Phase I will be invaluable here. The idea is for clients to be able to draw on coping mechanisms that have been practiced and have become well-established patterns even as they venture into new, scary therapeutic territory.

This work is not for the faint of heart, whether counselor or client. While clients will be limited as to the degree of healing they can obtain if they do not do the hard work of trauma processing, some choose to live out their lives within the constraints imposed as a result of this choice. However much we may want further healing for our clients, we cannot make this decision for them. Sometimes the emotional agony is simply not viewed as being worth it, even with the hope of something wonderful at the other end of the process.

Not every therapist is cut out for Phase II work. Even good counselors may not be able to handle their own emotional turmoil as they are forced to see the depths of depravity to which people created in God's image can go when they turn their backs on him and others. It is bad enough to witness the horror of abuses perpetrated by those who make no pretense of following Christ, but to see the destruction wreaked by individuals who purport to be Christians can be world-shattering. This counseling work somewhat resembles willingly diving into a dumpster of rotting garbage and staying there for long periods of time. It can be like entering hell and facing evil itself.

So why would any Christian counselor in their right mind be willing to walk on such unholy ground? It is because the light shines all the brighter the deeper the darkness. I have never been as aware of God's power as I have been when I have faced evil head-on. The horror and fear of entering the pit are more than compensated for by the Holy Spirit's presence, comfort, and guidance.

I have secular colleagues, wonderfully compassionate people and very skilled therapists, who do Phase II work. Honestly I do not know how they survive without relying on God for help and restoration, both for themselves and their clients. But as Christian counselors, we know where our help comes from: "My help comes from the LORD, the Maker of heaven and earth" (Ps 121:2). The knowledge that I have not been left to do this work on my own has made a huge difference. Many times I have drawn comfort and strength from Deuteronomy 31:6: "Be strong and courageous. Do not be afraid or terrified because of them, for the LORD your God goes with you; he will never leave you nor forsake you." It is when I solely rely on my own abilities, forgetting that God is the team leader, that Phase II work starts to feel unmanageable.

Phase III: Consolidation and resolution. Once symptoms are alleviated and trauma memories have been processed, there is still work to do. C-PTSD clients have to learn how to live as whole, healthy individuals. For some, this may involve further work on developing an integrated sense of self. For others, reintegration involves learning healthier relational patterns. Certainly Phase III provides an opportunity for the consolidation of the work of previous phases and an opportunity to end the therapeutic relationship well. After bemoaning the slowness of the healing process, one of my C-PTSD clients once remarked: "You know, as much as this is excruciatingly painful and seems to be taking forever, I think God knows what he is doing. If God had reached down and miraculously, instantaneously healed me, I wouldn't have known how to cope with being healthy! I think God knows that I need all these years to adjust to the changes. If they came any faster, I would be overwhelmed."

Wise words, are they not? Phase III work allows all the loose ends to be gathered up so that clients whose lives have been so shattered know how to face the world as whole individuals.

COMPONENT-BASED PSYCHOTHERAPY

A recently proposed alternate way of conceptualizing treatment of C-PTSD is component-based psychotherapy (CBP).[3] The developers of this approach argue that because skills and techniques used in one phase are re-utilized in other phases, it makes more sense to discuss the necessary components of treatment rather than identify phases. They describe four primary components: (1) relationship (focus on past and current relationships), (2) regulation (affect regulation and physiological regulation), (3) parts work (very similar to what I describe in this volume, where it is assumed that individuals have different parts of self that serve various functions or hold aspects of memory and can be accessed in therapy), and (4) narrative (trauma processing and meaning making). Ongoing attention to the therapeutic relationship is considered key to the success of working through each component.

I agree that these components are essential, but I would contend that CBP, for the most part, is still utilized within an implicit phase-oriented approach (which its advocates acknowledge). Proponents of most, if not all, stage- or phase-oriented models of psychology (e.g., models of development such as Erikson's psychosocial stages, Fowler's model of faith development, or Sue and Sue's model of racial and cultural identity

---

[3]See Hopper, Grossman, Spinazzola, and Zucker (2018) for a more complete description of CBP and its application to emotional abuse and neglect, and Pressley and Spinazzola (2017) for application of CBP in the Christian context.

development) caution that individuals move back and forth between stages; it is not a truly linear process.

The same is true of phase-oriented treatment of complex trauma. Attention to self-regulation, for example, is not only a Phase I task, but is also necessary in Phase II and will continue to be a focus to some degree in Phase III. However, if mental health professionals begin the counseling process with the component of narrative, a lot of damage can be done. While I have no argument with the components of CBP, I think that focusing on a phased approach is important. Therefore, I will be discussing all of these components, but I will place them within the phases in which they are generally most helpful.

WHAT COMES NEXT

In this chapter I have addressed assessment issues, including how to proceed in the case of a dual diagnosis and/or if the counselor is not clear whether or not a client has C-PTSD. I have also provided a rationale for using the three-phase trauma treatment model and outlined some of the dangers of not providing counseling for complex clients within that structure. In the next few chapters I will discuss in greater detail the logistics, techniques, and specific considerations of each phase of treatment.

4

PHASE I

Safety and Stabilization

PHASE I WORK REQUIRES CAREFUL ATTENTION as it lays the foundation for the other two phases. As mentioned in the previous chapter, moving prematurely into Phase II can be problematic, even dangerous. Some C-PTSD clients may not move beyond Phase I work.

When my children were little they loved to blow bubbles. Giggling, they would chase after some, cupping their hands in the hopes that one would float down and settle there. Of course, the bubbles almost always broke immediately upon contact. Once in a while, though, a bubble would last a few precious seconds before bursting.

Some C-PTSD clients are so wounded that they seem as fragile as those bubbles, in danger of imploding unless handled with extreme care. Others are more like diamonds. They catch the light, as do bubbles, and may look delicate but are actually very strong. Most are somewhere in between. The challenge for counselors is to identify and build on whatever strengths their counselees possess, while at the same time recognizing that in order to survive, such counselees often have had to hide any weaknesses behind a mask of pseudostrength. Laying a solid foundation of safety is the best way to ensure that fragile clients will not fall apart, that symptoms can be managed well, and that more resilient clients can shore up even greater strength in preparation for demanding Phase II work.

As safety—both actual safety and felt safety—is so critical to work with C-PTSD clients, the concept of safety will serve as the framework for this chapter. I will begin by examining safety within the therapeutic relationship, followed by safety from others, and finally, safety from self. Symptom management and emotional/physiological regulation will be discussed in the context of safety from self.

SAFETY WITHIN THE THERAPEUTIC RELATIONSHIP

■ Developing rapport
■ Becoming a safe person
■ Remaining a safe person

SAFETY WITHIN THE THERAPEUTIC RELATIONSHIP

The importance of establishing a solid therapeutic relationship is not restricted to C-PTSD clients; it is one of the foundational principles of counseling with anyone, regardless of presenting problem or diagnosis. However, work with C-PTSD counselees can present challenges to establishing and maintaining such a relationship, which we will discuss in terms of developing rapport, becoming a safe person, and remaining a safe person.

Developing rapport. There are unique challenges to developing rapport with those who have C-PTSD. For example, while war veterans or survivors of natural disasters might believe that the world is not a safe place, they may at least have derived comfort from others, even in the midst of the traumatic event. However, for C-PTSD clients, people such as parents, teachers, pastors, church members, friends, spouses, and sometimes previous counselors, all of whom were supposed to be safe, were the very source of their trauma and pain. Those who were not direct perpetrators may also be suspect because they did not serve as protectors. This could happen, for example, in the case of children who were not abused by their parents but who assumed that their parents knew what was happening to them and ignored it.

My colleague Robert Muller expresses the dilemma facing complex trauma survivors well in his book *Trauma and the Struggle to Open Up*. In the introduction he states, "We see what a double-edged sword relationships are. Trauma stems *from* them. Recovery depends *on* them. The most harrowing trauma happens in close relationships, but recovery can't happen in isolation. Relationships are both poison *and* antidote" (Muller, 2018, p. 2).

It makes sense, then, that C-PTSD clients often will not know how to distinguish between safe and unsafe people, including whether a therapist is safe or not. Understanding this may help counselors be patient with their clients rather than label them as uncooperative or resistant. Their past experiences have taught these counselees that even people who appear safe are actually dangerous. Therefore, the struggle to trust a therapist is not so much an attempt to avoid personal therapeutic work as it is a legitimate safety concern. Instead of pathologizing the difficulties with trust, counselors should normalize this struggle for C-PTSD clients so that the guilt many of them feel for their chronic difficulties in this area can be potentially alleviated.

One of the common errors counselors make when seeing C-PTSD clients is setting aside the foundational counseling skills they generally use, assuming that specialized techniques are necessary. Of course that is true to a point. However, any such advanced interventions will only be helpful if they are implemented by counselors who use well-developed, basic skills. Use of the facilitative conditions of empathy, respect, and authenticity are extremely helpful in developing a sense of safety. Empathy, the ability to fully enter into another's experience, can be communicated through accurate reflection of content and feelings. When counselees sense that counselors understand what they are going through and are fully present with them in the moment, rapport will steadily, even if slowly, develop.

Showing respect involves having a nonjudgmental attitude toward counselees. Rogers (1957) labeled this attitude "unconditional positive regard." Ultimately it means valuing counselees as people made in the image of God, however marred that image is. Sin is not condoned, but neither is the person condemned. As a general principle this sounds easy enough, but it may be more difficult to actually put into practice. For example, some C-PTSD clients may be promiscuous, perhaps even prostituting themselves. Others may be full of hatred or rage toward their perpetrators, which makes sense, but also toward others in their lives who unwittingly failed to help. Some may self-mutilate in repugnant ways. Counselors will likely have a harder time with some of these than others. Empathizing with counselees around these types of attitudes or behaviors can also greatly help counselors develop respect by allowing them to see past the problematic attitude or behavior to what motivates it.

An easy pitfall for counselors who already have some experience in treating C-PTSD is to assume that all C-PTSD clients are basically the same. This attitude shows disrespect; God created all of us uniquely, and we each have our distinctive stories. Counselees will balk at being forced into a box that does not fit their experience of themselves. This will impede the development of trust.

Finally, authenticity is important. C-PTSD counselees have very sensitive antennae for phoniness, even under the guise of professionalism. Being genuinely myself has been immensely helpful, particularly when working with this population. Sometimes allowing my tears to flow when clients are sharing intensely painful experiences does more than anything to show that I truly care for them. Of course, there are no guarantees as to how counselees might interpret high levels of authenticity, so it is important to process such interventions with them. For example, while most counselees have interpreted my tears as genuine concern, others have felt guilty for causing me pain.

Sensitive use of authentic humor can be of enormous benefit in developing rapport. C-PTSD clients are often in incredible pain—not a situation that is conducive to much playfulness in their lives. A little laughter can go a long way toward motivating clients to continue to come to sessions without totally dreading them.

Christ used the facilitative conditions masterfully. The story of Jesus and the Samaritan woman at the well is a good example (Jn 4:4-26). Christ showed profound empathy for this woman by discerning the deep spiritual yearnings that were masked by her promiscuous lifestyle. In offering her "living water" (Jn 4:10, 13), he not only recognized her need but also offered to meet it. Although her lifestyle was immoral, Christ did not condemn her. Instead, showing the utmost respect, he offered her an alternative but did not force her to choose relational and spiritual healing. Finally, Jesus showed authenticity. Not only was he genuine in the conversation as a whole, but at the end he revealed himself to her as the Messiah, the first time in the Gospel of John that he made this known to anyone. That Christ chose to share such significant information with a woman of ill repute is further evidence of his empathy, in that he must have recognized that she needed to know who he really was. It is also an indication of respect in that, despite her sinful choices, he saw her as worthy of this gift.

Finally, he risked authenticity despite the possibility of rejection. After all, she had not chosen to live in God-honoring ways in the past, and had even tried to start an argument about whether Jews or Samaritans were right about where they worshiped (Jn 4:19-20) in order to divert attention away from herself. Christ, however, did not allow himself to be sidetracked, but took the focus back to her need.

Christ interacted uniquely with different individuals, not placing them in boxes. How he interacted with the woman at the well, for example, was different from how he related to the rich young man (Mk 10:17-22). Jesus did not show the same level of authenticity with this man in that he did not reveal himself as the Messiah. In fact, by saying, "Why do you call me good? . . . No one is good—except God alone" (Mk 10:18), Jesus may have even steered him away from that thought. Through empathy, Christ must have known that this young man was not ready for that level of revelation. Jesus also understood that the young man's wealth was a barrier to following him (Mk 10:21). Yet Christ did not confront this directly, but respected him enough to let him make the choice to stay in pain and walk away.

While we cannot have the degree of insight into an individual that Christ had, a combination of sensitivity to the Holy Spirit and good training can certainly be helpful. Counselors who have not had adequate training in these foundational counseling skills, or who could use a refresher, should consult some skills-training books or take a course that focuses specifically on the development of counseling skills.[1] Without skilled application of these basic counseling principles, therapists are not likely to get very far with C-PTSD clients.

Becoming a safe person. Developing rapport with counselees serves the function of helping them feel safe within the counseling setting. However, even if counselees do feel safe, their trust may be displaced in that however well-intentioned, the counselor may not actually *be* a safe person for them.

Every client is unique. Respecting the God-given uniqueness of each counselee will go a long way toward not only developing trust, but actually being trustworthy. Unfortunately, in the absence of trust, damage can be

---

[1]*Skills for Effective Counseling: A Faith-Based Integration* (2016), a textbook that I coauthored with my husband, Fred Gingrich, and colleague Elisabeth Nesbitt Sbanotto, includes many exercises that individuals wishing to learn or enhance such foundational skills could go through on their own, checking their responses with the sample answers found in the appendix.

done. I know this firsthand. Flush with the excitement and sense of accomplishment from the successful completion of work with one of my first C-PTSD clients, I suggested to a new client, Rachel, that she could be healed within a year if she agreed to see me. Of course I had no business promising any such thing, but I wanted to give Rachel hope, and I thought I knew what I was doing.

BECOMING A SAFE PERSON
- Remember that every client is unique
- Know your limitations
- Give advance warning of change

We both worked diligently for many months to no avail. Rachel clearly wanted to trust me, and I was doing everything in my power to help develop a sense of safety so that she could. The problem was that I had blown it in that very first session. Because I had promised the impossible, and was thereby being disrespectful, Rachel, at some level, picked up that I was not a safe person for her to work with. Unfortunately she was right. Although the three-phase model had not been developed yet, I had been pushing Rachel toward trauma memory processing—that is, Phase II work. Looking back years later, I realized that had she been willing to go there, the high level of functioning she was experiencing at that time would have been severely compromised. Had I truly respected Rachel as a unique individual, I would have understood that she had a valid reason for her apparent therapeutic resistance. It is a serious error to assume that what worked well for one client will automatically be appropriate and helpful for other clients.

Know your limitations. While the source of much of my difficulty with Rachel was in my not recognizing that all C-PTSD clients are different, I also erred in another area: I lacked humility. While my knowledge of how to work with C-PTSD had vastly expanded over the previous years, there was a lot I did not yet understand. On the one hand, counselors who lack awareness of their limitations are not going to be safe for their clients. On the other hand, counselors who are inexperienced with C-PTSD but are honest with themselves and their clients about that and are willing to continue to get training or supervision can be of immense help to these clients.

Give advance warning of change. Part of what helps to develop a sense of safety is a sense of predictability. C-PTSD clients generally had little control over what happened to them in childhood. Both children and C-PTSD clients need structure and predictability. Therefore, any change in you, the counselor, or the structure of the counseling relationship is bound to be unnerving.

It took me awhile to realize that when a C-PTSD client commented on my haircut, or complimented me on a new outfit, they were not actually saying, "You look great!" but rather, "Are you the same person you were last week? I was starting to trust the counselor with longer hair, but now you look different. Maybe you've changed in other ways too!" Therefore, rather than saying "Thank you!" as I typically would under other circumstances, I now check it out further, saying something like, "What's it like for you to see me wearing something you haven't seen before?" Or, rather than a question, I sometimes make an intuitive empathic statement such as, "I'm guessing that you may feel kind of unsettled to see me in something new; maybe you're wondering if other things about me have also changed." It is important to listen for such subtle indicators that the therapeutic relationship may be in question. Explicitly addressing underlying concerns will help the survivor feel not only better understood, but also safer.

Similarly, it is important for counselors to give as much notice as possible if they are going to be away, if they need to adjust the day or time of a session, or if the counselor is moving and needs to refer the counselee to someone else. These kinds of situations are sometimes unavoidable but should be minimized as much as possible. When they do happen, counselors should process the change with the client. I sometimes dread telling C-PTSD counselees that I am going on vacation because it seems as though from the time I share the information until several weeks after returning, sessions are focused on anxiety that I might not come back. Over time, when I consistently reappear and reconnect, a sense of safety increases. What may at first glance seem like unhealthy dependency is actually a temporary but essential part of the healing process for these clients who may not have been able to rely on anyone previously.

Any change in the office setting is also crucial to process. I use office space in the counseling clinic at Denver Seminary where I am a professor. I always reserve the same room, but if counselees want to come in at a different day or time than usual I warn them that our usual space may not be available so that they are not caught off-guard.

Even apparently minor changes can create potential distress. Unbeknownst to me, the picture on the wall of the counseling room I generally reserve had been switched. Both of my clients that day immediately noticed it and were very disturbed. "Don't they realize that people with trauma backgrounds like me don't handle such changes well?!" one of them exclaimed. I mentioned the reaction of my clients to the clinic director who immediately apologized, saying she had not even thought about the potential impact on trauma survivors of such a minor change.

Remaining a safe person. Counselors may pay careful attention to the above safety conditions initially, particularly when counselees are obviously skittish. However, over time, with increased familiarity and a deepened sense of intimacy, counselors may not be as cautious about everything they say and do with these clients. It is also possible that counselors develop relational vulnerabilities as a result of difficulties in their personal lives, making them more prone to not recognizing issues of countertransference. Therefore, even counselors who have established good rapport with C-PTSD clients and who have previously been safe may become increasingly unsafe over time.

REMAINING A SAFE PERSON
- Keep appropriate therapeutic boundaries
- Consult
- Protect confidentiality
- Appropriately process therapeutic terminations

Keep appropriate therapeutic boundaries. Appropriate boundary setting is essential to both becoming and remaining a safe person for C-PTSD counselees. Seeing their neediness, even experienced counselors may be tempted to make exceptions for such clients, departing from their usual counseling practices out of their very desire to provide a sense of safety for their clients. Another true confession with regard to counselor error is a good example of this.

Simon did not present with any explicit posttraumatic symptoms. He was referred to me by his physician because of physical symptoms that were a nuisance, but for which no medical cause had been determined. He complained of tingling in his forearms, shortness of breath, heart palpitations, and sweaty palms, but had no subjective experience of emotional distress. I sensed that there was something amiss because of Simon's blunted emotional presentation, but as I was not very familiar with dissociation, I did not recognize it as dissociated affect (i.e., the "A" of the BASK model). I worked with Simon on recognizing feelings and inadvertently opened Pandora's box. Having blocked out his feelings for years, Simon now was overwhelmed with anxiety and depression to the point that he felt suicidal.

I wanted to keep Simon safe. I also felt somewhat responsible for his flood of emotion; after all, he had not been in this mess until he started working with me! So I gave Simon my home phone number to use when the suicidal impulses became severe. In my own defense, this was an era in which therapeutic boundaries were not as strongly encouraged. What I had intended as a temporary safety measure, however, turned into a nightmare of daily phone calls. I attempted to keep some semblance of boundaries, limiting the calls to ten minutes. However, I dreaded the hours before the phone inevitably rang, and after I hung up, I resented the fact that my privacy had been intruded upon. It took over a year (yes, I am sometimes a slow learner)—and the knowledge that if this pattern continued I would have to leave the counseling field altogether because of burnout—before I had the courage to set new boundaries. I had unknowingly set a trap for Simon and me. I wanted desperately to be a caring, Christian therapist for this hurting man. He needed safety, and I figured the onus was on me to keep him safe. Unwittingly I had tried to play God.

Simon did feel safe—that is, until I changed the rules and effectively turned his life upside down. Ironically, my very desire to be a safe person inevitably resulted in not remaining one. I learned two very hard but extremely important lessons from this therapeutic faux pas: first, do not promise what you cannot deliver, and second, if you make a mistake, rectify it immediately.

Degree of accessibility to the counselor is one boundary issue. While the example I gave had to do with phone contact, similar accessibility issues can be connected to text messaging, emailing, Skyping, reading client-generated written material between sessions, allowing for extended sessions, and adding sessions during crisis times. While counselees may desire unlimited time and attention, I have found that they respond well to the limits I set when those limits are explicit and clear, and alternatives are offered.

Christ modeled good boundaries. Even though Jesus had crowds of people clamoring for his attention, he at times left them with their needs unmet. For example, he often withdrew by himself to the mountains to pray (Mt 14:23; Lk 5:15-16; 6:12; Jn 6:15), and on other occasions, he left by boat to escape the crowds that were following him (Mt 8:18; 14:13).

Use of touch is another potentially dangerous boundary issue. Licensing laws vary, and mental health professionals differ with regard to what kind of touch is allowable under what kinds of circumstances, if at all. With C-PTSD clients this matter becomes even more perilous because the traumatic experiences they have encountered are often the result of inappropriate, destructive touch. Further complicating matters is that such counselees have often effectively lost any sense of personal voice or power, so that even if they give apparent consent to be touched, their agreement may be due to their inability to say no. After all, growing up they said what they had to in order to survive, including what their perpetrators wanted to hear. When it comes to physical contact, those with C-PTSD may be ambivalent—desperately craving touch, but at the same time feeling fearful of either being abused or having memories of abuse inadvertently triggered.

I sometimes use the analogy of a chainsaw with regard to touch. If there is a big tree to fell, a power saw can be of immense benefit. If, however, the chainsaw is not properly handled, both the one wielding the chainsaw and others in the vicinity can be injured or even killed. This does not mean that we should never use chainsaws. It does, however, behoove us to be extremely careful with them and make sure we are adequately trained in their use.

When counselees are in obvious distress, as C-PTSD clients often are, the impulse may be strong to spontaneously touch them in an attempt to show comfort or empathy. However, it is much better to use words of empathy in the moment, then afterward process what it was like for the counselee to *not* be touched. Conversely, if touch of any kind is used, it is important to talk about what impact it had on the client.

Years ago I came up with a spur-of-the-moment technique that allowed for some degree of physical contact with minimal risks. I named it a "pinky hug" (i.e., linking baby fingers together for a moment). I had forgotten all about it until Haley informed me that this had been one of the crucial turning points in the development of a trusting relationship with me. It allowed her safe touch with another human being that was not invasive, was not as formal as a handshake, and was also playful. I have used it since with other clients, also with positive results.

Consult. Due to the intensity of the work and its power to evoke countertransference in us as therapists, even seasoned professionals can lose perspective in their work with C-PTSD clients. Therefore, seeking consultation from others who are experienced in this type of work can be very helpful. Regular supervision is ideal, but if an ongoing relationship is not possible, then anything is better than nothing. When I first began doing this work, there were very few experts to draw on. I took advantage of any training opportunity I could and consulted by telephone when no one was available locally. For a period of time I met with two other female therapists in a peer supervisory relationship. We served as an accountability group, sharing both therapeutic concerns as well as our personal struggles to stay emotionally and spiritually healthy in the midst of seeing C-PTSD clients. Our times of prayer together were especially valuable. Asking for help when I needed it enabled me to remain a safe person for my counselees.

Protect confidentiality. It is not uncommon for many people to be involved in trying to help C-PTSD clients. Primary care physicians, psychiatrists, neurologists, pastors, lay leaders, friends, spouses, other family members, teachers, employers, and life coaches may all seek contact with counselors or vice versa. It is extremely important to ensure that informed, written consent is obtained before communicating with anyone not covered in the initial consent for counseling. Even an acknowledgment of seeing a specific client is a breach of confidentiality. Pastoral counselors or lay counselors who work within a church setting may be especially susceptible to inadvertently breaking confidentiality with church leaders who may expect that information is shared among pastoral staff. If this is the church policy, it is essential that counselees are explicitly informed of the limits to confidentiality and give their informed consent at the beginning of the process. Otherwise, counselees will feel betrayed, and the pastoral or lay counselor will not be perceived as safe. Of course, professional counselors are legally bound to keep confidentiality except where required by law to break it.

Appropriately process therapeutic terminations. I have seen numbers of complex trauma survivors who have felt abandoned by previous therapists because of the way in which terminations were handled. In each case the counselor decided to end the relationship, giving no more than two weeks' notice after having seen the clients for years. The counselors had often explicitly stated that they knew that healing from this kind of trauma would be a long-term process, and that they were willing for it to take as long as was necessary. In reality, they got impatient with the excruciatingly slow pace of change, blamed the client for not working hard enough, and ended the relationship. These counselors *had* been safe, sometimes for years, but had not remained safe. These prior retraumatizing experiences made my work with them so much more difficult, because no matter how long we had worked together, they were still waiting for me to similarly abandon them.

SAFETY FROM OTHERS

Trauma survivors, while they may be hypervigilant for some forms of danger, may not always recognize people or situations that put them at potential risk for retraumatization. Counselors need to help C-PTSD clients identify when they are at risk.

SAFETY FROM OTHERS
- Identifying healthy versus unhealthy relationships
- Helping clients find physical safety

Identifying healthy versus unhealthy relationships. As mentioned earlier, C-PTSD clients have particular difficulty distinguishing between healthy and unhealthy, safe and unsafe, or harm-free and toxic relationships. It is easy for them to discount their own internal warning signals with respect to individuals who have shown them some care and attention, in part because they are often so desperate for nurture, but also because they are aware that they could be sensing danger where there really is none.

I have found that intimate partner relationships within or outside of marriage are often unhealthy if not explicitly abusive physically, sexually, or psychologically. Asking about the nature of such relationships, or listening for indicators that all may not be well, can be important. I am a strong advocate for the sanctity of marriage, but there have been times that I have asked clients if they have considered a marital separation because the abusive cycles are so detrimental to them and their healing. I have found that they often feel indebted to their partners for "putting up" with them, or even saving their lives when they were highly suicidal. If abusive relationships are all an individual has ever known, he or she may not realize that there may be an alternative.

Those with C-PTSD tend to give up their personal power too easily, valuing others' perceptions over their own, even about what is best for them. This tendency makes C-PTSD clients especially vulnerable to spiritual and emotional abuse at the hands of pastors, lay counselors, and Christian leaders who are attempting to be helpful. When those in such positions of authority claim that God has told them what is best for C-PTSD survivors, especially when this conflicts with the survivor's intuitive sense of what is good for them, it can be very destructive.

If they are not careful, Christian counselors also can fall into a similar trap of unduly influencing their clients' choices, rather than helping them to discern the Holy Spirit's voice for themselves, thereby empowering them to make their own decisions. Counselors should certainly express concern for their clients' safety when they see indications that something is amiss. However, hard as it may be to watch people enter into or remain in destructive relationships, it is better to facilitate the process of helping such counselees to figure that out for themselves. For example, rather than tell a counselee that his mentor seems to be overly controlling, a therapist should ask him how he feels when his mentor makes certain demands. If he is able to express discomfort, the counselor could follow up the response with an empathic reflection that could help to reinforce the idea that perhaps something is wrong. Hearing their own words back from the counselor tends to have a stronger impact than merely verbalizing them in the first place.

Jesus did not always confront directly. In the Scripture passages discussed earlier we saw how Christ got his message across to the woman at the well and the rich young man in an indirect, gentle, yet clear way. Jesus also made good use of questions. In Mark 8:27-30, for example, Christ asked his disciples what others were saying about him, followed by whom they believed him to be, allowing them to come to their own conclusions. Jesus skillfully used parables as an additional means of conveying information in a way that would be less likely to illicit defensive responses. As these examples indicate, creative, indirect confrontation can sometimes be more powerful than a more straightforward approach. As relationships can be a sensitive issue around which C-PTSD clients often are confused and conflicted, such indirect approaches can be particularly helpful.

Helping clients find physical safety. Even when retraumatization is explicit, such as a counselee going to a family gathering and being raped by her uncle who also molested her as a child, counselors need to exercise caution in how they process this information in therapy. Insisting, for example, that the crime be reported to the police could destabilize clients who are not far enough along in their healing process to manage the posttraumatic symptoms that could be triggered through a police interrogation or court case. Of course, state or provincial reporting laws pertaining to a specific situation have to be taken into consideration in making such decisions.

It is difficult to see clients make decisions that put them at potential risk. For example, incest survivors may be conflicted about whether or not to attend a family gathering if a former perpetrator will be there. Counselors can help C-PTSD clients process the many issues involved in making a choice of whether to attend or not, but ultimately the decision has to be the client's, as either decision could have potential long-term consequences for them. Asking questions such as "What could help you to stay safe?" can provide opportunities for examining new options in respectful, noncoercive ways.

One of the most compelling reasons that counselors give for not sticking to appropriate therapeutic boundaries is that they are concerned for the safety of their clients. One such situation stands out in my mind due to the disastrous impact it had on the life and ministry of the counselor.

Cindy had been consulting with me for several months about her work with a C-PTSD client. She had been concerned about her client's safety from a religious cult the client had broken away from. The cult had been harassing her client, and Cindy was afraid that cult members might even kidnap her client in order to get her back. I, too, was concerned for her client's safety. But I was even more horrified to discover that Cindy had taken her client into her own home in an attempt to protect her. While currently this would be an offense that is reportable to the appropriate counselor licensing boards in the United States, in Cindy's context this was not an issue. It was, however, still a huge boundary violation.

I strongly expressed my apprehension to Cindy, advising her to help her client make alternate arrangements immediately. But then Cindy pulled the "God card." She informed me that she knew it was generally something to be avoided at all costs. In this case, however, Cindy and her husband had prayed relentlessly about her client's situation (her husband's involvement evidence of yet another ethical violation in that Cindy likely broke client confidentiality) and felt directed by the Holy Spirit to have her client move in with them. I continued to have deep reservations, but I left Cindy to make her own decision about this matter. Knowing that I disapproved, but coming up with a different excuse for her decision to stop contact with me, Cindy terminated our consultations.

Within six months I heard that Cindy had burned out to the extent that she left the counseling field completely. Several years later I had a chance to talk with Cindy again, allowing me to apologize to her for not having even more strongly insisted that she force her client to find another place to live. Cindy's response to me was that nothing I said or did would have changed her mind. She recognized that in her desperation to keep her client safe, and out of her own sense of helplessness, she had misinterpreted her own thoughts as God's voice. Hearing that I could not have influenced her decision, even had I been more insistent, assuaged my guilt to some degree, but did nothing for my sadness that the Christian counseling world unnecessarily lost an otherwise very good therapist.

While counselors need to do everything humanly possible, legally mandated, and ethically permissible to keep our clients safe, ultimately their safety is in God's hands. If we truly believe in the power of prayer, we need to put our beliefs into action. It may not always be appropriate to pray with C-PTSD clients in session, but there is nothing to stop us from praying for such counselees outside of session. When I have been particularly concerned for the safety of some of my clients, I have fasted as well as prayed for them.

Asking others to pray for our counselees potentially incurs the risk of breaching confidentiality, unless case material is appropriately disguised. A general rule of thumb is to ask yourself, "If prayer partners saw my client come out of my office, would they recognize him or her as the one they had been praying for?" Using pseudonyms, changing the gender of clients when you talk about them, and modifying other potentially identifying information are some ways to protect client confidentiality. Better yet is for counselors to ask for prayer for themselves and their work so that individual clients are not referred to at all. God knows who is being prayed for and what the specific situations are, even if those praying do not.

SAFETY FROM SELF AND SYMPTOMS

The most obvious threats to safety from self are self-destructive and suicidal tendencies. However, safety has a huge subjective component. If posttraumatic and other symptoms are out of control, clients are not likely to feel safe. Although symptoms may have originated and be currently triggered by external events, when symptom levels are chronically elevated, clients may feel that they cannot escape their symptoms, or even that their identity is defined by their symptoms. Such seemingly uncontrollable flashbacks, nightmares, thoughts, emotions, physical complaints, and behavior can feel like self-betrayal if not self-destruction. For these reasons the focus of this section will be symptom management.

SAFETY FROM SELF AND SYMPTOMS
- Making sense of symptoms
- Parts work: Therapeutic use of dissociation
- Suicidal and self-destructive tendencies
- Early symptom containment
- Concept of the "window of tolerance"
- Additional approaches to symptom management

Making sense of symptoms. While counselees are generally desperate to seek symptom relief, symptoms are not necessarily all bad. I think that it is helpful to interpret symptoms as self-induced, albeit ultimately dysfunctional, ways of coping. In a sense they can be viewed as warning signals, as a means of clients desperately trying to draw attention to the fact that something is terribly wrong.

The ability to feel physical pain is a fitting analogy. If, for example, our nerves did not quickly process the message that a plate is too hot to touch without burning our fingers, we would not instinctively let go of the plate, potentially resulting in serious injury. Similarly, clients' symptoms can be warnings that damage has already been done, and/or that they possibly are in imminent danger of further injury. Clients, however, are usually unaware of any potentially positive role their symptoms may play due to the overwhelming nature of the symptoms and the disruptive influence they often have on day-to-day functioning. Once counselees can be helped to recognize that their symptoms are not random but rather have meanings that can be discovered over time, and that they can even aid in their healing, initial progress has been made toward gaining control of them.

Parts work: *Therapeutic use of dissociation.* Cognitive-behavioral techniques are generally employed by most trauma therapists to help manage posttraumatic symptoms with clients who suffer from PTSD. Some of these techniques can also be beneficial with survivors of complex trauma, particularly in managing anxiety. So anything a counselor already knows about how to help counselees without obvious trauma histories better cope with their anxiety or other intense emotions will also be helpful with C-PTSD clients. However, because C-PTSD clients have usually been the victims of long-term, chronic trauma, the number of traumatic events that could potentially be reexperienced by them is staggering. Additionally, the related anxiety and other posttraumatic symptoms often profoundly impact their ability to cope on a daily basis. Fortunately, utilizing the client's own dissociative abilities to manage posttraumatic symptoms can be a life-changing (for the counselee) and practice-revolutionizing (for the counselor) addition to a counselor's repertoire of skills.

THERAPEUTIC USE OF DISSOCIATION
- The concept of parts work in the literature
- How I use parts work
- Contracting for symptom management
- Ideomotor signaling

Over the years, I developed a subspecialty in dissociative identity disorder (DID). As a result, I became adept at using specific techniques to help my DID clients have more control over their lives and symptoms. I found it frustrating, however, that it seemed so much more difficult to obtain the same results with my C-PTSD clients who did not use dissociative defenses to the same extent.

At some point it became clear to me that even if these other C-PTSD clients did not have DID, they were inevitably still dissociating, at least to some degree. The light bulb went on! If all of my C-PTSD clients were dissociating, then was there any chance that the techniques that were so helpful in therapy with my DID clients could be beneficial to other C-PTSD clients? I began to experiment and found to my delight that indeed this was true. In fact, it felt truly miraculous to be able to intervene in a way that brought almost immediate symptom relief to my C-PTSD clients. This discovery dramatically changed the way I conducted therapy.

There is a delightful irony to me in the idea that although C-PTSD clients developed a capacity to dissociate as a defense against horrific relational trauma, this same ability can be utilized to greatly aid in their process of healing. In other words, what Satan intended for harm, God is using for the good of these individuals (Gen 50:20; Rom 8:28).

The concept of parts work in the literature. As discussed above, I developed my approach to working with complex trauma survivors by taking what I had learned about working with DID and generalizing it to work with C-PTSD. Other authors have independently come up with similar approaches to working with complex trauma survivors, although they use varying labels to describe what they do. I will briefly mention some of these labels so that if you come across them, you will understand that they are all referring to similar ways of working.

A term that I find is becoming increasingly more common is *parts work*. The developers of component-based psychotherapy, for example, which I referred to earlier, use the label *parts work* to refer to one of the four primary components of treatment with C-PTSD clients. Although use of this term is more recent, working with parts of self has been around for a number of decades.

The sexual abuse literature has long talked about the importance of communicating with the *inner child* that had been abused.[2] In the 1990s it was common for public TV to broadcast John Bradshaw speaking about the "hurt inner child of the past," who he suggested may exist to some extent in all of us (see Bradshaw, 1990). Eric Berne's *transactional analysis* (TA) was a popular therapeutic modality for several decades and is still used, primarily in communication training (Berne, 1964). Proponents of TA talk about

---

[2]For example, a classic book on treatment of adult survivors of child sexual abuse, *The Courage to Heal* by Bass and Davis, originally published in 1988, uses "inner child" language.

various *ego states*—including adult, parent, and child ego states—out of which each of us function at various times. TA is not generally used in trauma therapy, but focuses, rather, on communication patterns between individuals in an attempt to get them to interact on an adult-to-adult level rather than parent to child, child to child, and so on.

More recently some authors have written about working with *ego states* (J. G. Watkins & Watkins, 1997) or *self-states* (Howell, 2005; Noricks, 2011) with both trauma survivors and other types of clients. Robin Shapiro's book *Easy Ego State Interventions* (2016) in particular is easy to understand and clinically very practical. Richard Schwartz's *internal family systems* (IFS) model has become increasingly well-known among therapists and, I believe, made the idea of working with parts more popular (Schwartz, 1997). Although I do not agree with aspects of Schwartz's theory, I am glad that the idea of parts work no longer seems as unusual as it did when I first began teaching about it.

How I use parts work. With DID clients I had become accustomed to using language such as *parts of self* in reference to various alter personalities. When the focus was the person as a whole, I commonly used terms such as *the whole system* or *all of the person.* These expressions were intended to help severely dissociated clients understand that they were, in fact, not separate people sharing one body, but different aspects of one person. The goal was to get dissociated parts of the person to work together, rather than at cross-purposes, to enhance overall functioning.

Most C-PTSD clients do not have DID or any other dissociative disorder. However, upon investigation, they will report feeling various degrees of fragmentation or compartmentalization. Using the term *parts of self* with clients who do not dissociate much could be a recipe for disaster; they would not likely come back for another session with a counselor who talked so strangely! But those with C-PTSD *do* dissociate. Rather than find such language weird or offensive, they more frequently express relief that someone is using terms that accurately reflect their subjective experience. Some will say things like, "Interesting that you talk about 'parts of' myself. I've never used those words before, but they ring true. It's always felt like I'm not really whole, like there are different pieces of me." Others will confess, "I've always thought that way, in terms of 'parts of' self. I've just never heard anyone else say that. Maybe I'm not so crazy after all!"

I have found it helpful to use this type of language from near the beginning of therapy, as soon as I pick up indicators that a particular counselee may be dissociating. This sets up a context conducive to initiating discussions about dissociation that can help counselees understand their symptoms. I find the concept of the dissociative continuum helpful for educational purposes. Often I will draw a rough sketch of the continuum on a piece of paper as a way of illustrating the ideas. I will not place the counselee at any particular point on the continuum, as premature diagnosis of a dissociative disorder can feel extremely threatening for a counselee and result in exacerbated symptoms. Besides, I may not yet know the counselee well enough to determine whether or not they have a dissociative disorder. Instead, I will indicate a broad range in which the counselee may be located, usually somewhere between dissociative episode and DID. If counselees press for a more specific diagnosis, I will put them off, informing them that treatment would follow the same general course wherever they were on the continuum. This explanation is generally satisfactory. Once there is even a basic level of understanding about dissociation, I can begin using contracting techniques.

Contracting for symptom management. As mentioned previously, C-PTSD clients are often unaware of why they are symptomatic because aspects of their memory, identity, or experience are dissociated (as described in the BASK model). Psychodynamically oriented therapists would label such lack of awareness *repression*. To me the image invoked by this term is one of deeply buried, unconscious material that is difficult to access. *Dissociation*, however, works differently. I think a good metaphor is one of finding the key to a locked room. Admittance to the room and its contents is simply a matter of turning the key in the lock and opening the door.

With C-PTSD clients the challenge is connecting with whatever dissociated part of the person holds the key. For DID clients, this could be an alter personality. For other C-PTSD clients, it is some other aspect of self or experience. I do this by addressing the client as a whole and simply requesting that the part of the client who has knowledge of what is going on be willing to communicate that information somehow. Let me give an example from a case study I wrote that was originally published in the *Journal of Psychology and Christianity* and was recently expanded and updated for publication in a secular trauma journal (H. D. Gingrich, 2002, 2018).

Ahmee was a missionary to a Muslim tribe that lived on a remote island in the southern Philippines, a people group that included religious and political extremists. One day she was traveling with a friend, a young Filipino woman, when men jumped out from nowhere and shot Ahmee's companion at close range in an execution-style killing. When I met with Ahmee, less than a week after the incident, she showed no emotion (i.e., dissociated "A"). After a couple of days, she began to experience severe intrusive PTSD symptoms. Particularly disconcerting were the nightmares she was suffering, which were terrifying and severely impacting her ability to sleep and function the following day. It was clear that the nightmares would continue to impede Ahmee's healing process unless they could be contained.

I did not know Ahmee well enough to determine whether or not she was a complex trauma survivor. However, I had observed her dissociated affect, so I decided to approach symptom management in the way that I would with someone who had C-PTSD. Addressing Ahmee as a whole, I simply requested that the part of her who knew why a particular symptom was manifesting be willing to communicate that information somehow. I then negotiated an agreement, or therapeutic contract, with respect to the identified symptom so that it would not continue to be problematic.

The nightmares were the target of my first such attempt at a contract with Ahmee. First of all, I demystified the process for her. I said something like the following:

> Ahmee, I know that you are really distressed about the nightmares. I wonder if what's happening is that some part of you is trying to communicate that the murder really impacted you, and that you need to deal with it. Of course it's true that you do need to process what happened. But it can't happen all at once. I think that the nightmares are coming from someplace inside of you, that some part of you is allowing the nightmares to manifest. Would it be okay with you if I addressed the part of you that controls the nightmares?

I do not dissociate easily myself, so if a counselor said that to me (and I was not a therapist), I would be quite leery. Frankly, I do not think that this technique would work well on me. But remember, I had already seen Ahmee dissociate, although I did not know to what extent she used dissociation. Ahmee had no hesitation whatsoever. She was desperate to try anything. So I continued in the following fashion. Ahmee's responses are in parentheses.

Ahmee, you can keep your eyes open if you want to, but most people find it easier to concentrate if they close their eyes. What are you most comfortable with? ("I think I'd like to close my eyes.") Okay. I want you to know that you can open your eyes any time you wish to, as well as stop the whole procedure at any time you want. Now just take a few moments to relax and let me know when you're ready. ("Okay, I'm ready.") I would like to invite all parts of Ahmee to listen in right now. Ahmee, do you have a sense that the whole of you is listening? ("Yes.") My name is Heather, and I'm a counselor. Ahmee has been very upset about her friend getting killed and has asked if she could talk to me.

You will notice that I introduce myself. I do this as a matter of course. I cannot assume that all dissociated parts of a counselee have been aware of what has been happening in a session, so some may not have a clue as to who I am or what is going on.

Ahmee has been having a lot of nightmares. Is the part of Ahmee that knows what is going on with the nightmares listening in right now? What's your sense of this, Ahmee? ("Yes, I think so.") Okay. There must be some reason for the nightmares. Maybe you want to make sure that Ahmee knows that this is very upsetting to you and that you want to make sure she doesn't just forget about it? ("Yes, that feels like it fits.") Well, I'm hearing you. And Ahmee's hearing you too. There's a problem though. While I know you want to help by making sure that Ahmee deals with things, the opposite is happening. Ahmee is exhausted because she isn't sleeping, and that makes it even harder to cope. I'm wondering if you would be willing to make an agreement. If Ahmee agrees to deal with things, but does it gradually during the day when she's awake, would you be willing to temporarily stop the nightmares? You're right that she does have to look at what happened, but it needs to be slower. Then, if she doesn't live up to her end of the bargain, you can allow the nightmares to come again. What do you think? ("I'm not totally sure, but I somehow feel calmer. I think there's been agreement.") Thank you so much for agreeing to this. It will really help Ahmee a lot. Okay, Ahmee, you can open your eyes. What was that like for you?

Believe it or not, the nightmares that had plagued Ahmee stopped from that night on, allowing her to process the trauma without feeling so overwhelmed. So what actually happened here? This was not some kind of New Age phenomenon; it is fully understandable using the lens of dissociation. I found the "key," the part of Ahmee who controlled the nightmares. While in Phase II work such a key can be used to unlock the figurative door, in this case we were still in Phase I and I was asking this part of Ahmee to tempo-rarily place the trauma memories into a room and use the key to lock the door until she was ready to do Phase II work. In effect, I was asking Ahmee to dissociate out the traumatic material. This is, of course, not a permanent solution. Ultimately Ahmee would need to process those memories. This technique just bought us time.

In a similar fashion, any symptom can be brought under temporary control for someone who dissociates. Let me give you additional examples. Ruth woke up one morning in a jail cell wearing a leather miniskirt and facing a charge of solicitation for prostitution. I suspected that this behavior was associated with past trauma, and that suspicion was confirmed during Phase II work. However, we were not at a point where it would be helpful to process the memories of child prostitution that we found out later were actually at the root of this behavior. I just needed to help Ruth stop this potentially dangerous behavior until Phase II work was appropriate.

So I asked to talk to the part of Ruth who had been selling her body. I told her that Ruth and I were concerned for the safety of the body, and that Ruth was very disturbed that her body was being used in this way. I told this dis-sociated part that at some point it would be helpful to find out why she felt the need to prostitute herself, but that Ruth was not ready to hear about that yet. Until that time, would she be willing to stop the behavior? She agreed, and it stopped. In this case the BASK component "B" had been dissociated out from the other components. Using the room and key analogy, I merely asked that part of Ruth if she would be willing to go into the room for a while, taking the key with her so that she could unlock it from the inside at a future date.

I have not addressed much so far about dissociated sensation, or "S," so this example has to do with a physical symptom. Rachel came into a session looking awful. She told me that during the night she had started hemor-rhaging vaginally at an alarming rate and had been rushed to the ER to see if physicians could stem the flow of blood. Tests had shown no apparent cause for the bleeding, so the doctors had merely packed her with gauze, at least slowing things down.

As Rachel talked, I could not help but wonder if this was a "body memory," an example of a sexual abuse memory being reexperienced physically. But Rachel had been in the middle of some other Phase II work. If there was a memory attached to this physical symptom, now was not the appropriate time to deal with it. So, in a similar fashion to what I described above, I asked "all of the parts of Rachel" to listen in, checking to make sure that the "part of Rachel that knew what was happening with the body" was there. I asked if the bleeding had any connection with a past event. When the response was affirmative, I explained that Rachel was too overwhelmed to deal with anything else right now, but that she would be willing to look at what had happened at some point in the future. Would that part of Rachel agree to stop the bleeding? Agreement was reached. In this case the bleeding did not stop immediately, but it began slowing down and stopped completely within a couple of days. Months later we processed the associated memory.

Dissociation can also be used to help contain overwhelming affect (A). Counselors can ask C-PTSD clients if they can visualize some place inside them that they could temporarily store the emotion until the next session. I have had clients place feelings in internal cupboards or locked chests, which are then unlocked again in the therapist's office. There have been occasions when the intensity of rage has been so strong that counselees have preferred to "leave" the rage in my office rather than someplace inside themselves. In these instances I have asked counselees to "place" the anger in my hands, and I have physically walked over to my filing cabinet, "put" it inside and locked the drawer. While this would not be effective for nondissociative clients, the process feels very real to individuals with C-PTSD. Of course the emotion is not actually in my filing cabinet; the client has just internally dissociated out the particular affect to a greater extent. If it feels as though the rage is in my office, it is more likely to stay contained and less likely to erupt. Again, this is not a permanent solution. The rage needs to be "taken out" during the next session or two and explored (usually in Phase II), or a longer-term solution needs to be negotiated until Phase II work is appropriate.

Occasionally there are glitches in the negotiation process. This can happen when the part of self that has control of the symptom does not want to cooperate. If there is resistance, there is generally a good reason. In such instances I ask for more information so that I can understand what is behind the block. Once any concerns can be alleviated, contracting for management of symptoms can progress. An example of this would be suicidal ideation in a client named Mary. When contracting for "no suicide," I made sure that "all parts of Mary" were listening in, then asked for either direct or indirect communication with the "part of Mary who is suicidal." When I did not have initial success in negotiating a no-suicide agreement with her, I investigated further, discovering that decades before, her perpetrators had threatened her by saying, "If you ever say anything about what I've done to you, you will have to die." When Mary entered counseling, the dissociated fear (A) that she would reveal carefully guarded secrets was activated, and the dissociated behavior (B) of hoarding pills for a suicide attempt was triggered. I told Mary that her abuser was mistaken. When she was little she had no choice but to do what he demanded, but now that she was an adult, she was no longer bound by his rules. With this new information, Mary's perspective was altered, and the suicidal feelings went away.

I have found that using this kind of parts work approach while integrating cognitive-behavioral techniques into the process is much more effective than relying solely on the cognitive-behavioral techniques that are typically used in such cases. There are still cognitive-behavioral principles at play here, in that Mary had a cognitive distortion (i.e., that she *must* kill herself if she reveals her abuse), which when challenged lessened her self-destructive behavior. The difference between regular cognitive-behavioral techniques and what I have been describing is the ease with which the erroneous cognitions are recognized, as well as the speed with which the cognitions can be altered for the better. This can be explained by the increased suggestibility that is characteristic of being in a dissociative state, which makes counselees like Mary more amenable to suggestions made by their counselors. For this reason, great care must be taken not to lead the client.

Ideomotor signaling. I often use ideomotor signaling to help with negotiating the kinds of agreements discussed above. It is a kind of nonverbal communication shortcut that makes use of "yes" or "no" finger signals. This helps to minimize the potential confusion that can arise when counselees try to verbally describe their vague sense that "I think all of me is listening" or "I believe there is agreement inside" but are not quite sure. This technique makes use of the inner sensing or intuition we all have about what is happening inside ourselves but is difficult to articulate. For example, we may have an uneasy feeling that something is wrong even if we cannot identify specifically what that is. Or we may "guess" correctly the right answers to multiple-choice exam questions even if we do not always consciously know why we chose a particular answer. I believe that sometimes this kind of knowing is the direct result of the Holy Spirit revealing truth, and other times it is knowledge that we already have but that is not accessible to our conscious minds at a given point in time.

I want to make sure that Christian clients understand that there is nothing mystical or magical about this process. Therefore, since this technique is new to most clients and may seem initially strange, it is not something I generally suggest in the first couple of sessions. I wait until basic rapport and some level of trust have been established. If I do decide that ideomotor signaling could be helpful, and determine that the timing is right, I always prepare clients well for this procedure, making sure I obtain informed consent before proceeding. I might say something like the following:

> *I sometimes use a kind of shortcut to get in touch with aspects of people's experiences that they aren't aware of. I believe we all have things we aren't conscious of, but which we know about at some level. I've found it helpful to have some of my counselees use finger signals to respond to some of my questions about things they wouldn't have an answer to if I asked them right then. If you agreed to try this, what the finger signals would do is allow the part of you that knows the answer to respond using your body, but bypassing your conscious mind. That way, you don't have to try to figure out what the answer is, you can just let your fingers respond. What do you think?*

It is sometimes amazing to me that I can suggest something like ideomotor signaling to C-PTSD clients without them thinking it is totally bizarre! But I believe that their ability to dissociate explains their positive reaction. They intuitively seem to accept that this kind of a process could work, perhaps because they so much identify with the idea that their experiences are not fully integrated. If prayer has already been used appropriately and effectively with particular clients in previous sessions, I will sometimes pray that the Holy Spirit will guide the process and bring clarity to the situation.

Once I have informed consent to begin, I will continue:

> *While any finger signals can be used, I tend to get people to use the same ones all the time so that I don't get confused. I use the index finger for a "no" signal and the baby finger for a "yes" signal. We should also have some kind of "stop" signal so that if for any reason you want to pause, ask a question, or stop, I will know it. What would you like to use as a stop signal?*

Most counselees use an upraised, palm-side-out hand signal for this. While an "I don't know" signal could be negotiated, I tend to not assign one as "I don't know" could become an easy default response, limiting the amount of information that could be obtained through this technique. I have found that clients, of their own accord, will raise both "yes" and "no" fingers, either simultaneously or alternately, if they really do not know the answer.

Once a stop signal is agreed on, I will continue in the following way:

When I ask you a question, the idea is not to think to yourself, "I have to figure out if the answer is 'yes' or 'no' so that I know which finger to lift!" Instead, just let your fingers respond how they want to. Some people describe feeling a tingle in a finger, or your finger may twitch. (I will usually demonstrate my finger moving ever so slightly.) You may want to exaggerate the movement so that I can see it, but you will clearly know which finger to move. Do you have any questions?

At this point the most common concern expressed is, "What if nothing happens?" I just take the pressure off counselees by saying, "If nothing happens, nothing happens! This is just a shortcut. If it doesn't work well, we'll simply do something else. So it's really no big deal if it doesn't work. There's nothing to lose, and potentially something to gain by trying." This usually helps alleviate their concerns.

At this point, I proceed in much the same way as outlined above in the "contracting" section. I give counselees the choice to keep their eyes open or closed, reminding them that they can open their eyes or stop the process at any point. I then tell them that once they are ready, I will invite all parts of them to listen in, introduce myself, and go over the finger signals again. This sounds repetitive, and is, but when counselees are dissociative one cannot assume that communication has filtered all the way through to all parts of their system.

The advantage of ideomotor signaling over clients responding to my questions verbally is that it increases the level of certainty that the responses of the dissociated parts are not misunderstood. When not using the finger signals, some clients wonder whether they were accurately answering. However, counselees tend to trust the finger movements because it is usually such a definitive response. I always ask afterward whether the answers to my questions came cognitively followed by the physical response, or vice versa. Almost always clients tell me that when they tried to figure out the answer cognitively they just felt confused, whereas when they relaxed and let their fingers respond, the responses may have been surprising but rang true.

A disadvantage of ideomotor signaling is that the finger signals only work for closed questions. If, for example, I am asking for agreement to stop cutting behavior and the index finger indicates "no," we have a problem. In that event I ask if that part of the person would be willing to somehow communicate their concerns, and I give some suggestions as to how that could be done. For example, I will let them know that they could talk to me directly if desired, that they could speak to the client through his or her thoughts, that they could give the client a visual image that would help him or her to understand the concern, or that the concern could be written down. I then ask if that dissociated part will agree to one of those methods. If I get a "yes" response, I go through the options one by one until we get to the chosen means of communication. If there is a "no" response, I take a deep breath and give more information about why it is important. Generally this will result in an appropriate contract. If there is still resistance, I will ask whether there is any other part of the client that could help to shed some light on the issue and go from there. Sometimes some creativity is required, but I have found it rare to come to a total stalemate.

Suicidal and self-destructive tendencies. Self-destructive and suicidal tendencies are all too common in C-PTSD clients, although the reasons for these impulses may vary from one individual to another and from one situation to another. The principles of contract negotiation discussed above apply to these symptoms, just as they do to any symptom. However, the damage that can be done through these two behaviors merits some additional discussion.

Suicide. The reasons behind suicidal ideation can be complicated. In many instances thoughts of suicide are related to a sense of hopelessness that their suffering will ever be alleviated. Sometimes clients battle direct suggestions from former perpetrators that they should die, or their self-loathing is so strong that they feel they deserve to die. For C-PTSD clients who dissociate to the extent that they fit criteria for dissociative identity disorder (DID), suicidal impulses may actually be subjectively experienced as homicidal impulses. This can happen when a dissociated part of self wants to get rid of another dissociated part of self, usually not recognizing that there is only one body, and if that is killed, all parts of the client will die.

It may not be possible to fully work through the underlying motivations behind suicidal impulses until Phase II, in that they may be tied up with specific trauma memories. Nevertheless, no-suicide contracts must be made in Phase I. In many ways the process of developing a no-suicide contract with C-PTSD clients will look much the same as setting up a contract with any suicidal client in that it must be for a specified period of time (e.g., until the next session or until at least talking directly to the counselor on the phone) and include alternative suggestions to suicide if the impulses seem unmanageable (e.g., call a crisis hotline, go to the ER, call a friend). No-suicide contracts may need to be renegotiated regularly. As with other suicidal counselees, it is important to try to not leave any loopholes open. For example, rather than negotiating for no suicide until "next week's session" it is better to contract for "the next time we get together in person," in case something prevents the session from taking place as scheduled.

NO-SUICIDE CONTRACTS
- Ensure all "parts of self" agree to the contract
- Set a realistic, specified period of time
- Include alternative suggestions to suicide
- Look for loopholes
- Regularly renegotiate if necessary

As mentioned previously, C-PTSD clients tend to dissociate to some extent or another. If they have limited awareness as to why they are feeling suicidal, they may also have a decreased capacity to abide by a no-suicide contract. For example, alter personalities of DID clients may argue that "Susan is the one who made the contract. I never agreed to it!" For this reason it is important that the whole system—that is, "all of" the client—consents to any agreement made. Ideomotor signaling can be a particularly helpful way to ensure that all parts of an individual are onboard, minimizing the potential for sabotage by a dissociated aspect of self.

Self-destructive behaviors. It is not always possible to make a C-PTSD client totally safe from self-harm; that is a longer-term goal to work toward. Therefore, counselors need to choose their battles in their attempts to minimize the harm their clients inflict on themselves.

I have found that self-induced, injurious behaviors fit into two general categories for this clinical population: attempts to numb emotional pain, and trauma reenactments. Into the first category fit behaviors such as abuse of drugs and alcohol, and self-mutilation or cutting. Substance abuse often needs specialized attention. I have found twelve-step programs such as Alcoholics Anonymous and the evangelical offshoot, Celebrate Recovery, to be very helpful sources of outside support. In-patient rehabilitation programs are an option when addictions are out of control. However, if such programs do not deal adequately with posttraumatic and dissociative symptoms, the benefits need to be weighed against the possible risks to C-PTSD clients. Contracting for containing self-mutilation can be done in the same way as any other negotiation; for example, asking something like, "Is the part of Terri who has been cutting the body listening in?" If there is a "yes" response, either through the "yes" finger moving or the counselee indicating assent verbally, the process has begun.

Trauma reenactments can take many forms, but some examples I have encountered are promiscuous unprotected sex, prostitution, initiating physically aggressive behavior toward others, self-administered electric shocks, staying with a violent spouse or partner, and apparent voluntary contact with perpetrators who continue to abuse. Viewing these behaviors through the lens of dissociation helps to make better sense of them. They can be seen as posttraumatic intrusive reexperiencing symptoms that have been dissociated. According to the BASK model, these are behaviors (B) that have been dissociated out from all or some of the other components.

For example, Ruth, whose story was introduced earlier, was not aware that she would occasionally sell her body on the street until she was arrested for solicitation. Ruth was neither aware of her current behavior (K, B) nor was she aware that she had been a victim of child prostitution (K) in the past. The former became apparent when she woke up one morning in a jail cell wearing a leather miniskirt and facing a charge of solicitation for prostitution. That this was a type of trauma reenactment became clear during trauma memory processing in Phase II. While Phase II work is necessary for resolution of the underlying trauma issues, the kind of behavioral contracting discussed previously can be essential in Phase I.

Early symptom containment. While symptom management can be difficult at any point in therapy, it is particularly challenging early on in the process. For one thing, it takes time for safety within the therapeutic relationship to be developed, yet at least a minimal degree of safety is a prerequisite to negotiating around symptoms. The good news is that as counselees experience relief from symptoms, the trust level in the therapeutic relationship increases. In a sense the initial sessions become a kind of dance between working on safety within the therapeutic relationship, making sure that the client is not in current danger (i.e., safety from others), and contracting around symptoms to increase the level of safety from self.

This process is further complicated in that counselees often experience a greater number of symptoms upon entering therapy. A common scenario is one where counselees enter therapy because of intrusive symptoms, such as flashbacks or nightmares, that are negatively impacting their ability to function. Some clients have been barely holding on until they find a counselor willing to work with them. It is almost as though they have been doing their utmost to hold emotions and memories down, but then the pressure becomes too great and they erupt, similar to what happens when a car becomes overheated and pressure from the building steam causes the radiator cap to blow off.

For others, relief at finally finding someone to talk to about symptoms that could seem bizarre to the average person can result in exacerbated symptoms. Some of my C-PTSD clients have described it as getting so excited that someone is finally "getting it" that they just want it to all come out at once, hoping that the process will be shortened. The reality is that unless such clients can become stabilized, the reverse will actually happen. Therapy may feel like a constant battle to keep counselees alive or out of the psychiatric ward of the hospital. There really is no time to waste if counselees present with such exacerbated symptoms.

For example, after educating a client named Susan about dissociation, I asked "all parts of Susan" to listen in. I then said something like the following, similar to what I described in the case of Ahmee:

My name is Heather, and I'm a counselor. Susan has come in to see me because she is having a hard time coping with life. When she first made the appointment she was seeing some images in her mind of terrible things that were happening to a little girl. But now Susan says that this is happening even more frequently, and that she is now having nightmares every night as well. I realize that these images and nightmares likely mean that Susan needs to pay attention to some things. Is that right? ("Yes" finger signal or spoken word). I want you to know that Susan and I are listening. The problem is that Susan cannot do it all at once.

*First she needs to be able to function better at school and work, and she needs
to get regular sleep. She really won't be ready to look at the pictures or nightmares
for quite a while, so she needs your help. Would you be willing to stop the images
and nightmares as long as Susan agrees to continue to work toward being ready
to look at things?*

The negotiation process then can continue as discussed previously. If
clients do not feel safe enough to agree to this kind of contracting process,
counselors have no option but to continue to work on developing rapport
while letting counselees know that there are things that can be done to help
control the symptoms once they are ready. Sometimes just telling counselees
that it is possible for them to negotiate with themselves around symptoms
can help, even if they are not willing to risk having the counselor's direct
involvement in the process. For instance, if explicit work with parts of self
initially feels too threatening for clients, counselors can simply address their
clients and ask that the "message be passed along to all of Susan." Ultimately,
the key to successful navigation of these tricky situations is creativity on the
part of the counselor. Once counselors understand how dissociation works,
and how the dissociative capabilities of their C-PTSD clients can be used in
the contracting process, they can tailor specific techniques to fit the needs
of specific clients.

Concept of the "window of tolerance." In chapter two we looked at some
of the neurophysiological changes that are the consequence of living through
trauma. This included a discussion of the *fight, flight,* or *freeze* responses that
involve either increased or decreased arousal of the sympathetic or parasympathetic branches of the autonomic nervous system (ANS), as well as sometimes activating the dorsal-vagal response.

What this means is that, even in the first session, the nervous systems of
counselees may be either overly excited (i.e., *hyper*aroused) or underacti-
vated (i.e., *hypo*aroused). Hans Selye, one of the early pioneers with respect
to the neurophysiological consequences of stress, used the analogy of a
guitar when discussing the optimal level of arousal within the autonomic
nervous system that is required for physical and mental health (Selye, 1974).
When the tension in the guitar strings is too high, they snap; when the
tension is too low the strings go slack and it is not possible to play music.
It is only when the tension is just right that the guitar will function properly
and be in tune. Similarly, we need an appropriate balance between the

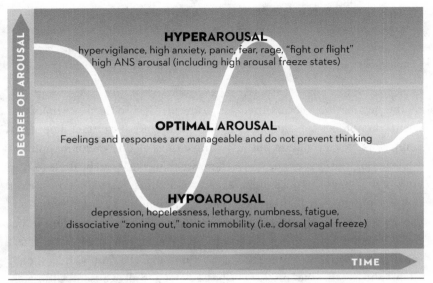

Figure 4.1. The window of tolerance

sympathetic and parasympathetic nervous systems in order to function well physically and psychologically.

Figure 4.1 illustrates the idea of the *window of tolerance*, also referred to as the *zone of tolerance*, or the *window of affective tolerance*. The area between the two horizontal lines labeled "optimal arousal" represents the window that we want to keep our clients within. While it can take a long time for survivors of complex trauma to learn to live within this optimal zone on a regular basis, for counseling to be effective it is imperative that we help our counselees stay within this optimal arousal zone within the therapeutic hour, or doing any real work will be impossible.

If there is not enough ANS arousal, there is not enough energy available to engage in meaningful dialogue. For example, I have worked with counselees who have been severely depressed and lethargic without success until they were prescribed antidepressants that moved them even slightly within the optimal window. Only then was it possible to work therapeutically with the issues underlying their depressive symptoms. Similarly, if clients are hyperaroused they are too distracted by their heightened physical and emotional states to be able to focus.

Techniques for staying within the window of tolerance. There are specific things you can do to help keep your counselees within the optimal window of arousal during sessions. The first step is to develop awareness of when clients are outside of this zone, after which you can experiment with techniques to see which work best to bring particular clients into the desired window.

Observing client states. Babette Rothschild has developed a comprehensive system of what to look for to assess when clients are at various levels of hypoarousal (including "hypo freeze") or hyperarousal (including "hyper freeze"), or are in danger of moving outside of the optimal zone of tolerance (Rothschild, 2017, p. 38). For example, she suggests that some of the indicators of hypoarousal are slack muscles, shallow respiration, low blood pressure, smaller than usual pupil size and heavy eyelids, and hands and feet warmer or cooler than usual. If these are directly observed, or upon questioning, if counselees report such symptoms, Rothschild recommends that counselors find ways to activate the parasympathetic nervous system in order to gently increase energy.

TECHNIQUES FOR STAYING WITHIN THE WINDOW OF TOLERANCE

- Observing client states
- Grounding techniques
- Creating internal safe places and anchors
- Developing body awareness and relaxation
- Trauma-focused yoga
- Not judging emotions

Conversely, some signs of hyperarousal are tense muscles, fast and shallow breathing, quick heart rate, elevated blood pressure, dilated pupils and tensed or raised eyelids, cold hands and feet, and pale skin tone. When these symptoms are noted, Rothschild (2017) proposes stopping to bring the arousal level down ("putting on the brakes") before continuing in a particular therapeutic direction.

I have found that sometimes these arousal states are fairly obvious once you tune into them, but not all of them are readily observable. When affect is dissociated, clients may appear calm, even if physiologically their nervous systems are overly excited. As a means of survival, one of my clients had learned to control many of the external indicators of hyperarousal by keeping her face impassive and always speaking in a composed manner. It was not until I asked her specific questions about her physiological state that I discovered that her heart was continually racing, she was breathing shallowly, her hands were cold, and so on. Upon learning (to my dismay) that she had actually been operating well outside of the optimal window of tolerance for many months, both within and outside of session, it became clearer why few therapeutic gains had been made.

Grounding techniques. Helping clients to ground themselves in the here and now can be immensely important if they are having trouble staying in the present during a session because of flashbacks or are overwhelmed by fear or anxiety. These situations can lead to highly activated nervous systems that are outside of the window of tolerance. Grounding techniques make use of any of the five senses to help counselees focus on the present and not get lost in past traumatic experiences. For example, if it seemed as though a counselee was paralyzed by fear, or not able to focus well, I would say something like the following in a calm, gentle voice:

> *Listen to my voice (hearing). This is Heather. You're in my office. Look around (seeing). See the green paint on the walls? Look at the picture over there. You see the trees and flowers in it? Now look at me. Do you recognize me? (In the midst of a flashback counselees will sometimes assume that you are their perpetrator, so it is important to check out their perceptions). Now feel the fabric of the chair with your hands (touching). You brought in a cup of coffee. See it on the end table? Go ahead and have a sip of the coffee (tasting). You are wearing perfume. Can you smell the scent (smelling)?*

Physical movement can also help ground clients in present reality. Having them move their hands and arms or getting them to stand up and move their whole bodies can be quite effective in helping clients to contain symptoms. Rubbing bare feet on a carpet utilizes both movement and sensory stimulation. You may need to experiment to see what works best for a particular client. Sandy always brings ice water into sessions so that she can press the cold bottle against her face as well as drink the water. The cold temperature relatively quickly brings her more fully back to current time and place. I simply remind Sandy that she has her water bottle with her. Sandy also keeps sour candies in her car that she can suck on if she needs to further ground before driving home.

While it is beneficial to have someone give these kinds of prompts, clients can also learn to practice grounding techniques on their own outside of sessions. Appendix B includes a list of coping mechanisms that was compiled by a group of complex trauma survivors and is used with permission. Counselees can also teach friends or family members what to say that can help pull them out of a crisis when they are in obvious distress.

Creating internal safe places and anchors. Individuals who dissociate tend to have good imaginations, an ability that can be tapped in order to help those with C-PTSD cope with intense feelings of fear or anxiety. Counselors can ask such clients if there is any place that has felt safe to them or potentially could be experienced as safe to them, and then have them imagine that they could go to that place when they are feeling unsafe.

Babette Rothschild (2017) coined the term *anchor* to describe a similar principle. According to her, an anchor is anything that helps an individual connect to the here-and-now when the nervous system is becoming overly activated. An internal safe place could serve as an anchor, but a client could also think about a good memory, a safe person, or anything that brings comfort.

The transcript below utilizes the idea of a safe place, but the language could be changed slightly if you prefer the concept of an anchor. The conversation could go something like this (client responses are in italics):

Mary, is there any place that has ever felt safe to you?
Well, when I was in my uncle's blue pickup truck I always felt safe. Nothing bad ever happened when he was with me.

Could you imagine this truck as being inside you so that it could become a safe place that you could visualize going to when you start to panic?
I'm not sure. The real truck was a good actual place, but I don't think it would work to imagine it.

Okay. Let's see if you can imagine what a safe place that is inside of you would look like. Maybe it would be a safe room, or maybe it would be outdoors somewhere.
Hmmm. Well, a room might work. But how could I be sure that no one could break into it?

Well, you could lock it from the inside, or post a guard at the door.
That's a good idea! But I'm afraid of the dark so there would have to be some light.

You can create the room to be any way you like!
That's true! So I'll make my room have windows so that light comes in and I can see if there's any danger coming. But there can be bars on the windows so that no one can break in. Then the room can have a light for when it gets dark out.

Is there anything else that would help the room to feel safe?

Maybe it could have a bed and some soft blankets and some stuffed animals inside that I could cuddle with. Then if I'm really tired I could rest.

Counselors should follow the lead of their clients in developing safe places or other anchors, because what feels safe will vary among individuals. Some feel safe with windows in a room, and others need a room to be windowless. Some have bad memories associated with enclosed spaces, while others might desire a small space that is entirely theirs.

Once a safe place has been created, clients can prepare for situations that might cause them to feel fearful by inviting the vulnerable parts of themselves to go to their safe place during the scary event. This empowers other parts of the person to deal with the demands of daily life without being overwhelmed by the fear and anxiety that are now safely contained. A doctor's visit, for example, could potentially be triggering for clients who associate abusive incidents with a physician's office. However, if the child parts of self that hold memories of the abuse go to their safe place, an adult part can get through medical procedures without reexperiencing the past traumatic event.

While most counselees with a complex trauma history can benefit from creating safe internal spaces, there are a minority who have never felt safe so cannot even imagine a place that would be safe. For these clients, a sense of safety likely will come only through developing safety within the therapeutic relationship. Finding a different kind of anchor (e.g., holding an object, thinking about a special place or a good memory) may be a better option with such clients.

Developing body awareness and relaxation. In order for counselees to learn to live within the window of tolerance, they need to know when their nervous systems are outside it. The problem is that C-PTSD survivors often have limited awareness of what is happening in their own bodies. This makes sense when you consider that their bodies have been hurt, perhaps even tortured as part of their trauma. We talked earlier about the BASK model of dissociation and how traumatized individuals can dissociate out the physical sensation component (S) of a particular memory. If this happens often enough, people can learn to ignore physical sensations altogether—in other words, dissociate from their bodies on an ongoing basis.

One way you can begin to help a C-PTSD client develop body awareness is to ask them specific questions. For example, "How fast or slow does your pulse feel right now?" or "What is the temperature of your hands?" Eventually they can learn to scan their bodies, beginning at the top of their heads and going gradually down to their toes to notice any points of tension or indicators of distress that are there. It may take a lot of in-session practice before some counselees will have much success with attempts to do it on their own. There are phone apps, many of which can be downloaded free of charge, that can help. One of my colleagues recommends the app *Calm*.[3] There is a moderate cost for this app, but a free trial is available, and it comes with many tools. Apps could initially be used in session to help counselees become familiar with them, after which they could download the apps onto their own phones and practice as homework. Such apps help individuals become aware of what is happening in their bodies but also lead into relaxation and deep-breathing exercises which help to regulate the nervous system.[4]

When highly aroused, individuals tend to hyperventilate, breathing shallowly and quickly from their chests, or sometimes they forget to breathe at all. I have found diaphragmatic breathing to be helpful with such clients. I ask them to place their hands on their abdomens so that they can feel their diaphragms expand when they are breathing properly. After practicing this way over a series of weeks, I can often merely say "Breathe!" and the counselee will be able to immediately change their breathing patterns. Because breathing is unobtrusive, it is something that clients can do even in public settings to help themselves regulate emotionally.

While relaxation exercises or breathing exercises are generally an obvious way to help C-PTSD survivors go from a hyperaroused state to one that is within the optimal window of tolerance, there are some counselees for whom relaxation backfires; it actually increases their activation levels. It may be that relaxed muscles feel unsafe—that if danger suddenly appeared they would not be ready to run. Instead of the focus being on relaxing muscles, exercises that work on toning muscles can be helpful for such clients. The

---

[3]See www.calm.com.
[4]There are also mobile apps that help to track and manage PTSD symptoms for the trauma survivor, as well as apps to support family members who are living with an individual with PTSD. The National Center for PTSD in the United States has many apps available free of charge at www.ptsd.va.gov/appvid/mobile/index.asp.

goal is calmness rather than relaxation, which physiologically are not necessarily the same things.[5]

Trauma-focused yoga. According to Bessel van der Kolk (2014), trauma-
focused yoga (TFY) can be very beneficial to C-PTSD survivors as both a
way to develop greater body awareness and to regulate the ANS. He points
out that while all yoga practices involve a combination of focus on breathing,
doing particular stretches or postures, and practicing meditation, the
amounts of time and intensity given to these three aspects vary among particular approaches.

In the TFY programs that van der Kolk has developed, the focus is on
becoming aware of breath (e.g., paying attention to breathing in and out,
whether the breathing is fast or slow, etc.) and paying attention to which
muscles are being used for particular classic postures. Awareness of when
particular muscles are tensed and when they are relaxed is also emphasized.
Meditation is not emphasized in his TFY approach, but some mindfulness
exercises are substituted.

Although TFY is not something with which I have had first-hand experience, I have gotten reports from students I supervise about its benefits with
some of their trauma clients. Particularly helpful was a case in which my
supervisee was in regular contact with her client's TFY instructor (with the
appropriate consent for release of information given by the client). This
enabled the instructor to further adapt yoga postures that would be less
triggering for the C-PTSD survivor, as well as allow for better processing of
the TFY experience in counseling.

Not judging emotions. Intense emotions are often viewed by clients as
negative. This is particularly true for Christians who may feel that their
hatred or anger are against the biblical principles of love and forgiveness.
Clients who believe that their emotions are bad or wrong will almost invariably try to suppress them or pretend that they do not exist. This type of
denial is detrimental to the healing process because it increases inner division rather than supporting inner connection. While angry or fearful parts
of self can be driven into hiding for a short time, all parts of self will need
to be embraced and owned before full healing can occur. Instead of denying
or disdaining their emotions, counselees should be encouraged to take a

---

[5]Rothschild (2000, 2017) discusses more fully "relaxation-induced anxiety" and toning of muscles
as an alternative to relaxation training.

longer-range view of these emotional symptoms. They can be reminded that they chose to come to counseling to work on issues in their lives and that God, who knows all things, is aware of their desire to honor him. Clients can better accept the reality of where they are at the present time by knowing that they can expect to feel differently in the future as long as they remain committed to the process of healing.

Some third-wave CBT techniques such as *mindfulness* can help clients learn to accept their negative feelings by helping them to become aware of them without automatically judging their rightness or wrongness (Segal, Williams, & Teasdale, 2013). This allows individuals to step back and observe what they are feeling so that they do not become so easily overwhelmed.[6] *Acceptance and Commitment Therapy (ACT)* is one therapeutic model that makes use of mindfulness as a technique. The focus within this approach on accepting whatever emotions are present in the moment as well as the emphasis on self-compassion can be helpful to C-PTSD clients who are often so hard on themselves. *Mentalizing* is another recent therapeutic approach that involves teaching counselees to become aware of their own thoughts and feelings and to reflect on them in a way that helps distinguish between their own experiences and those of others (see Bateman & Fonagy, 2012).

Additional approaches to symptom management. I mentioned earlier that cognitive-behavioral approaches to trauma treatment are the most commonly used to treat PTSD, but that working with C-PTSD requires additional considerations. While there are clinicians who treat C-PTSD and identify as primarily cognitive-behavioral therapists, they acknowledge that modifications to the CBT approaches used for PTSD are necessary (Jackson, Nissenson, & Cloitre, 2009).

One CBT approach that is intended specifically for use with C-PTSD is *Skills Training in Affective and Interpersonal Regulation Plus Modified Prolonged Exposure (STAIR-MPE;* Levitt & Cloitre, 2005). As the first part of the title implies, a core aspect of this model is skills training in affect regulation, which is key to functioning. *Contextual Behavior Trauma Therapy (CBTT)* combines aspects of behavioral analysis and ACT in pre–trauma processing

---

[6]Christian counselors may have concerns about these approaches because some of the concepts originated in Eastern religions. I believe that they can be helpful therapeutic tools without a Christian worldview being compromised. I mention them here because they are increasingly popular. For more information about mindfulness as a technique, see Koerner (2012). For a Christian perspective, see Tan (2011).

stabilization work (Follette, Iverson, & Ford, 2009). *Trauma-focused CBT (TF-CBT)* was originally developed for use with traumatized children and adolescents but has more recently been adapted for treating adult survivors (childwelfare.gov/pubs/trauma). The TF-CBT protocol includes teaching relaxation techniques, working on affective expression and regulation, and cognitive coping and processing, which are all applicable to Phase I work.

Dialectical Behavior Therapy (DBT), originally developed for use with borderline personality disorder, has been found to be effective with many different client populations (Mara, 2005). Its main focus is regulation of affect and behavior, with particular attention to reducing suicidal risk, which can make it of particular help to C-PTSD clients during Phase I. In my experience, most in-patient programs, whether specifically trauma-focused or not, conduct mandatory DBT groups, probably because difficulty with managing overwhelming feelings or self-destructive impulses is what lead to their hospital admissions.

I had a counselee with C-PTSD roll her eyes at the mention of DBT groups or CBT approaches that have not been modified, because she had previously been through such treatments and had found them wanting as primary treatment modalities. However, when she felt particularly overwhelmed she admitted that the tools that she gained through attending such groups had been very helpful.

FURTHER CONSIDERATIONS

Phase I work is the most crucial of all the phases, because if adequate attention has not been paid to safety issues, the rest of the therapy process will be problematic. A solid therapeutic relationship is essential, not only as a base from which to launch into Phase II work, but in and of itself. In chapter two we saw how torture at the hands of intimate others in childhood invariably impacts the ability of C-PTSD clients to develop healthy attachment relationships to caregivers, God, and others. When counselors can help these clients to both *feel* safe and *be* safe—within the counseling relationship, from potentially dangerous others, and from themselves and their symptoms—the result can be healing at a very deep level. Even if counselees are not willing or able to go on to Phase II, Phase I work can be hugely beneficial. Posttraumatic and other symptoms may continue to be an issue for those who do not continue on to Phase II. If, however, counselees have learned good symptom management skills, overwhelming symptoms can sometimes be held at bay for a long time, if not permanently. For example, some individuals could possibly contract with themselves to continue to use dissociation to keep aspects of experience compartmentalized. There is, of course, a price to pay for not ever dealing with the roots of the symptoms. But for some clients, the limitations on healing placed on them as a result of not processing the trauma memories are less than the perceived cost of doing the excruciating Phase II work. Ultimately it has to be the client's decision. We can simply pray that the Holy Spirit will guide and direct the choices.

5

PHASE II

Trauma Processing—Integrating the Components of a Traumatic Experience

THE COUNSELOR'S GOAL IN PHASE II is to help clients process and integrate specific trauma memories into a deepened awareness of their life story, identity, and relationships. I will first focus on assessing readiness for Phase II work, after which I will discuss how to access and reintegrate the various components of specific memories and how to incorporate those memories into a new sense of self and identity.

TRAUMA PROCESSING
- Readiness for Phase II work
- Memory work
- Facilitating integration of self and identity
- Working through intense emotions
- Keeping perspective

READINESS FOR PHASE II WORK

Trauma-processing work requires a lot of courage for both counselors and clients. Not all counselors are capable of bearing witness to atrocities day after day, week after week, while remaining appropriately emotionally engaged with their counselees and still continuing to be psychologically and spiritually healthy themselves. Some counselors may be personally triggered due to their own trauma histories or emotional sensitivities. Others may be skilled at approaches such as problem-solving, solution-focused, or cognitively oriented therapies, but shy away from working with intense emotions.

While growth is certainly possible in these areas, it is also okay to admit to yourself and others that you may not be cut out for this particular aspect of trauma work. God created us as unique individuals, with specific gifts and abilities (see Ps 139:13; 1 Cor 12). While some counselors may immediately recognize that they are not well suited for such grueling work, others may need to dive in and give it a try under supervision before knowing whether it is a good fit for them. Certainly this decision should be made a matter of prayer and significant personal reflection.

Some clients should not enter Phase II work. Not all trauma survivors are able to develop the inner strength necessary to allow them to delve into the unspeakable horrors of their past experiences. Others are not willing, at least at a particular point in time, to face the horrors they sense are there. The proper timing is crucial. The writer of Ecclesiastes recognized this as he wrote, "There is a time for everything, and a season for every activity under the heavens: a time to be born and a time to die, a time to plant and a time to uproot, a time to kill and a time to heal, a time to tear down and a time to build" (Eccles 3:1-3).

I used to put some pressure on counselees to enter Phase II work. I knew that trauma processing was necessary for full healing, and I desperately wanted health and wholeness for these people who were so obviously hurting. My reasoning was that if they just gritted their teeth and got through it, however difficult it was, they would come out the other side so much better off. This may have been a sound rationale if the timeframe for the work was weeks or a few months. But the reality is that Phase II can take several years of excruciatingly difficult work that is not confined to sessions but spills over into the whole of life. I realized that it was much more respectful to be brutally honest about all aspects of Phase II, giving the counselee full freedom to consent to begin this work, delay it to a future date, or opt to not go there.

Counselors can reassure their clients that even though Phase II work will be very difficult, they will not be alone in the process. I put it this way:

There's good news and bad news. The good news is that it really is possible to be healed. I have witnessed the transformation in people's lives as they come out

*the other end of this process, and they tell me it is worth it. Another positive is
that you are an adult now, so you have resources to deal with whatever happened to you that you did not have when you were a child.*

*The bad news is that it can be a very long process and that it is very painful.
I wish there were a way around it, but I haven't discovered one! What I can tell
you is that we would pace things so that you do not get overwhelmed by too
many memories at once. But the reality is that the process will shake up your
world. While I will help you consider the issues involved, ultimately you are the
one who needs to decide if you're willing to go through it, or if now is the best
time to do this work.*

*One of the factors to consider is whether the support system you have in place
is strong enough to help sustain you between counseling sessions. You might
want to talk to some other people about this decision, and, of course, make it a
matter of prayer [if appropriate for the particular client]. If you choose not to
do memory processing now, I will continue to work with you on safety and will
do my best to help you to manage your symptoms. However, the symptoms are
unlikely to fully go away without doing Phase II work.*

While counselees undoubtedly will struggle with the decision, I have found
that they appreciate that I am not sugarcoating the reality of the process.
Sometimes it is obvious that the timing is right to enter Phase II work, while
for others many sessions may be devoted to discussing the pros and cons.

MEMORY WORK

The trauma processing that is at the core of Phase II work is often referred
to as "memory work." In this section we will briefly examine some of the
characteristics of memory, after which the discussion will focus on the spe-
cifics of how counselors can go about working with the traumatic memories
of C-PTSD clients.

The nature of memory. In 1992 an organization was formed called the
False Memory Syndrome Foundation (FMSF).[1] The founder, Elisabeth
Loftus, developed a theory that false memories of sexual abuse could be
implanted by therapists, intentionally or otherwise, through the use of sug-
gestion (Hyman & Loftus 1997). The FMSF does not deny that abuse happens,
but it is strongly opposed to any notion of "repressed" or "recovered" memories. Findings from research studies conducted by the FMSF purportedly

---

[1]Retrieved from www.fmsfonline.org on Aug. 20, 2011.

showed that memory is fallible and that people can be persuaded that something happened to them that, in actuality, did not.[2] The organization developed a lot of political clout, particularly impacting the decisions of judges with regard to defendants accused of child sexual abuse. One of my clients, Tara, was negatively affected in this way by a judge saying, "How can I know whether these memories are real or fabricated?" and therefore not convicting her perpetrator. This was despite her sister's report that she too had been abused by their father and had repeatedly witnessed my client being raped by him.

MEMORY WORK

- The nature of memory
- Accessing dissociated memories
  - Deciding where to start
  - When specific memories do not surface
- Is memory recovery the goal?
- Facilitating the integration of experience

While I believe that many victims like Tara experienced further harm because they were even less likely to be believed during the heyday of the FMSF era, the FMSF's claims did have some positive effects. For one thing, they forced counselors to be much more careful while doing Phase II work, taking great pains to guard against suggestibility in the process. They also served as a catalyst for good research on the nature of memory. Research studies have shown that there are differences between regular and traumatic memory. For example, the brain mechanisms between the two are different: the hippocampus is the part of the brain involved in regular memory, and the more sensory and affective parts of the brain are involved in storing traumatic memory (van der Kolk, 1997). Amnesia is also more likely to be experienced for traumatic memory. While all memory is fallible, the central themes of traumatic memory tend to be quite reliable even if peripheral details may not be accurate. However, false memories can be created for both regular and traumatic memory.

---

[2]See Blizard and Shaw (2019) for a critique of the original study on which Loftus based her concept of false memories.

If you are interested in learning more about memory, including the differences between traumatic and nontraumatic memory and how reliable memory is, I recommend the Blue Knot Foundation's well-researched, comprehensive, very clear article on memory, which is available on their website (Stavropoulos & Kezelman, 2018). Much of their article is based on Levine's (2015) book on memory, but they incorporate many other sources.

The research findings on the accuracy of memory could be briefly summarized in the following way: It is clear that memory blocks for traumatic events do happen. However, memory is not infallible. Both regular and traumatic memories can be distorted or created. Therefore, the accuracy of any given memory cannot be determined without corroborating external evidence (Chu, 2011b).

 For these reasons it is important that counselors recognize that what their clients say about what happened to them is not necessarily 100 percent accurate. Clients also need to be aware that memory is fallible. Fortunately, therapeutic success does not depend on having corroborating evidence for the details of clients' trauma. Developing a narrative that helps them make sense of their experiences, and working through the subjective components of the memories as they perceive them, is healing.

Recognizing that memories can be created or distorted, counselors need to make sure that they are not adding to the potential problem. One of my favorite examples of therapist "errors" was portrayed on an old television documentary (Mierendorf, 1993). It showed a counselor doing memory work with a client who was traumatized as a child. The client appears to be in a regressed state and is experiencing a flashback. In this segment she screams, "There's a man coming into my bedroom!" after which the therapist asks, "Is there a beard on his face?" According to the FMSF, this question could have been enough for the client to then believe that she sees a beard on the face, even if there had not been one there previously. The question is potentially a dangerous one, because it is leading. An appropriate, nonsuggestive counselor response would have been, "What does he look like?" Notice how this question is open, rather than closed, and allows the counselee to furnish the details without undue interference. What I appreciate about the video clip, however, is that the client answers "no" to the question about the beard. In other words, even though the question was inappropriately leading, the client did not allow herself to be led!

Nevertheless, it is very important in Phase II work for the counselor to avoid even a hint of suggestibility.

Suggestibility should be avoided both with respect to whether potentially traumatic events happened at all, as well as with regard to the details of a specific memory. For example, it is not appropriate to say to a client, "You are exhibiting a lot of symptoms that could be explained by a history of abuse in childhood." Rather, a counselor could say something like, "You seem to have a lot of anxiety in certain situations. Some part of you probably understands why the anxiety (or memory gaps, or physical pain, etc.) is there. Is that something you would like to find out?" Notice that in this last example there is no reference to abuse or trauma that could be suggestive.

Similarly, when processing a dream or a flashback, it is important to ask nonleading, open questions, such as, "What are you seeing?" or "What's happening now?" Closed questions—that is, questions that can be answered with a "yes" or a "no," such as "Are you alone in the room?" "Is your mother watching?" or "Were you scared?"—can inadvertently result in memory distortion. Any information needs to be offered freely by the client, untainted by the assumptions or hypotheses of the counselor.

Accessing dissociated memories. It is possible for counselees with a complex trauma background to have full, conscious access to their trauma memories. However, as mentioned in previous chapters, either full or partial amnesia for trauma is common. These clients have dissociated, or compartmentalized, the cognitive knowledge (K in the BASK model) of their trauma from the rest of their experience.

I have seen clients, for example, who have presented with an issue such as anxiety or an eating disorder, but have had no clue upon entering therapy that they have been victims of trauma. A trauma history often presents itself through intrusive symptoms that appear as counseling progresses. It is almost as though these clients sense at an unconscious level that they have found a safe place to get help, so they finally allow the information to seep, or sometimes explode, into conscious awareness.

Bringing unconscious material into conscious awareness is the key goal of psychoanalytically oriented therapies. From this theoretical framework, the memory blocks of C-PTSD clients would be viewed as resulting from the defense mechanism of repression. Free association, dream analysis, slips of the tongue, projective assessment techniques, and so on are all intended

to break through the client's resistance in order to allow repressed psychological material to surface. These techniques can be very helpful in doing
just that. However, the process is not an easy one. The analogy that comes
to my mind is a therapist with shovel in hand, working very hard at "digging"
for the repressed material.

Using the lens of dissociation, unconscious content is viewed differently.
Rather than unearthing what has been buried deep within the mind of the
client, gaining access to dissociative material is more like getting permission
to open a locked room in a house. It is a more collaborative process that is
dependent on the trust and safety that has been developed in Phase I. Once
the key is available by gaining the trust of the dissociated part of self who
holds it, unlocking the door is a relatively easy process. Since traumatic
memories are created through the abuse of power and limiting of freedom,
the therapeutic process needs to be one of high respect for the client's
freedom with regard to the timing and method of accessing dissociated aspects of self or experience.

Deciding where to start. Similar techniques to those discussed in chapter
four for symptom management can be helpful in determining an appropriate place to begin. However, rather than seeking the help of known and
unknown aspects of the client in order to reduce symptoms, the idea is to
access all parts of self in order to help assess whether or not Phase II work
is appropriate at this juncture and, if so, the best way to proceed.

My conversation with Mary went something like the following:

> *Mary, we have been talking for a number of months now about the possibility*
> *of entering a different phase of therapy, one where we would be looking in detail*
> *at some memories that could be extremely painful. You have said that you feel*
> *you are ready, but with your permission, I'd like to check in with all parts of you*
> *to make sure that there isn't something else we should be considering before we*
> *move on. Is that okay? (Mary gives her consent.) Mary, we can either use the*
> *"yes"/"no" finger signals that we have used before, or I can invite all parts of you*
> *to listen in and you can indicate verbally what you sense the answer to be.*

Let us assume that Mary chooses the finger signals because we have used
them frequently in Phase I work. This being the case, I will skip some of the
preamble to ideomotor signaling that I wrote about in the previous chapter,
because I am assuming that Mary already understands the process well and

is therefore able to give informed consent. Otherwise I would explain it all in more detail.

To introduce the Phase II work to Mary's "parts," I would say this: "I would like to invite all parts of Mary to listen in right now. Is all of Mary listening? (Fingers indicate yes.) My name is Heather, and I'm Mary's counselor." I introduce myself every time I use this kind of technique, as not all parts of Mary may know who I am.

> *I know that some of you have been working hard to help Mary control some of her flashbacks and nightmares. Mary is feeling more stable now and thinks she is ready to know more about what has happened to her. Of course, it wouldn't be good for all of it to come back at once. We will have to go one step at a time, working together to make sure that Mary isn't overwhelmed. Are all parts of Mary in agreement about allowing the memories to begin to come back in a gradual, planned way?*

Occasionally, there will be a "no" response at this point. If that happens, I ask the parts of Mary that have concerns if they are willing to let us know what their hesitations are. It is rare that there would be other than a "yes" response to continuing the dialogue. If there has been a "yes" response, I then invite that part of Mary to communicate to Mary and me, in a way that feels comfortable, what the concerns are. Often the reluctance to begin memory work has something to do with fears that Mary will not be able to handle the information. If this happens I would address it in the following way:

> *I certainly don't want Mary to be overwhelmed either. If it really is the case that Mary wouldn't cope well, then it would be better to wait. However, the way we would go about it would be to go very slowly. It would be up to all of Mary to decide which memory to look at first. We would also have a "stop" signal (usually an upraised hand) that any part of Mary could use at any time that they had a question or concern.*
>
> *If I were to see the signal, I would immediately stop what we were doing and find out why a part of Mary wanted to stop. We will go at a pace that is okay with everyone. It could take us several sessions to go through one memory. All of Mary would have input into how things go. Also, you have to remember that Mary is an adult now. Even if some parts of Mary feel younger, her body is big, and her adult self can handle things that she couldn't handle when the body was little.*

Often these types of reassurances quell any doubts. I am not merely attempting to placate the client, however; I mean what I say. If the client really is not ready for Phase II work, it is a grave therapeutic error to go there. At some level, the client will know better than I will whether or not she is ready. The safety mechanism in this process is the sense of shared responsibility between all parts of the client and me. I am entering territory that is uncharted for me, but for at least some parts of the client, the territory is known. I would be unwise not to take any concerns seriously.

If Mary indicated that all questions had been dealt with, I would then tell "all of Mary" that it was up to her to decide where to begin. If Mary was having difficulty managing a particular symptom, I might suggest that as a starting place. But I would ask Mary to think about it during the following week, cautioning all parts of her to not bring any of the material to Mary's awareness until the next counseling session. Generally, clients will come to the next session with an idea of where to start. Allowing clients to make these choices not only empowers them but helps to ensure that Phase II work is progressing in a way that maximizes the potential for healing while minimizing the risk of unnecessarily precipitating a crisis.

When specific memories do not surface. Some clients have a sense that they were traumatized in childhood but have no actual memories and do not have clear intrusive reexperiencing symptoms. This can be extremely frustrating because such individuals do not have any idea how to validate their intuitive sense that something was greatly amiss in their childhood. If the counselees are Christians who believe in the power of prayer, I suggest that they come before God and say something like: "Lord, you made me and you know me. You know what has happened to me, even if I don't. I feel like I'm ready to find out if there is something there, but maybe I'm not. If there are things I should know about, and if this is the right timing, please allow things to surface. If this isn't a good time, then help prepare me for what will come in the future. I want your will for my life and your healing."

I also encourage clients in this position to attempt to communicate with themselves in whatever way they wish. Some find journaling helpful, while others will talk to themselves by using internal dialogue. Basically, the idea is to say, "If some things happened when I was little, I think I'm ready to know about them. I'm an adult now, and I can handle things that I couldn't when I was a kid. Maybe you can somehow let me know."

Through this process, clients are both giving themselves permission to heal and giving consent for God to work in this area. If nothing comes of it, then I believe the answer is, "You're not ready."

There are clients who are convinced that they are ready to enter Phase II work because the part(s) that make and keep counseling appointments are eager to begin the process. However, there may be strong internal opposition from another part(s). This is why it is important to address "all parts" of a client before beginning that work. I remember clearly the frustration a client, Margaret, and I both experienced as we worked exceedingly hard, but got nowhere, in attempts to delve into blocked memories that were partially leaking out in her journal entries and nightmares. Eventually we mutually agreed to terminate therapy, recognizing that we were spinning our wheels and could not find a way to get unstuck. As I am not a fan of failure, this situation haunted me for many years until I figured out what likely was happening. Margaret—a mother with young children, including one with chronic health problems—was the primary breadwinner of the family. She had to function well or her whole family would suffer. I believe that the parts of her that had kept the trauma states dissociated from her day-to-day functioning states knew that the timing was wrong and kept me from making a huge therapeutic blunder. My prediction is that after her children are grown and her husband has a steady job, Margaret will be at a point where she can successfully benefit from Phase II work.

Is memory recovery the goal? The answer to the question, "Is memory recovery the goal?" is both "yes" and "no," depending on how one defines "memories." If the BASK model's K component—cognitive knowledge of what has happened—is what is meant by memory, then retrieving the K is important but is only one aspect of trauma processing. Full memory involves awareness of every aspect of experience, that is, of every BASK component. Therefore, a key goal in Phase II is the integration of various aspects of a memory, not just cognitive recovery. Figures 5.1, 5.2, and 5.3 illustrate various levels of integration of BASK components. The solid lines in figure 5.1 are representative of an experience for which there is no awareness of the connection between various behaviors (B), certain feelings (A), specific sensory experiences or physical sensations (S), and a specific event (K), of which there may or may not be amnesia. In figure 5.2 there is partial integration as represented by breaks in the solid lines. An individual in this situation might understand that he has feelings of anxiety that are connected to having been tortured while a prisoner of war, but not be aware that some of the anger and depression he experiences are also connected. He may realize that some of the random physical pain he feels is directly connected to the torture, but he may be puzzled by why he occasionally sees flashes of white light that are so intense that he cannot keep his eyes open, only to discover that no one around him is experiencing the same thing. He may also have no idea that the reason he suddenly lost interest in attending baseball games is that the bright stadium lights trigger a trauma response.

VARYING DEGREES OF INTEGRATION OF BASK COMPONENTS

NO INTEGRATION		**PARTIAL** INTEGRATION		**FULL** INTEGRATION	
Behavior	Affect	Behavior	Affect	Behavior	Affect
Sensation	Knowledge	Sensation	Knowledge	Sensation	Knowledge
Figure 5.1		Figure 5.2		Figure 5.3	

In contrast to figures 5.1 and 5.2, figure 5.3 has dotted lines between all BASK components. This represents the free flow of information between components as an individual chooses to attend to them. If the former prisoner of war mentioned above has fully integrated an experience in connection to an incident in captivity, he will remember, for example, that bright lights were used by his captors as a means of torture (K). He will also be able to recall how much his eyes hurt because of the intensity of the lights (S), as well as his feelings of anger and frustration that he was helpless to escape from the situation (A). He will also understand that the reason he currently avoids baseball games is directly connected to this experience of torture because the stadium lights serve as a trauma trigger (B). At the end of Phase II, the hope is that each trauma experience has been integrated in this way.

Facilitating the integration of experience. Developing a cohesive, verbal trauma narrative of a particular memory (i.e., being able to talk about what happened in a cohesive way) is essential to the healing process. In part this is thought to be a way of moving the trauma memory from the "right brain" emotional systems (e.g., amygdala) to the "left brain," which involves more verbal, logical processing (Siegel & Bryson, 2011).

The importance of details. In order to develop such a narrative, the counselor must walk through every detail of the traumatic event with the client, from beginning to end. If some details are left out, there can be gaps in the narrative, leaving the client with a sense that things are incomplete. The details are also important for their power in combatting the intense shame that C-PTSD clients feel, even for existing. Because they feel that they are somehow responsible for what happened to them, if they hold back some of the details, it leaves a loophole for them to believe, "My counselor hasn't abandoned me yet, but if he *really* knew *everything* that happened, he would tell me he doesn't want to see me anymore." Conversely, to put every aspect of the trauma out there and have someone (i.e., the counselor) remain in relationship is incredibly powerful. It challenges their sense of unworthiness.

FACILITATING THE INTEGRATION OF EXPERIENCE

- The importance of details
- Titrating the process: Staying within the window of tolerance
- The extent to which reexperiencing is necessary
- Ensure the memory is complete
- Further reflections on grounding techniques
- Checking in
- Memory containment
- Structuring the session and counseling relationship
- Is it necessary to process all traumatic memories?

When I first began doing this work, I thought that I was protecting my clients by allowing them to talk in only general ways about their experiences. Later on, however, I realized that the only person I was protecting was me! Frankly, I did not want to have to listen to the gory details because they were too disturbing. I will never forget a telephone conversation I had with a former client who had transferred to another counselor because she moved to another city. Giving an update on her therapeutic process, she told me, "I've been able to talk about the details of my abuse to my new counselor. I needed to do that." I admitted to her that I now understood the necessity for going into the details, although I had not fully realized that at the time she was seeing me. I did not make the same mistake again.

Titrating the process: Staying within the window of tolerance. Do you remember conducting experiments in science class that involved titrating one solution into another one drip at a time? The speed with which the one solution drips into the other is the crucial factor in the success of the experiment. If the solution drips too fast, the whole experiment could be ruined. Trauma processing also needs to be titrated—that is, done at a step-by-step, gradual pace. I alluded to this above when I talked about seeking permission from a client to proceed with Phase II work. However, I continually let clients know that we will only proceed at a pace that is comfortable for them.

One of the ways to ensure that this will actually happen is to remind counselees that they can stop in the middle of processing a particular memory at any point in time. This can be done either verbally or by using a prearranged nonverbal signal. I think the latter is important because it is possible for clients to become so paralyzed by fear or so lost in the memory that they find themselves unable to speak, but they retain the capacity to move their bodies, at least enough to signal. It also allows parts of self who are preverbal or who do not have executive control to express their concern about the pace of the work.

When clients signal that they want to stop, they sometimes merely have a question, after which they are immediately able to proceed with the memory. At other times, they need a breather from the intensity, after which they are willing and able to once again enter the fray. Everything we discussed in chapter four about staying within the optimal window of tolerance is relevant here. The techniques that were used and practiced in Phase I to help clients self-regulate become essential with respect to the appropriate pacing of processing a particular memory in Phase II. It is the counselor's job to continually assess the client's level of ANS arousal and to "slam on the breaks" (Rothschild, 2017, p. 43) if the arousal level appears to be too high. It should ultimately be the client's decision whether to continue on with the processing of the memory or whether they have had enough for one session, in which case it is better to pick up where they left off in a future session. Later on, I will describe how to contain the rest of the memory between trauma-processing sessions.

After a particular experience is integrated, it is sometimes helpful to take a session or more to continue to process it before moving on to another memory. This is a decision that should be made between the client and counselor. As Phase II work potentially can extend over many months or years, it is important to resist the temptation to push ahead in order to get to the other end more quickly. The extra time spent on stabilization between bouts of memory work helps counselees stay within the optimal zone of tolerance both within session and in their daily lives. This enables clients to function well between sessions so that they are able to continue Phase II work over the long haul. It also builds confidence in their ability to process disturbing memories and then regain stability.

Once clients have demonstrated over many rounds of trauma processing that they can manage well between sessions, trauma processing potentially can be sped up. Although I have never done this myself, I have colleagues who have facilitated the processing of two or three traumatic memories in one session with good success. Each client will differ with respect to the pace that works best for them.

The extent to which reexperiencing is necessary. While it is important for all four BASK components to be reexperienced to some degree, the goal is not abreaction or catharsis (i.e., having an intensely emotional experience, getting the feelings "out," or releasing the built-up emotions). What happens in the therapy room needs to be substantially different from merely reexperiencing a full flashback. After all, some C-PTSD clients have had nightmares or flashbacks of specific traumatic experiences dozens of times over the years. That kind of reexperiencing becomes retraumatizing rather than healing. Instead, the aim is to be, in effect, in two places at once: "back there," reexperiencing what happened, and "here and now" in the counselor's office. The here-and-now focus allows clients to stay grounded so that they do not lose touch with reality while they are remembering past trauma. It is essential that they be able to hear and respond to their counselor's voice as well as to recognize that the trauma is not currently happening.

The goal is to maintain an appropriate balance between reexperiencing at an intensity that allows integration to happen and at the same time not overwhelming the client. While all BASK components ultimately need to be addressed, awareness of them can be either concurrent or consecutive. When either client or counselor is concerned that the emotional intensity could be too great, I recommend the latter option. Although I do not find that it is always necessary to do so, some of my colleagues make it a practice to help their C-PTSD clients initially process traumatic memories cognitively, after which they add the remaining components.

There are a number of ways to process the cognitive (K) components of a memory first. One technique involves encouraging clients to visualize temporarily placing all of the emotions and physical sensations connected to a specific memory into some kind of internal container (e.g., bucket, chest, room). They are then encouraged to give a detailed blow-by-blow account of each aspect of the traumatic event, possibly putting it into words for the first time. Once the cognitive component is processed in this way, the client walks through the narrative once more, this time adding in what they are experiencing emotionally (A) and physically (S) at each moment. Finally, how their behavior has been impacted by this particular incident (B) can be reintegrated.

Another way to prevent affect from being overwhelming during trauma processing is to suggest that clients "watch" the memory as though it were on a television or movie screen. The counselor can let them know that they can use a virtual remote control, which will allow them to start, stop, pause, and mute the story as it unfolds on the imaginary screen. This allows the client to have increased control over the pace of the work. While clients with other types of problems may not be able to make good use of such visualization techniques, dissociative clients typically can due to the high level of suggestibility I discussed previously. For many C-PTSD clients, an imaginary object such as a screen will seem as real as anything in the counselor's office. Use of visualization techniques is a way of making constructive use of their capacity for derealization.

In a similar fashion to what I discussed above, clients will then be asked to give a detailed account of what they are seeing and hearing on the screen, while being reminded that they do not have to feel any of the related emotions and physical sensations, that they can use their remote to turn down the volume and so on. The "movie" can then be replayed, perhaps with a bigger screen, and the emotions and physical sensations integrated into the memory as a whole. Or perhaps no screen is used during the second telling of the trauma narrative so that it feels more real.

Eye Movement Desensitization and Reprocessing (EMDR) is a set of specific memory processing protocols utilized by some counselors who have received specific training in its use. It is often utilized to help victims of natural disasters or those with PTSD to integrate their traumatic experiences. Exactly how EMDR works is unknown, but proponents believe that it directly affects how the brain processes information.[3] EMDR involves reexperiencing of trauma, but to a lesser extent than some other approaches to memory processing. Some good research has shown support of its effectiveness for single-event traumas.[4] However, while it can be helpful for working with some individuals with C-PTSD, a caution is in order. Regular EMDR protocols are generally not recommended for clients who are highly dissociative, particularly for clients with other specified dissociative disorder (OSDD) or DID. The potential danger for these clients is that they can become more easily emotionally overwhelmed through the process in ways that other clients do not. Of course, the premise of my whole treatment approach is that all C-PTSD clients dissociate to some extent! Therefore, the counselor has to have adequate training in EMDR and enough understanding of dissociation to make a decision about the appropriateness of using it with those who have C-PTSD. There are now advanced EMDR training levels that deal specifically with how EMDR can be used effectively with dissociative clients. Without this very specialized training and good supervision from someone who understands the potential dangers, I would recommend that great care be taken in how EMDR is used with C-PTSD clients.

Ensure the memory is complete. For resolution of a traumatic memory to occur, all aspects of the memory must be processed. While some memories may have resided in a particular dissociated part of self in their entirety, there may be a number of different parts who have held particular aspects of an event. For example, one part of self may remember the perpetrator entering the room and feel afraid but then remember nothing else. Another part may hold the memory of the perpetrator ripping off his clothes, another remember being cold and naked, and still another remember being raped. Sometimes the memory gaps are for short fragments of time, so can be easily missed. It is always a good idea, therefore, to ask if any other part of the person has anything to add to the narrative in any BASK component.

---

[3] See the EMDR International Association website at www.emdria.org.
[4] See https://emdrresearchfoundation.org for links to research summaries and more information about EMDR.

Further reflections on grounding techniques. Some of the scariest thera-peutic moments for me have been when clients are in full flashback mode, "lost" in their traumatic memories. Sometimes it is obvious that the client is terrified because they are screaming in terror or yelling something like, "Get away from me!" Equally, if not more, disturbing have been instances where clients have been unresponsive, slouched over in their chairs, and I have wondered momentarily if they are still breathing. In either case, it is im-portant to get the client grounded again and back within the optimal window of tolerance. What works well will vary depending on the client, but following are some suggestions.

As mentioned previously, sometimes verbally reminding clients of who you are and where they are in time and space is enough to enable them to "snap out of it." For example, I might say, "Mary, this is Heather. You're in my office in a counseling session. It's the year 2019. I would like you to come back to my office again." If that does not work I will add, "I'm going to slowly count to three, and you will gradually come closer and closer to being back in my office. By the time I count to three you will be able to open your eyes and you will see me and my office. One . . . you are starting to come back, two . . . you are getting closer, and three . . . you are back in my office." Re-member that dissociative clients are highly suggestible, which is what allows a technique like this to work. This is all in the context of severe agitation or unresponsiveness on the part of the client. Though I've often wondered in the heat of the moment whether this was really going to work, the vast ma-jority of the time it has.

On one occasion a client—Norman, who had DID—remained unre-sponsive, slouched over in the chair with his eyes closed, and not moving or making any sound. In desperation I asked if some part of Norman could tell me which dissociated identity was there, and the response was "nobody." I interpreted that information as an attempt to let me know that the client was in some kind of indeterminate state, where no particular part of him was out, but it was clear that he was in a severe hypoaroused state, perhaps in a post-traumatic dorsal-vagal "freeze" state. Eventually I found out that a dissociated part of Norman was present, and that this dissociated identity was named Nobody! Apparently Nobody's job was to appear when no other part of him wanted to deal with a situation, or when being unresponsive was an attempt at safety. Since Nobody was nonverbal and could not move, it was not until

I asked to speak to another dissociated identity that I could help Norman ground and eventually be in a safe enough space that he could get home.

Prayer can certainly be important at such times. However, I do not recommend praying out loud, as the client is not in a position to give informed consent for explicit prayer under these circumstances. Also, because you do not know what the client is experiencing at that moment, you cannot predict how the client will respond to the prayer. It could potentially put the client at greater risk, triggering harmful reactions that could further complicate the situation and leave the person further ungrounded. However, in such times of crisis, counselors can pray internally. For me, these prayers are of the most basic kind, usually taking the form of, "God, help! Please help!" God, who knows what is going on, can give the counselor direction on how to proceed.

As mentioned in the previous chapter, another way to orient clients is to help them connect to their sensory experiences. For example, "You're sitting in a chair in my office. Feel the arms of the chair with your hands. Can you feel that? Now open your eyes. Look at the green paint on the walls. Why don't you stand up and move your body. Stretch your arms above your head. Can you feel your feet on the floor?" It may be tempting to use touch as a way to get clients to realize that you are there with them. When clients are not aware of current reality, however, touch can be particularly dangerous, even if well-intentioned. Rather than helping "bring them back," the counselor's touch can instead become incorporated into the traumatic memory, with counselees confusing the counselor's caring touch with their abuser's intent to harm. As you get to know particular clients, you will discover what works best for them and be able to get them grounded more easily.

Checking in. The only way counselors can know whether they are moving forward at an appropriate pace is to continually check in with clients in the midst of working on a particular memory. The idea is *not* to just keep going without pause from the beginning to the end of the memory, hoping that discussing it later will be helpful. If the content is not particularly overwhelming, sometimes no break is necessary. However, usually it is best to interject from time to time, asking clients if they need a break or reminding them that it is important to talk about what is happening. Long periods of silence are not generally helpful because counselors have no way of knowing what is happening and so are limited in their ability to prevent the memory work from becoming retraumatizing. Regularly checking in also keeps clients connected to the here and now rather than getting lost "back then." Clients can respond either verbally or through ideomotor signaling, depending on what has been agreed to ahead of time.

An illustration of how some of these principles could be used in a trauma-processing session follows. See if you can identify how I am attempting to titrate the process, where I check in with the client, and the way I use open questions to avoid suggestibility. Also notice how I ask for details, as well as the way in which I use grounding techniques to keep the client from reexperiencing the memory too intensely. In this case the memory has taken the form of a recurring dream.

I am assuming that Mary and I have already determined that now is an appropriate time to look at a particular memory, and that she has been given assurances that we will only proceed at a pace that feels manageable for her. I have asked all of Mary to make a decision about where we should begin. She informs me that she thinks it is time to examine a nightmare that we had negotiated about in Phase I of counseling a number of months before. At that time, the part of Mary that was allowing the distressing dream to repeat night after night had agreed to stop the dream from reappearing until a later date. Now she is ready to look at the content of that dream. In the following sample transcript, Mary's words are italicized.

Mary, let's just double-check that all parts of you still agree that this is the place to begin. (Through ideomotor signaling Mary responds "yes.") Okay, we will proceed then. Is the part of Mary who has control of this dream listening? (Mary indicates "yes.") Go ahead, then, and allow yourself to remember the dream. Tell me what's happening, Mary.

Well, I can see my mother putting her coat on. I know she's going to go out. The doorbell rings, and my Uncle Jim comes in.

How old are you, Mary?

I'm not sure . . . I think I'm about eight though, because I remember I wore that dress in second grade.

Okay, Mary. You said your Uncle Jim came into the house. What's happening now?

I'm feeling afraid, but I don't know why. My mom gives me a kiss and a hug goodbye, and I whisper in her ear, "Please don't go, Mommy." She tells me not to be silly, that I know she has Bible study and that she'll be home in two hours. (Mary stops talking and starts to cry. I wait for a few minutes and then ask her if she's okay with going on.)

I don't know! I just feel like something bad is going to happen. I'm not sure I want to find out! (I let her know that this is her choice. If she wants to take a break, or if she wants to go only that far today, she can. Mary decides that she wants to continue.)

I hear the car door slam shut. The engine turns on, and I can hear the sound of the car as my mother backs out of the driveway.

What are you feeling as you hear your mom drive away?

I feel like I want to throw up! I look at my Uncle Jim, and he's smiling at me. But it's not a nice smile. I don't know how to describe it. He tells me that it's time for my bath and that I should go and start the bath water. But I don't want a bath! I tell him that I had a bath the night before and I don't need one tonight. Then he starts to get mad and calls me a "dirty little girl."

How are you feeling when he calls you that?

I feel ashamed . . . and scared.

What's happening now?

He tells me that he'll tell my mom what a disobedient child I am if I don't hurry up. (Mary is silent, but I see tears rolling down her cheeks.)

I see your tears, Mary. You seem upset.

Yeah. I'm so confused. I'm afraid to do what he says because I just know something bad is going to happen, but I'm also afraid to disobey him. I don't know what to do!

What do you do?

I do what he says, because I don't really have a choice. But I lock the bathroom door first. Maybe if I lock the door I'll be okay. I'm shaking, but I get undressed and get into the bathtub and start to wash myself. I'm thinking that maybe I'm just being stupid, that everything will be okay after all. But . . . oh no! He's pounding on the door! Jesus, please don't let him come in! Please, Jesus. But I hear him . . . the doorknob is jiggling! He's trying to unlock it! Oh no! It's opening! Please, Jesus! (Mary is obviously distressed. She is shaking in her chair, talking rapidly, and breathing shallowly.)

Mary, this is Heather. You're in my office. Can you hear me? (There's no response. I speak more firmly.) Mary, can you hear my voice? (No response.

Mary is still shaking. I sense that she is lost in the memory and is not aware of her present surroundings.) Mary, I want you to feel the sensation of the chair against your legs and the armrests against your arms. Wiggle your fingers. You're not in the bathtub. You're in my office. Now open your eyes. (Mary is wiggling her fingers, and I see her eyelids flutter and then open.) Hi, Mary. How are you doing?

I'm not sure . . . I'm still shaking . . . It really felt as though I was eight years old again. Thanks for getting me out of there. I could hear your voice, but it sounded so far away that I couldn't do anything for a while. The doorknob rattling was just so much louder than your voice was.

I could tell you were really scared, Mary. While you need to experience those feelings again, I want you to be able to do that while being aware that it isn't actually happening right now. The idea isn't to retraumatize you. I have an idea of something that might help. Instead of feeling it as intensely as you just did, you could visualize a TV screen and watch the rest of your dream on that. Then if you start to get too scared, you can press the pause button, or turn down the volume, or even turn the TV off. That would give you a sense of greater control. Would you like to try that? Another option, of course, is to stop here for today.

Well, in one way I'd rather stop here, but then I'd just have to come back to it next week. I think I'd rather get it over with. I like your idea of the TV. Maybe we could try that.

While the above is a fictitious example, it gives a realistic picture of how memory processing works. Notice that I asked Mary for step-by-step details about what she was experiencing, using open-ended questions that were not suggestive. In terms of BASK components, Mary was able to tell me what was happening (K), share her emotions (A), and react physically (S). Later on we would look at how her behavior (B) had been impacted by this event. She is well on her way to integrating all aspects of this particular experience.

As Mary continued her narrative she began to reexperience the event in the form of a total flashback. This is to be avoided, which is why I called her back to the here and now. Some clients are more prone to getting "lost" in the past during Phase II work than others. Every client is unique, so counselors need to be prepared for any eventuality.

Memory containment. If work with a particular traumatic memory extends over more than one session, the danger is that the rest of the memory will come back as an intrusive symptom (e.g., nightmare, flashback, somatic symptom) between sessions. It is important that "all parts" of the client understand the dangers inherent in allowing that to happen without the counselor present to help mediate the process. This is another time that the dissociative abilities of C-PTSD clients can be constructively used to manage symptoms. The counselor can help the client use dissociation to "put the memory away" until the next counseling session, enabling the client to function normally without intrusive feelings or memories. If Mary had decided that she wanted to put off the rest of the memory processing of the incident involving her Uncle Jim until the following week, I might end the session in the following way. I would either use ideomotor signaling, or allow Mary to verbally respond, whichever method had worked best with her previously.

> *I would like to invite all parts of Mary to listen in, particularly those who were part of the incident that Mary was just remembering or who know about it. As you know, it is not easy for Mary to remember these things. I know that some of you might want to just get it all out now that it's been started. But Mary can't handle any more today (or, our time is almost up for today). It is very important that she not remember anything else that happened until we are together again next time. Mary needs to be able to work, go to school, and take care of her kids. If the rest of the memory comes back when she's not in a counseling session, she may have trouble doing those things, and that wouldn't be good. Does all of Mary understand that?*

I would wait for some kind of indication that this was understood and agreed to. If there was a "no" response I would then give that part of Mary more information about the potential negative impacts of not waiting and then negotiate with that part of her. If that part of Mary does not care about those consequences, perhaps not seeing that they are relevant, I would try to find a way to show how that part of Mary could be negatively impacted. For example:

> *I realize that you are angry at Mary and think she deserves to suffer. However, even if you don't really feel like you are part of Mary, you do share the same body. So if Mary ends up in the hospital in the psych ward, you will end up there too.*

This is where counselor creativity comes in, because no particular way of negotiating will work with every part of every client. The goal, however, is to get voluntary consent from the client system as a whole to prevent memory leakage. In a worst-case scenario, if you cannot get the agreement of a particular part of the client, you can elicit the help of other parts of the client to intervene in the process.

Structuring the session and counseling relationship. Memory work is unpredictable, as neither counselor nor client will know what to expect going into a particular incident. Therefore, predictability with regard to session structure and the counseling relationship helps clients to be certain about at least some aspects of the process. Keeping session times the same from week to week whenever possible is helpful, as are meeting in the same office and not changing session length. Knowing that therapeutic boundaries will remain consistent is also reassuring for clients. One of my clients was relieved to see no loveseat or couch in my office, as she had previous experiences of therapists "flying" across the room and sitting beside her in an attempt to bring comfort in the midst of a particularly difficult memory. This invaded the client's personal space and caused her to fear what the counselor might do next. Everything discussed with regard to safety in Phase I work is relevant here, particularly the issues related to "remaining safe" as a counselor.

Adequate time should be allowed for debriefing clients, allowing them to become reoriented to their current reality before leaving the session. At the beginning of Phase II work, and assuming a fifty-minute session, I would suggest that twenty minutes be allowed. This time can be decreased as clients are able to make more efficient use of grounding techniques. Even then, ten minutes should be an absolute minimum. It can be tempting to skimp on the time allotted for debriefing, particularly if the memory retrieval of a specific incident appears to be nearing its end. It is best, however, to resist that temptation, as what appears to be the end may not be, and debriefing is so important.

Keeping to a regular session length is important. I have found that extended sessions can sometimes be helpful, particularly when processing a new memory. The extra time can allow the client some time at the beginning of the session to prepare for the difficult work ahead. Having increased time to allow for debriefing and grounding is another benefit. With some clients, however, I have found that the same amount of actual work gets accomplished, whether the session is fifty minutes or two hours in length, with much of the session time being wasted. So it is best to experiment with what works best for a particular client. One and one-half to two hours is the maximum time I would recommend for an extended session. Longer than that is too exhausting for all concerned.

If a particular session is extended, it is essential that it be preplanned so that both the client and the counselor can prepare. To spontaneously extend sessions without the client's knowledge and consent is bad practice. One of my DID clients told me of a previous counseling experience where sessions could range from an hour to four hours in length without his knowledge or consent. He had amnesia for the times in session that other dissociated parts of himself were out, so he could not watch the clock himself (which is not the client's responsibility anyway) and only found out at the end of the session that hours had gone by. This was so disconcerting that in our sessions even a minute over the prescribed session length became a point of contention.

An alternative to extended sessions is to contract for more than one session per week. Some C-PTSD clients find it easier to manage between sessions if they are spaced closer together. So consider carefully whether extending the length of sessions, increasing the frequency of sessions, or perhaps both, might best benefit the client.

A tricky issue with either of the above possibilities is how fees will be negotiated if more of the counselor's time is being taken up. While this may not be an issue for some survivors with C-PTSD, others may not be functioning well enough to work or may be at low-paying jobs. If the client cannot afford to pay more, you as the counselor will have to decide if you are willing or able to take up more of your time for a reduced fee.

I have already discussed the importance of predictability in the scheduling of appointments, the counseling room, and the counselor's behavior within the session. But predictability is also important with respect to counselor availability between sessions. C-PTSD clients need to know what the rules are and that the rules will change only with much discussion. If, for example, I allow email communication (regarding issues other than appointment times) from a client between sessions and I do not set a specific boundary about how many emails I will read, it would be irresponsible of me to blame the client for sending too many emails if I begin to resent the extra time that it takes to read them. The appropriate way to handle these situations is to brainstorm with the client about alternatives (a certain number of emails a week, paying more per week to cover the extra time spent, or finding additional support people, etc.).

Is it necessary to process all traumatic memories? While ideally all memories should be processed in order to minimize the likelihood of intrusive posttraumatic symptoms being triggered, the decision is ultimately the client's to make. Processing trauma can be horrendous. While there is ultimately relief and healing around a particular incident once it is processed, it takes some of my clients weeks to recover from the impact of particularly difficult sessions. While much of the processing gets done in session, it is not uncommon for other aspects of the particular memory or similar memories to come to awareness in the following days and weeks. Even if no new content comes to mind, it takes time and energy for clients to work through the full impact of a particular memory. As discussed in more detail in the sections that follow, every new memory means that C-PTSD clients have to shift their views of their personal histories, themselves, their families, and their worlds.

Some clients get to the point that they are satisfied with who they are; they enjoy their relationships with friends, family, and coworkers; they feel fulfilled; and posttraumatic symptoms are manageable. They may be aware that other memories exist, but in weighing out the advantages and disadvantages of continuing to process them, they decide that the cost is too high. In such cases I move on to Phase III, leaving the door open to go back to trauma processing in the future if they decide they wish to do so.

FACILITATING INTEGRATION OF SELF AND IDENTITY

So far our discussion has focused on the integration of the BASK components of a particular experience. However, most individuals with C-PTSD have many such traumatic experiences. While understanding and experiencing specific traumatic incidents in their totality is important, it is perhaps even more essential for clients to be able to integrate these experiences into their overall sense of self and identity. Therefore, while verbalizing a trauma narrative is an essential aspect of Phase II work, it is incomplete unless the client is able to work through the personal ramifications of what comes to light.

The following poem—included with the permission of Dan, the client who wrote it—illustrates both how damaging abuse can be to an individual's sense of self and how intense the accompanying emotions can be.

Try to Imagine

Try to imagine being caught in a rainstorm, and the heavy drops have soaked through to your skin . . . you head for cover, some kind of protection from the rain, you shake yourself . . . but you're soaked . . .

Now suppose those raindrops are razor blades and you can't escape them, and there's no protection from them at all . . . and you can't rub your skin or shake them off . . . and wherever a raindrop has kissed your skin a razor blade will cut a part of your very soul away and leave a gaping, weeping wound . . .

All your dreams, hopes have vanished and your ability to scream and cry have been stripped from your life . . . and you survive . . .

Try to imagine.

Adults with C-PTSD have already formed some sense of self, however incomplete, distorted, or fragmented. As the BASK components of individual experiences are integrated, individuals find that their life history is different from what they thought it was. Therefore, they have to be willing to set aside their previous self-perceptions while they struggle to weave together their traumatic experiences with the rest of their lives.

Think for a moment of Dan, the client who wrote the above poem. Dan was a young adult who was living with his mother because he experienced too much anxiety to hold down a job. Until a few months before entering counseling, Dan had thought of his childhood as pretty normal, although when pressed, he would not have been able to tell you any details about his growing-up years. He appreciated that his mother allowed him to live with her rent-free.

When Dan came for counseling, his world had been turned upside down by nightmares and waking flashbacks of sexual, emotional, and physical abuse that was perpetrated by both his now-dead father and his very-much-alive mother. In time, Dan and I did the excruciating work of going through each memory in turn, allowing the details to come to mind (K); feeling the terror, anger, shame, and horror of what was done to him and what he was forced to do (A); reexperiencing the physical pain and pleasure involved (S); and understanding his own behavioral reactions (B). In the process, his whole view of his childhood, his family, his world, and himself was severely challenged because his personal history was so changed from what he had always believed it to be. Gradually acknowledging that he had been horribly abused, he began to identify himself as a childhood trauma victim. I hoped, however, that his life script would not remain that of victim but could be rewritten as that of a survivor and a healthy, resilient human being who was created by and deeply loved by God. For that to happen, not only did each of Dan's traumatic experiences have to become integrated units, but it was necessary for each of those experiential units to become woven into the fabric of Dan's sense of self and identity.

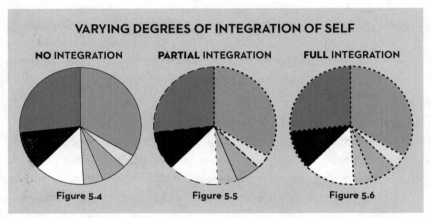

VARYING DEGREES OF INTEGRATION OF SELF

NO INTEGRATION   **PARTIAL** INTEGRATION   **FULL** INTEGRATION

Figure 5.4   Figure 5.5   Figure 5.6

Earlier in this chapter, figures 5.1, 5.2, and 5.3 represented aspects of experience that were dissociated from each other to some extent. For some clients, each quadrant of the rectangle (i.e., B, A, S, or K) could be representative of a distinct aspect of a traumatic experience, with the larger rectangle representing the experience as a whole. Figures 5.4, 5.5, and 5.6 have some similarities to the earlier figures; however, rather than the outer circular boundary of the pie representing an entire experience, in these figures the outer circle represents the whole person. The segments of the pie, then, are symbolic of various aspects of personality and identity. For example, a particular segment could represent a specific role, such as the part of self who is a parent or the part of self who functions at work. Another segment could represent a traumatized inner-child part who is frozen in time and who holds memories of abuse. Still another segment could be made up of pieces of various experiences that all relate to a particular emotion, such as shame.

The solid and dotted lines between slices of the pie denote varying degrees of integration. In figure 5.4, the solid lines represent no awareness between various aspects of self. This, however, is purely theoretical, as no one, not even someone with dissociative identity disorder, is compartmentalized to the extent that there is absolutely no information that crosses over from some parts of self to some other parts of self, even if it is quite limited. Figure 5.5

is representative of some degree of compartmentalization, as some information can flow between the spaces in the lines. Complex trauma survivors who dissociate to some extent are more aware of some parts of self (i.e., segments of the pie) than others. Figure 5.6 indicates a free flow of information between all parts of self—a fully integrated individual.

I will use myself as an example of what figure 5.6 represents. When I am teaching a class, I am in my professor mode. However, if the content of a particular class relates to children, I may be reminded of my youngest son and wonder for a moment how he is doing. For those few seconds I am operating out of my mother part, symbolized by a different segment of the pie. Later on, as I am processing the events of the day with my husband, or as I am snuggling with him while we watch television together, I am in my wife state. While one is more predominant at any point in time than another, I am aware that the other parts of me exist. I also remember what I said, did, and experienced when operating out of each of these aspects of myself.

In actuality, I am not fully integrated. None of us will ever attain full integration this side of eternity, as we tend to not want to acknowledge some of the parts of ourselves that we label as negative or think of as sinful. As Jeremiah 17:9 states, "The heart is deceitful above all things and beyond cure. Who can understand it?" It is difficult to be fully honest with ourselves. But even if complete healing is not possible, we can work at increased self-awareness so that we can come closer to what figure 5.6 represents.

Figure 5.7 combines the previous sets of figures, linking the concepts of integration of experience and integration of self. Notice that each slice of the pie in figure 5.7 contains full and partial boxes. These boxes represent various experiences, either in their entirety (a complete box) or partially (as

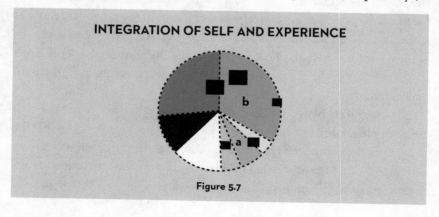

INTEGRATION OF SELF AND EXPERIENCE

Figure 5.7

one or more BASK components). This shows how larger components of personality or various aspects of self are influenced by discrete experiences or components of experience. Segment "a," for example, could consist of the "A" BASK components from separate, dissociated experiences, all of which are related in some way with the emotion of anger or rage. As this is a very specific function, it makes up a smaller slice of the pie, while segment "b," representing a more complex part of the person—such as the role of employee, student, parent, or musician—will be correspondingly larger.

Let's say that figure 5.7 represents Mary as a fully integrated individual, with segment "a" symbolizing a fearful state of being and segment "b" representing Mary in her student role. The square box that is partially in segment "a" and partially in the section of the pie between segments "a" and "b" represents the particular memory (BASK) with Uncle Jim and the bathtub discussed previously. One aspect of that memory is the fear (A) that she experienced. Another aspect of the memory is the knowledge of what Uncle Jim did to her (K), which is contained in the segment between "a" and "b." However, segment "a" also includes fearful responses associated with other situations, and the segment between "a" and "b" includes cognitive knowledge of other incidents with Uncle Jim. If there was room on the diagram, segment "a" would be composed of numerous partial boxes, all representing the emotion of fear from various incidents.

Segment "b," on the other hand, is bigger than segment "a" because being a student is a large part of Mary's identity at the present time. Since she is enrolled in full-time studies, a lot of her time and energy is focused on her education. In her role as a student are many experiences, represented by the boxes within section "b." While Mary experiences fear from time to time (segment "a"), her fear is not nearly as significant to her sense of identity as is the part of her that is associated with studying. After Mary graduates, the student part of herself may become smaller and the mother part of her larger as she decides to devote most of her energies to parenting her preschool-aged children.

For integration between dissociated aspects of self to occur, not only is it necessary to go through each memory of a traumatic experience so that the dissociated aspects of the experience become reintegrated, but it is also essential to spend time processing the *meaning* of particular memories. Many counselees have questions such as the following:

"How does knowing this change who I am?"

"If God really loves me, why didn't he stop them from hurting me?"

"What does this mean for my relationships with my family?"

"Were my siblings hurt too?"

"Are my children safe?"

"Do I really want to find out more, or should I terminate therapy?"

"Will my spouse desire to stay married to me if he or she finds out the horrible truth?"

"What if I really wanted it? After all, my body responded."

Addressing these kinds of questions can take up even more session time than going through the memories themselves.

Each new memory brings fresh information that has to be integrated into the client's sense of self. This may require old ground to be continually reworked. Dan, who was introduced above, had come a long way toward accepting that he had been emotionally, psychologically, and physically abused by his father. However, as new memories of his mother's abuse came to light, his world and view of self were once more shaken to their very foundations. Remember that although his father was now dead, Dan and his son were currently living with his mother. This meant that every day he had to try to come to grips with a dual reality: his present-day experience of her as kind and helpful, and his childhood experience of her in which she participated in torture. The challenge to Dan's view of self was not only the discovery that he had a mother who had hurt him so badly, but also the realization that he was now an adult stuck in a dependent relationship with one of his perpetrators from which he did not see a way out.

This aspect of Phase II work is not unique to working with clients with C-PTSD. Much of the healing process for clients in general involves helping them come to grips with bad things that have happened to them, grieving losses, managing affect, working with cognitive discrepancies, and so on. Therefore, many general counseling skills will be helpful here. Cognitive-behavioral techniques, psychodynamic approaches, person-centered interventions, and use of narrative therapy and other postmodern/constructivist approaches are examples of potentially helpful ways of working with counselees as they grapple with the implications of the trauma memories that have surfaced.

WORKING THROUGH INTENSE EMOTIONS

In this section I will first examine some of the general principles counselors should keep in mind to help their clients work through the intense emotions that tend to arise during Phase II work. I will then discuss some of the specific emotions that are commonly experienced by C-PTSD clients and offer some tips for helping clients deal with them. Finally, I will address the internal struggle counselors may experience when they are faced with the intense emotions of their clients.

WORKING THROUGH INTENSE EMOTIONS
- General principles
- Understanding and dealing with specific emotions
- Roadblocks for counselors

General principles. Counseling can provide a safe place for C-PTSD clients to express their emotions. Counselors, in effect, serve as a container for these emotions, helping them to be less scary for clients. The nonjudgmental, compassionate acceptance of these intense feelings, whatever they may be, is a gift the counselor can offer.

The rules of safety, of course, are still in effect. My basic rules are that neither the client nor I get hurt and that my office does not get destroyed. Inside of this basic framework, I tell clients that they do not have to censor what they say, because if intense emotions continue to be pushed down rather than expressed, it is as though poison will continue to infect them. For some clients, physical movement is helpful. They may pace the room, tear pieces of paper to shreds, pound on a chair cushion, hug a stuffed animal, or rock themselves.

Sometimes a Gestalt two-chair technique can be a useful way of eliciting feelings or helping to work through them. For example, clients may want to visualize their perpetrator in the empty chair and tell them how they feel about the trauma that was inflicted. The intention is not to necessarily ever say those things directly to the perpetrator, because few perpetrators respond to such confrontations with true repentance. They tend to either deny the abuse altogether or greatly minimize it. Rather, the purpose of such a technique is to enable the client to express emotion without fear of reprisal.

As identifying emotions is new to some C-PTSD clients, they may need to learn how to accurately label certain feelings. Helping them connect physical sensations with emotional states is one way to do this. For example, clients can learn that a certain type of tension in their stomach is indicative of feeling anger, while a tightening of the throat may mean they are feeling sad. If you fear that someone is getting out of control and is in danger of hurting themselves or you, use the same interventions that were discussed previously to pull someone out of a memory. For example, firmly talk to the client, orienting him or her to time and place, and tell the client to stop and calmly sit down. If there is no response, you can use the counting procedure (i.e., "At the count of three you are going to stop and sit down—one, you're starting to relax . . . two, you are much more relaxed . . . and three, you are feeling calm and are ready to sit down.").

It needs to be clear to clients that the intense affective work is to take place in the sessions and not outside of their counselor's office. It would not be productive for clients to lose their jobs, for example, because of anger outbursts at work. C-PTSD clients often have not developed appropriate tools to deal with their emotions, having relied on dissociation to compartmentalize them. Counselors can assist survivors in learning some skills in this area by encouraging them to journal, talk into a voice recorder, use exercise as a way of releasing some emotional energy, and develop the ability to use positive self-talk. Clients also can be encouraged to acknowledge what they are feeling without making judgments about their emotions.[5] This may allow them to gain enough distance from the emotion so that they do not feel so out of control. It will take time for clients to learn to appropriately regulate their affect as this is one of the areas that likely has been damaged as a result of the attachment deficits in childhood. In a sense, the counselor takes on the role that the client's primary caretaker should have performed years before: teaching the client how to handle their emotions.

While these skills are developing, the ability of these clients to dissociate can be used to help them contain their feelings between sessions, just as they did during Phase I. Intense emotions, for example, can be left temporarily in the counselor's office. This can be visually played out, as we discussed in

[5] As mentioned in chapter four, a term that is increasing in popularity is the principle of mindfulness. Dialectical Behavior Therapy (DBT) emphasizes mindfulness as does Acceptance and Commitment Therapy (ACT), both more recent developments of cognitive-behavioral approaches to therapy.

chapter four, by having the client literally hand the emotion, with out-stretched arms, to the counselor. The counselor physically "takes" it from the client and "places" it in a filing cabinet. Of course, the counselor has to remember to take it out of the drawer in which it was stored for safekeeping and hand it back to the client during the next session. In a slightly modified fashion, clients can also find a safe place within themselves to store poten-tially problematic emotions. So, for example, they can visualize an internal locked chest or a locked closet and make sure that a reliable part of them holds the key. These are simply stopgap measures that can be used until the feelings can be fully worked through and longer-term, healthy ways of regu-lating feelings have developed.

In our discussion so far, it has been assumed that accessing emotions that have been previously dissociated is the main challenge. There are, however, instances where the reverse is true—that clients are well aware of their feelings and are emoting too much. Ultimately, the goal is the same, because these clients, too, must learn healthy ways of regulating their affect and con-taining their feelings.

When the process goes as it should, emotions will gradually be worked through. While there is no specific timeframe that is normative, and some-times the process seems very long, counselors should be able to sense that progress, however small, is happening. While it is important to get the "in-fection" out, there are the occasional clients who want to continue living in the muck of their hatred and self-loathing.

I remember a client, Chris, who entered therapy because he felt so angry all the time. Chris had good reason to be angry about the emotional abuse and neglect that he had experienced as a child. The problem was that after doing memory work and affective work, no change was apparent. As I prayed about this stalemate, I got the clear sense that Chris was making the decision to hang on to his anger; he was not willing to "let it go" (an overused but appropriate Christian aphorism in this case). I suggested this to Chris during the next session, and he admitted that he realized he was holding on to his anger. He felt that by doing this he was sinning, but he was afraid that if he let go of his anger, his perpetrators were somehow getting away with what they had done. We worked for some time on this false belief but eventually decided to terminate therapy as it became clear that Chris was not willing to work toward letting God have control of his life and the healing process.

Counselors should not easily come to such a conclusion, as clients could feel abandoned by a counselor who is apparently giving up on them. Usually with continued therapeutic work over time, counselors can help their clients get to a place where they are able to work through such feelings. Occasionally, however, progress will be stuck to the point that it may not make sense to continue counseling until the client really desires change.

Understanding and dealing with specific emotions. So far in this chapter, we have examined the importance of doing more in Phase II than working through each memory. The importance of integration of self has been emphasized, as well as the place of working through intense emotions in this process. We have also looked at how to help C-PTSD clients identify, access, and experience their emotions, as well as contain intense affect between sessions until they learn better emotional regulation on a continual basis. In this section we will focus on specific emotions that are commonly experienced by C-PTSD clients.

UNDERSTANDING AND DEALING WITH SPECIFIC EMOTIONS

- Mourning: denial, anger, and depression
- Guilt, shame, and self-hatred
- Fear of abandonment
- Anxiety, terror, and fear

Mourning: denial, anger, and depression. I have found that one of the most difficult aspects of Phase II work for C-PTSD clients is letting go of what they thought reality was, or what they hoped it would eventually be. Incest survivors, for example, have to eventually grieve the loss of the fantasy that they would ever be children who were loved in healthy ways by their parents. Acknowledging other childhood losses, such as the loss of innocence, the loss of the dream of entering marriage a virgin, and the loss of a sense of safety, can be equally as hard. There can also be loss associated with a changing perspective of who God is. For example, individuals whose theology encompasses a view of God's love and protection as being synonymous with nothing bad ever happening to them may have a hard time accepting that God allowed them to be hurt. Over time, Christian counselors can help C-PTSD clients work through their spiritual angst and come out the other end with a realistic, healthy view of God, but mourning the loss of their unrealistic view is an essential aspect of this process.

While mourning these losses, counselees can alternate between denial, anger, depression, and the beginnings of acceptance of what was. It is not uncommon for C-PTSD clients to enter the counseling room after months or years of therapy and say, "I wasn't really abused, was I?" Immediately afterward they will usually admit to knowing it is true, although they desperately want it not to be reality. The novice counselor working with clients in Phase II can be caught off-guard by this emotional roller coaster, because what seemed like a breakthrough of acceptance a few days earlier has once again become denial. This is to be expected.

Cathy, a C-PTSD client, expressed it this way:

> The worst thing is facing the anger and sorrow . . . so I deny them, push them aside.
>
> It's really very easy, because if you deny them it won't be real and the pain [will be] false.
>
> The mourning inside cannot surface, so it can't be real, and then it won't hurt . . . turn the noise on and just forget, push away the sorrow and pain, suppress them and ignore them, and be sure to deny them again and just maybe, just maybe it won't hurt to the extent of this . . .

Depression and anger can be seen as two parts of the same coin. Some Christians view depression as more acceptable than anger, while for others, particularly male clients, anger becomes the emotional outlet of choice. Some have bought into the lie that Christians must always be happy, and so push away both anger and depression.

I am so glad that Scripture gives many examples of individuals feeling intense emotion, because for counselees who value the Bible, these passages can be used to illustrate that there can be an appropriate place for hard-to-acknowledge emotions such as depression and anger. Mark 14:32-36 shows the agony that Christ experienced in the Garden of Gethsemane as he wrestled with the knowledge that his crucifixion was imminent. Clients can be encouraged to read this passage, and perhaps to watch the scene from the movie *The Passion of the Christ* in which the struggle is vividly portrayed (Gibson, 2004).

The psalmist expresses both intense anger and intense pain. C-PTSD clients can relate to the psalmist's desire for revenge on his enemies (e.g., Psalms 10,

28, and 55, to name a few) as they, too, will often desire that their perpetrators suffer for what they have done. C-PTSD clients can also identify with the psalmist's despair and hopelessness (e.g., Psalm 42) because they too, at times, become mired in their current circumstances and despair of a way out.

The challenge for Christian counselors is to not short-circuit the mourning process. It is easy to fall into the trap of thinking, "Okay, my client has been intensely angry now for eight sessions. It's about time he got over his rage!" When trauma has been chronic, lasting years if not decades, there can be a lot of grieving to do and much to feel angry or depressed about.

Guilt, shame, and self-hatred. Guilt and shame are not identical but are often associated. One way to think of the difference is that guilt tends to be experienced in response to personal behaviors one chooses, whereas shame is one's sense of unworthiness in the context of relationships. When people feel shame, they focus on their feelings of powerlessness, worthlessness, or the sense of being exposed. When people feel guilt it is usually associated with something they have done or not done. Guilt is more a response to doing, while shame is a response to being (Martin, 1990). Shame can be viewed as being more central to identity, although both guilt and shame can feed feelings of self-hatred.

C-PTSD clients may struggle with guilt for behaviors connected to their abuse. Sexually abused children, for example, may feel guilty for having been involved sexually with their abuser, even though they had no choice. Some may have initiated sexual activities with their perpetrator simply because it was the only means by which they could get affection or gain attention. Others may feel guilty because they were forced to physically or sexually abuse others.

While guilt is a struggle for some, those with C-PTSD inevitably feel deep, pervasive shame. Their belief, though irrational, is that they are to blame for what has been done to them. Perpetrators will often explicitly tell their victims that they deserve what is happening. But even if this is not the case, victims often take on the responsibility, as though attempting to make some kind of sense of why they are being tortured. But because there is no valid reason, the only option they are left with is that something is terribly wrong with them. For others, the belief that they somehow caused what happened to them gives them a sense of control over their life. If they caused it, then perhaps in the future they can prevent it from happening again.

The challenge for C-PTSD clients is that they so often feel intense shame, assuming that there is something fundamentally wrong with them that is deserving of being hurt. It is a pervasive and chronic emotional experience from which they rarely, if ever, have felt relief. In that sense it may actually be the most familiar emotion they experience in life. This results in self-hatred that infiltrates the core of their beings. It can take a very long time and much hard work for such clients to get to the place that they truly understand, with both their heads and their hearts, that the trauma was not their fault, and that in the aftermath of such abuse, the shame and guilt they feel is neither necessary nor healthy.

In the following poem, Dan describes the insidious nature of the shame he felt:

By Accident

By accident I got some black marker on my hand, and I tried to wash it off, and I scrubbed at it, but it wouldn't come off, but inside I knew that it would eventually wear off,

As I looked at the black marker on my hand, it symbolizes to me the "abuse" that somehow "got on me," that intruded into my life, not by accident, but planned on, by my parents. It's black and ugly, and I've tried to scrub the blackness away . . . my skin has been raw many times, trying to get the ugliness off,

And I keep hoping that eventually it'll fade away too . . . hoping that it isn't always going to be a part of my life . . .

While it is necessary for counselors to repeatedly tell such clients that they are not to blame, counselors need to have no illusions that they will be believed. Similarly, for clients who are open to use of explicitly spiritual interventions, meditating on Bible verses that describe God's love for them can be helpful reminders of the truth. One particularly powerful verse is 1 John 3:20: "If our hearts condemn us, we know that God is greater than our hearts, and he knows everything."

The problem is that head knowledge (K) and heart knowledge (A) are not the same. Many of my Christian clients are well aware of such Scripture passages, having been encouraged to study them by well-meaning church leaders or Christian friends. The problem is that the adult parts of them are often the ones that are engaging in these disciplines, while the feelings of guilt and shame are compartmentalized in child trauma states, remaining stuck there. Ultimately, the child parts of a person have to be listened to, nurtured, and loved before heart truth can be experienced. Often this begins with God's agape love that is mediated through the therapeutic relationship. In other words, clients may not automatically believe what a counselor says, but over time, if the counselor is consistently safe, caring, and nonrejecting, counselees will begin to believe in their depths that maybe they have some value after all.

One of the advantages to narrating all of the details of multiple traumatic events is that doing so combats shame. Time and again, clients have been convinced that I will terminate therapy with them upon hearing their stories. When I do not react in the way they anticipate, but instead look them in the eye and remain consistent in my way of relating to them, shame begins to ebb away. In the sexual abuse literature this is often called "breaking the silence." However, I believe the concept also is helpful for survivors of any form of relational trauma, including child physical, emotional, or spiritual abuse and neglect, or chronic abuse as an adult, including intimate partner violence, kidnapping, and torture. When something as horrendous as relational violence, in whatever form, is kept hidden, the weight of the shame only grows. When the horrible secret is exposed—that is, when the silence is broken—major steps toward the healing of shame can occur.

While the counselor is often the first person to whom C-PTSD clients reveal their trauma histories, many C-PTSD clients find it helpful to "break the silence" with other people in their lives as well. Sometimes the relief is so great that counselees go overboard and begin to share their story indiscriminately, both privately and even publically. Counselors can help clients make healthy decisions about disclosing at the proper time, under the best circumstances, and to individuals who are safe. Certainly the gritty details of abuse should not be shared in a public setting such as a church service. However, publicly acknowledging that they are survivors of abuse in a more general way and revealing something of their healing journey with others can bring further healing with regard to shame.

Fear of abandonment. An ongoing theme throughout the counseling process is the fear of abandonment. This is universal to C-PTSD clients. If you recall the discussion in chapter two about the process of attachment, I discussed how traumatized children often are not able to develop a sense of safety and security in relationships. One of the ways in which this lack of a secure attachment reveals itself is in the fear such clients experience that everyone, including the counselor, is going to abandon them. Reassurances, while important, only go so far. It is the consistent, empathic, genuine, respectful, and structured stance of the counselor over an extended period of time that will ultimately help. A lot of energy will have already gone into dealing with this area during Phase I, but even if much progress has been made, with the emotional intensity of Phase II, the fight for trust and safety will continue.

Fear of abandonment tends to get triggered when the counselor has to miss a session or more due to illness, planned vacation, or conferences. As mentioned previously, it is important to give notice of such absences ahead of time so that clients are not caught off-guard. With such advanced warning, preparation can also be made to help clients cope while the counselor is away. For example, the counselor can leave a voicemail on the client's phone that the client can listen to over and over again as a reminder that the counselor exists and is coming back. An email message can serve the same purpose, as can a small symbolic object taken from the counselor's office that the client can "take care of" until the next session.

When the counselor makes a geographical move and has to refer clients elsewhere, the abandonment issues are particularly heightened, with good reason. While this is always an unfortunate situation given the length of time it usually would take to develop a strong therapeutic relationship with another counselor, it is sometimes inevitable. While never ideal, this circumstance allows C-PTSD clients the opportunity, probably for the first time, to experience a healthy ending to a relationship. The longer the therapeutic relationship has been, the more notice is necessary; certainly months, rather than weeks, is preferable.

When I moved from Canada to the Philippines, it was a very difficult time for both my clients and me. Session after session for many months, all I was doing with clients was processing abandonment issues. At the same time, I was working through my own feelings of loss at having to prematurely end treatment with my C-PTSD clients, preparing to say goodbye to friends and family, and looking ahead to many personal adjustments.

I found out later that one of my C-PTSD clients called her new therapist "Heather" for the first year after I left! The transition was very painful for her because we had worked together for seven years and she was almost through Phase II, with just a few very early memories left to process. In the months prior to my leaving, I remember saying to her, a woman of strong faith, "Haley, two things are clear to me: God brought us together and God is now calling me to a different ministry. I do not believe that God has brought you this far in the healing process only to forget about you now. While working with your new counselor will be different from working with me, I know that God has a purpose in this for you as well as for me, and that he will continue to heal you." Years later Haley revealed that she had finally come to realize why God had apparently ripped me from her life. If she had completed the whole process with me, her tendency would have been to rob God of some of the glory by putting me on a pedestal as the only one who could have helped her. Instead, she came to realize that God was the ultimate Counselor and that he could use many others in her life to come alongside her in the healing journey. This was wonderful confirmation to me, as well, that I am not indispensable—that God will bring other people to serve his purposes in someone's life.

Some clients will not be at a place where they can take comfort from Scripture, but for those who are able to let the truth of the Word infiltrate their hearts, Bible passages promising that God will be with us can be beneficial. Romans 8:35 can be immensely reassuring: "Who shall separate us from the love of Christ? Shall trouble or hardship or persecution or famine or nakedness or danger or sword?" After all, they have experienced some of these very things. Then they read on in Romans 8:38-39, "For I am convinced that neither death nor life, neither angels nor demons, neither the present nor the future, nor any powers, neither height nor depth, nor anything else in all creation, will be able to separate us from the love of God that is in Christ Jesus our Lord," and they are offered further assurance that no matter what their abuse entailed, God will not forsake them.

Anxiety, terror, and fear. When someone has been chronically traumatized in the context of a relationship, it is very difficult to feel safe with anyone. Even if trauma narratives have been verbalized and the associated fear (i.e., the "A" component of BASK) integrated, it can take a long time for hypervigilance to totally go away.

Behavioral and cognitive techniques such as relaxation training, systematic desensitization, and cognitive self-talk are examples of possible types of interventions, as well as the mindfulness techniques and other third-wave cognitive-behavioral interventions that were discussed in chapter four under symptom management. Physical exercise can help to relieve overall stress, as can the development of good sleeping and eating habits. Sometimes antidepressants or antianxiety medication can be of benefit in managing these symptoms, particularly if used in conjunction with therapy.

Sometimes, however, the commonly used methods of dealing with anxiety and fear are only moderately successful with C-PTSD clients because the feelings have been dissociated. A clue to the source of the anxiety can often be found by asking a client, "How old do you feel right now?" Much to their surprise, once they pay closer attention to their current experience, even C-PTSD clients who do not have a dissociative disorder will realize that they feel like a child or a teenager. This part of self can then be accessed through talking to all parts of the person, perhaps using ideomotor signaling so that the root of the emotion can be found. Adult parts of a person can then communicate with the scared child and offer to help in whatever way they can. Often this involves simply offering the information that the body is bigger now and that the adult parts will take care of things. Such "conversations" help to remove some of the amnestic barriers that are represented by figure 5.5. One "slice" of the "pie" is sharing information with another slice, thus furthering integration of self.

Roadblocks for counselors. As we have just discussed, Phase II work tends to elicit some very intense emotions for C-PTSD clients. While working with feelings is not, of course, restricted to this client population, the intensity of the feelings expressed by C-PTSD clients could be unsettling to some counselors. Hearing the horrific stories of C-PTSD clients and helping those clients work through the accompanying emotions is extremely difficult for counselors. Never have I been reminded of the depths of depravity to which human beings can fall as when I have seen what one human being is capable of doing to another, particularly when the victim is a child. However, if counselors are not able to handle intense emotion, they risk compromising the healing of their C-PTSD clients, because consciously or unconsciously, clients will pick up on what their counselors can handle, and they will not say more than their counselor can hear. Unfortunately, counselors are often not even aware of the signals they are inadvertently giving their clients. This is one of the ways in which ongoing supervision can prove very valuable.

I remember working with a client on a particularly gruesome, intense memory that had not been completed during the session. As the next session approached, I realized that I was dreading it. I just was not sure that I could handle more of that intensity so soon. However, I prayed about it, gave myself a good talking to, took a deep breath, and greeted my client. When she told me that she wanted to put off the rest of that memory work for another week, I was very relieved. Imagine my surprise when at the end of the session she revealed that she actually had been prepared to continue that piece of memory work, but she immediately sensed that I could not handle it, so she changed gears! To this day I do not know how she was able to pick up on my feelings, but I do know that C-PTSD clients often have highly developed antennae for others' reactions toward them, probably as a learned survival mechanism.

This same sensitivity can be used by clients to determine if the intensity of feelings they are expressing in sessions is okay with their counselor. Frankly, it is not easy to hear a client say that she hates her perpetrator so much that she would like to stab him one hundred times, then cut his body into little pieces! If our clients are Christians, such admissions can be even more disturbing. After all, Scripture commands us to "Get rid of all bitterness, rage and anger" (Eph 4:31). Could we potentially be leading our clients into sin by encouraging them to acknowledge and express such emotions? If the intention is to help clients work through such emotions, I believe that counselors are actually helping their clients to obey this verse. Let me illustrate this point by using the following analogy of an infected physical wound.

I used to live in the tropics, where wounds got infected very easily. It was not uncommon for a deep cut to close over on the surface and appear to be healing properly, only to fester underneath. If true healing was to occur, it meant that the wound needed to be lanced, allowing the pus to come out, after which it had to be carefully cleaned, antibiotic ointment applied, and the dressing changed regularly. C-PTSD clients need counselors to be able to help them open up their wounds to allow the infection to come out. If the full emotional intensity is not acknowledged and allowed expression, it is the equivalent of closing a physical wound back up that has not been thoroughly cleaned. In time that wound will once again fester. Similarly, if emotional wounds are not properly attended to, they will not heal. However, if appropriately dealt with, resolution can occur and those emotions will no longer have conscious or unconscious control over the afflicted individual.

If my counseling students express concern that such affective work may be dishonoring to God, I share the wound analogy with them. I help them to see that we are simply bringing to the light of day emotions that are already there and that are preventing the client from healing. I may refer them to Luke 16:15, where Christ confronts the Pharisees, saying, "You are the ones who justify yourselves in the eyes of others, but God knows your hearts." I tell students that in my experience, when clients are pushed, they acknowledge that God knows them better than they know themselves; he already knows what they are feeling. Even if they would rather deny some of the feelings that they label as negative or perhaps even sinful, not acknowledging them does not change the reality of their existence. I may also remind students of some of the Bible verses discussed above that show Scripture as full of honest, explicit expressions of emotion. Certainly counselors will need to have worked through any of these questions themselves before entering into Phase II work with their C-PTSD clients. It is also important for counselors to not shy away from the emotional intensity that is part of this work, or the process of healing for their clients will be hampered.

ADDITIONAL APPROACHES TO TRAUMA PROCESSING

All approaches to treating trauma in adults, with the possible exception of some body therapies, emphasize developing a trauma narrative in some form. Proponents of some approaches—for example, *cognitive processing therapy* (Resick, Monson, & Chard, 2017) and trauma-focused CBT, mentioned earlier—encourage trauma clients to write out the details of a particular traumatic experience before discussing it in session with their therapist. *Exposure therapy* or *prolonged exposure therapy* (Foa et al., 2018) may involve various types of exposure to the traumatic incident. For example, exposure could include taping survivors' narratives so that they can listen to them repeatedly both within and between sessions, as well as exposure to safe situations that are avoided because they are somehow associated with the trauma (i.e., in vivo desensitization). The theories referred to in the section on symptom stabilization in the previous chapter all have specific approaches to trauma processing.

Any approach to trauma processing potentially could be utilized during Phase II work with C-PTSD. My caution would be, first, to ensure that all BASK components are being reintegrated through whichever approaches are used, since theoretical conceptualizations behind specific approaches to trauma processing vary. Prolonged exposure therapy, for example, is based on a behavior therapy model of desensitization to the trauma. Therefore, the focus is on repeated exposure to the trauma, without any attention necessarily being given to having all of the BASK components at play. Second, counselors would need to make sure that it is appropriate to begin Phase II work with an individual suffering from C-PTSD, since authors describing a particular trauma-processing approach may not place it within phased treatment.

KEEPING PERSPECTIVE

While integration of experience and integration of self, including working through intense emotions, are the primary tasks of Phase II, the process actually begins in Phase I and continues on through Phase III. Just like any stage model, there is not necessarily always a clear distinction between phases. Phase II work is long and arduous. I have tried to outline some general principles as well as give some specific tips to help counselors navigate these difficult waters. The reality, however, is that there will be need for creativity in the process, as nothing can totally prepare you for every eventuality. Supervision and consultation with others who are doing this work can be literally a Godsend. Do not hesitate to ask for input from others when necessary.[6]

---

[6]If you do not know a supervisor who understands complex trauma and dissociation, see chapter ten for possible resources.

6

PHASE III

Consolidation and Resolution

WHEN NO NEW TRAUMA MEMORIES SURFACE, Phase II comes to an end. However, the emotions resulting from such memory work may not be fully worked through by this time. Therefore, while integration of experience may be complete, integration of self and identity will continue into Phase III. Phase III also involves further integration of clients into the community. While C-PTSD clients should be encouraged to develop supportive relationships from the outset of counseling, in Phase III counselees will have experienced enough healing that they can develop a greater number of healthy, mutual relationships, and perhaps even work on repairing previously damaged relationships. The ultimate goal is to prepare clients to live fulfilled, productive lives without a counselor.

CONSOLIDATION AND RESOLUTION

- Consolidating changes
- Developing new coping strategies
- Learning to live as an integrated whole
- Navigating changing relationships
- Evaluating employment
- Confronting the perpetrator
- Practicing forgiveness
- Ending the therapeutic relationship

Overlap between Phases II and III is normal. The important thing is to avoid the temptation to believe that the healing process is complete after the difficult Phase II work of trauma processing is finished. In Phase III, clients consolidate their changes and resolve remaining individual and relational issues.

CONSOLIDATING CHANGES

Both counselors and clients tend to hope that growth will take place in a straight line from point A to point B, as in figure 6.1. In reality, the process of change is much more irregular. As demonstrated by figure 6.2, a forward step toward the end goal is often followed by two steps backward or worse. At other times things seem to plateau.

This is all the more true in work with C-PTSD because of the magnitude of adjustments that these clients are forced to face in their perceptions of themselves, others, God, and the world around them. While much of this is worked through in Phase II, C-PTSD clients require additional time for these changes to become consolidated so that they begin to feel normal. Emotions that had apparently been worked through in Phase II will often resurface in Phase III. This does not mean that Phase II work was done inadequately; rather, it is to be expected because these issues can have multiple layers.

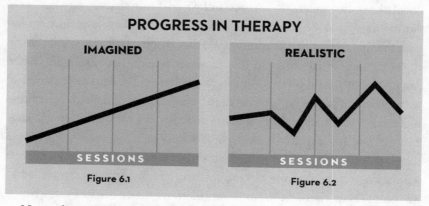

PROGRESS IN THERAPY

IMAGINED

SESSIONS

Figure 6.1

REALISTIC

SESSIONS

Figure 6.2

Normalizing the process for clients can keep them from getting discouraged when they feel as though they are regressing. I sometimes use the common counseling analogy of peeling back the layers of an onion to illustrate how a reemerging issue does not mean that it has not been resolved at all, but rather that they are merely dealing with a different aspect. Although I may not always wait until Phase III to do so, I will frequently draw rough sketches of figures 6.1 and 6.2 to help clients gain perspective on their healing process.

DEVELOPING NEW COPING STRATEGIES

C-PTSD clients who have used dissociation as a primary defense mechanism now need to develop other coping mechanisms. While the benefits of having integrated their experience and their sense of self and identity are readily apparent to counselees at this point, there are also some frightening aspects. For instance, in a stressful past situation, C-PTSD clients may have dissociated affect as a way of coping. But now, when faced with an anxiety-producing situation, they find they have lost the ability to compartmentalize their emotions and are stuck with feelings of anxiety they do not know how to handle. This is due to the fact that the more integrated they have become, the less they are able to make use of their ability to dissociate to even temporarily contain their feelings. For example, they may find that they can no longer "lock" their anxiety in a chest they visualize internally or "leave it" in a filing cabinet in their counselor's office, techniques that they may have found extremely helpful in Phases I and II.

This is where counselors can use everything they know about helping clients learn to regulate their affect. In Phase III this process may look very similar to work done with non-C-PTSD clients who have difficulty coping with their feelings, with the additional task of helping C-PTSD clients grieve the decrease in their ability to dissociate on demand. For example, clients can be taught relaxation techniques and positive self-talk to help them deal with anxiety. When depressed, they can be taught some cognitive-behavioral techniques, or encouraged to journal or seek out relational support. They can also be encouraged to find physical outlets such as exercise, wringing a towel, or tearing a piece of paper into shreds when they feel angry. Clients who acknowledge the role of God in their healing process can be led to Scripture verses that talk about these emotions. These are just some of the many techniques that are associated with various counseling theories and that are discussed as part of therapy training programs.

LEARNING TO LIVE AS AN INTEGRATED WHOLE

Other adjustments to living as a more integrated individual will vary depending on the degree to which the client dissociated in the first place. DID clients feel the difference the most keenly, often mentioning having to get used to being aware of their own thoughts rather than hearing a constant melee of voices inside their heads. While the reduction in internal chaos is reported as positive, no longer having separate parts of themselves to talk to results in feelings of loneliness for some DID clients. Taking full responsibility for their action or inaction is another big change. Formerly, if one part of the counselee did not want to do a task, it was possible for another part to come out and do it. I have heard mothers with DID tell me, for example, that they had no pain during childbirth because another part of them took the pain. Upon integration, these women report a very different experience of labor and delivery with subsequent children.

On the positive side, integrated DID clients retain abilities that formerly only specific parts of them had. So, for example, a nonmusical man discovers that he now has the ability to play the piano, or a nonathletic person suddenly develops proficiency in certain sports. While other C-PTSD clients may not experience the same magnitude of change, there will still be adjustments as they wrestle with a new self-perception and view of the world.

NAVIGATING CHANGING RELATIONSHIPS

Some might assume that as C-PTSD clients become more whole, their relationships will automatically improve. Nothing could be further from the truth. As clients change, even if for the better, they upset the equilibrium of their relational systems. For better or worse, people tend to prefer the familiar. If one person changes, it imposes change on his or her relational systems, including marriages, children, friends, God, church congregations, other community groups, and families of origin. Even changes that counselors would consider positive will most likely be resisted, consciously or unconsciously, by others within these systems.

Marriage and parenting. Andrew was a C-PTSD client who was able to function quite well with a lot of help from his wife. He fit diagnostic criteria for panic disorder with agoraphobia, as he had a great deal of difficulty leaving the safe environment of his house due to fear of having panic attacks. He was able to function in his job as an engineer as long as his wife drove him to and from work and was available by telephone during the day in case he started to feel anxious. While, to some degree, his wife resented Andrew's dependence on her, at a more unconscious level she welcomed it because her identity revolved around being needed. Therefore, as Andrew became more healthy and whole, becoming able to drive himself back and forth to work and reveling in his newfound independence, his wife felt threatened. Unfortunately, her attempts to sabotage his healing process eventually resulted in divorce.

NAVIGATING CHANGING RELATIONSHIPS
- Marriage and parenting
- Friendships
- Relationship to God and church congregations
- Community
- Family of origin

This is not an unusual situation. On the surface, Andrew's wife appeared to be psychologically healthy, while Andrew obviously struggled with mental health issues. However, spouses find each other for a reason, and they are often fairly evenly matched in their overall emotional health, even if one's pathology is more hidden than that of the other. When one spouse becomes healthier, he or she is, in effect, challenging the unconscious marital contract.[1]

Similarly, as C-PTSD clients become more integrated, their ways of relating to their children change. Parenting is difficult at the best of times. While struggling with flashbacks and other intrusive symptoms, as well as doing exceedingly difficult Phase II work, clients may find it is impossible to provide consistent, involved parenting. By the time parents are in Phase III of the recovery process, they may have enough emotional energy to become more engaged with their children. While this is obviously a good thing, with children benefiting from the increased attention, the change can also be confusing to them. Children entering their teen years may become particularly resentful of what they perceive to be intrusiveness on the part of a parent who may have been uninvolved but now is beginning to set boundaries right at the time that they want increased independence.

Due to the stress that healing causes the client's relational systems, concurrent marital or family therapy may be helpful during Phase III. While it

---

[1]See Taylor (2017) for a more thorough discussion about the marital dynamics when one of the spouses has a history of sexual abuse.

may be tempting for counselors who have been working with complex trauma survivors to also see the spouses or families of these clients, it is important to resist the temptation. After a counselor has worked so intensely with an individual, a spouse or other family members will have a hard time trusting the counselor to be impartial, a justifiable concern. Instead, it is better for the trauma counselor to continue with Phase III work, referring to an outside marriage or family therapist for the systemic work. Sometimes it can be helpful to obtain written consent for information to be shared between the counselors so that one process can inform the other.

Friendships. As C-PTSD clients get healthier, any friendships they have may become strained due to shifts on the dependency/independency spectrum. If changes in roles can be renegotiated, friendships can become stronger. However, if clients' friends have not been on a similar growth trajectory, or if clients are unable to communicate their changing needs, their friends may not understand why the rules are shifting and may feel threatened or abandoned. Counselors can help their clients understand why there may be increased strain in their relationships, as well as point out the options at their disposal to either work on their current friendships or to pursue new, healthier ones. Some C-PTSD clients have had little experience with mutual friendships in the past and so are learning for the first time what they can expect from diverse relationships, how to set appropriate boundaries, how much personal disclosure is appropriate for different levels of friendship, and how to handle conflict.

Relationship to God and church congregations. One of the more exciting and fulfilling aspects of my work with C-PTSD clients has been to watch them grow spiritually as they heal emotionally. As mentioned previously, individuals who have been traumatized, particularly if the trauma was the result of abuse in childhood, often have a distorted view of God.

Phase II work will often involve intense spiritual struggle as clients ask questions such as "If God loves me, why did he not stop the abuse? Why were my prayers not answered? My father hurt me, so is God going to hurt me too?" While these issues have likely been resolved to some degree in Phase II, the ongoing challenge in Phase III is for clients to learn new, healthier ways of relating to God.

Just as individuals choose spouses and friendships who will meet their needs at a specific point in time, so people choose church congregations

according to what currently fits for them. It may be, therefore, that a body
of believers that does a good job of ministering to clients in Phases I or II of
the counseling process may not be flexible enough to accommodate the
degree of change presented by a C-PTSD parishioner in Phase III. Another
possibility is that the view of God and theology espoused by the church no
longer fits the client's new perspective. This could happen, for example, in
the case of a fundamentalist church that focuses more on God's judgment
toward sinners than God's grace. The client might have resonated with that
view earlier in treatment but now finds it to be limiting, having come to
embrace God's compassion, mercy, and forgiveness.

Part of Phase III work for Christian clients, then, might involve helping
them to struggle with difficult decisions around whether to continue to
worship within their current church system, hoping to bring about change,
or whether they need to search for a different church home. If clients con-
clude that they need to make a transition, that knowledge is often accompanied by a sense of grief, loss, and guilt, particularly if church members had
accompanied them through difficult earlier phases of the healing process.

Community. Relationships with other people in the community may also
shift. Previous ways of dealing with health care systems (both physical and
psychological), school systems, government departments, self-help groups, and
neighbors may no longer be appropriate. For example, C-PTSD clients who
previously had not been functioning well enough to support themselves financially may have used government-assisted health care plans or social assistance
for food or housing. As they become healthier psychologically and are able to
get a job, they will no longer be a part of some of these systems and will have
to learn about others. For example, they may now need to learn how to navigate
private health care systems. Having developed a better sense of their own personal power, they may also have to learn how to be appropriately assertive with
authorities in the education system or with their bosses. It also may be that
C-PTSD clients previously have avoided dealing with some of these systems, so
are having to learn for the first time how to appropriately engage them.

Family of origin. Particularly when the perpetrator was a member of the
client's immediate or extended family, relating to the family of origin is a
complicated and emotionally intense issue. As memories surface during
Phase II, clients sometimes avoid interacting with family members, thinking
of it as a temporary solution until they have a better understanding of what

happened to them. But in Phase III, clients must make decisions about how to negotiate those family relationships. Some clients will disclose the abuse to their families for the first time. They must then navigate through their families' reactions, which can vary widely from believing the client's story and supporting the client's healing process to disbelieving the story and rejecting the client. The family also might minimize the impact of the trauma, even if they acknowledge the incidents themselves. Often clients will discover that others have also been abused by the same family member, adding validity to their own experience.

If the perpetrator is still alive, matters become even more complicated. Survivors have to figure out if they currently feel safe being around the person who abused them and if their own children are safe. These situations can pull families apart as members are forced to choose sides. If, for example, the client's brother was the perpetrator and the client is not comfortable in his presence, which one of them gets to attend Christmas dinner? Counselors need to help prepare clients for the potential reactions of family members and to support them while they struggle with the complex issues involved. There are sometimes additional losses to grieve as clients come to grips with rejection from family members they had hoped would support them but instead blame them for creating waves in the family.

EVALUATING EMPLOYMENT

As individuals become healthier psychologically they may be able to reenter the job market, or perhaps even become employable for the first time. Evaluating their employment situation, therefore, can become an important aspect of Phase III work. While this can be an exciting time full of new possibilities, it can also be overwhelming for clients to figure out what kind of job they would like to have. After identifying a specific direction, they may need to obtain further education or training in the chosen area. Some may realize that the field they would like to pursue is no longer realistic because of their age, the time it would take to prepare, or lack of finances. For example, a fifty-year-old client may discover that she has the interest and ability to become a physician. However, the physical, mental, and financial cost associated with the years of medical school, relative to the few years that she would be able to practice before retirement, may make such a goal unrealistic. Grieving such lost potential is also part of Phase III work.

CONFRONTING THE PERPETRATOR

Some counselors strongly encourage C-PTSD clients to confront their per-petrator either within or outside of the judicial system. In other cases, it is the clients who are eager to face their abuser, or friends or church members who push them to face their perpetrator in person.

I recommend erring on the side of caution. In their fantasies, clients usually visualize their perpetrators falling on their knees before them, tears streaming down their faces, as they repent and beg for forgiveness. In reality, attempts to confront usually end in more pain for the client. Perpetrators frequently totally deny the accusations, minimize the number of incidents or their impact, and want quick forgiveness. Similarly, if charges are brought against the perpetrator, victims often feel as though they are on trial when defense lawyers attempt to discredit their testimonies. Justice is not always served through the courts. Therefore, I spend a lot of time helping clients go through every possible outcome before acting on a desire to confront their perpetrator either in person or through the courts. If they still determine to go ahead, knowing that in all likelihood the perpetrator will not truly repent, at least the damage might be minimized.

An alternative to confronting the perpetrator in person is to confront them symbolically. Using the Gestalt two-chair or empty-chair technique, clients can visualize the perpetrator sitting in the empty chair and can ex-press what they want to say to the perpetrator without fear of reprisal. Many times, these role plays are unidirectional, with clients merely imagining talking to their perpetrator. Sometimes, however, it can be helpful for the client to change seats, "becoming" the perpetrator and expressing what they would want the perpetrator to say, even if they know that in reality it probably would not happen that way.

Another tool that can be helpful is writing letters to the perpetrator in a journal. The key to using this technique is giving clients permission to not censor what they write. It is not the intention for such letters to ever actually be sent, but rather for clients to express, in a safe way, what they are really feeling. Although I think it is a potentially dangerous idea, some clients choose to confront their perpetrator in writing. If they insist, even after having been cautioned against it, I will help them revise such a letter so that it expresses what they want to say in as constructive a way as possible. This letter will look quite different from the uncensored journal entries.

PRACTICING FORGIVENESS

If we are to help our clients forgive others we need to have an understanding of what forgiveness is. I have met many Christians who have a simplistic concept of forgiveness that does not encompass the complexity of the biblical view. I have found Steven Tracy's discussion of three types of forgiveness helpful in understanding what Scripture says about this concept. Tracy (2005) talks about judicial forgiveness, psychological forgiveness, and relational forgiveness. Judicial forgiveness cannot be offered by humans as it involves the pardoning of sin by God. Psychological forgiveness involves both letting go of hatred and revenge and extending grace to the one who wronged them. In the case of abuse survivors, Tracy mentions that extending grace may be most appropriately offered by desiring and praying for the healing of their perpetrators. Relational forgiveness involves restoration of the relationship or reconciliation with the perpetrator. A typical scenario with a survivor of C-PTSD may be to leave the judicial forgiveness to God, work on psychological forgiveness in counseling, and recognize that the relational forgiveness may not be possible.

A very real danger, particularly in Christian circles, is pushing C-PTSD clients to forgive their perpetrators before it is really healthy or even possible for them to do so. I have heard story after story of survivors who have been told that they are sinning if they refuse to offer forgiveness, particularly if the perpetrator has asked for forgiveness. The problem is that perpetrators so seldom really accept responsibility for the devastation resulting from their actions. Rather than truly acknowledging their sin, their repentance is really an attempt to assuage their guilt or to satisfy others around them. Their tears can be convincing but should not be mistaken for a true change of heart (Tracy, 2005). Often what perpetrators are sorry about is getting caught. They regret that their relationships, finances, freedom, reputation, or self-image may be impacted (Anton, Fortune, & Gargiulo, 1992). People who are unaware of the depths of deceit practiced by perpetrators are easily fooled. Therefore, Christians may push for reconciliation when there has been no true repentance on the part of the perpetrator, and the trauma survivor may still be in danger. Unfortunately, this can result in the revictimization of survivors by well-intentioned believers.

I believe that before they can offer either psychological or relational forgiveness, counselees need to have progressed through to at least the end of

Phase II of therapy. I say this because in order to truly forgive, one has to know *what* is being forgiven. If, for example, clients have a vague notion that they were abused in childhood but have no specific memories, saying "I forgive you" is not nearly as meaningful as it would be after having finished Phase II work, including remembering the details of traumatic incidents and fully understanding the impact of those events on their life.

Similarly, a generic request for forgiveness on the part of the perpetrator is much different from a request that clearly outlines an understanding of the full consequences of his or her actions. I sometimes tell clients that if their perpetrators had read their victims' journal entries and had watched recordings of counseling sessions that reveal the agony their victims have experienced as a result of their trauma, perhaps, then, perpetrators would be in a position to understand what they are really asking for when they request forgiveness from their victim.

I see forgiveness as a process rather than as an event at a particular point in time, a process that begins early in counseling. Some clients, including Christian ones, cannot even fathom wanting to forgive their perpetrator because their desire for revenge or their feelings of hatred are so strong.

Christian clients have often felt pushed by other Christians to forgive and are afraid that I will do the same. For this reason I tread very carefully around this issue. I tell them that the first step may be praying that God would help plant in their hearts a seed of desire to even want to begin working on forgiveness. However, even this can be threatening for some clients who need to first process the emotions that arise in Phase II and to feel understood by the counselor before even considering that forgiveness could be an option.

I have found that psychological forgiveness is often a natural outcome of the healing process. As clients process the emotions connected to their trauma in Phase II work and continue to consolidate changes in Phase III, they often realize that they no longer harbor ill will toward their perpetrators and have been able to let go of any feelings of hatred, anger, or desire for revenge. Others, though, may feel the need to consciously make a point of more actively working on forgiving their perpetrators and others who did not protect them. There are a number of approaches to forgiveness that have been outlined by Christian authors and researchers that could be helpful to counselors working with C-PTSD clients. A good summary of these models is available in a chapter on forgiveness in the book *The Long Journey Home: Understanding and Ministering to the Sexually Abused* (Sells & Hervey, 2011).

The role of the Holy Spirit in preparing clients for the process of forgiveness should be recognized. As their relationship with God develops, clients are increasingly able to respond to the Holy Spirit, trusting that God has their good in mind and will deal with their perpetrator. I have found that the issue of forgiveness comes up naturally in sessions when the timing is right, without me initiating or forcing the discussions.

While I believe that getting to the point where they can experience psychological forgiveness is possible for any trauma survivor, restoration of relationship is not always possible, particularly if there is still risk of harm to survivors or their children. Pedophiles, for example, are similar to alcoholics in that they can learn to control their addiction but are always at risk for temptation. Sex offenders, therefore, should never be placed in a position where they have easy access to children, including family gatherings where children are present. Extended family or church members who do not understand the continued risks will sometimes not recognize that a healthy, ongoing relationship with the perpetrator may not be possible this side of eternity.

ENDING THE THERAPEUTIC RELATIONSHIP

Often C-PTSD clients cannot conceive of ever being ready for the counseling relationship to end and are therefore surprised to find that a time does come when they actually do feel prepared to face life without the input of their counselor. Early on in Phase III, I will sometimes introduce the topic of the future end of the counseling relationship in a very general way, recognizing that the initial response of the client is likely to be panic. I will offer reassurance in the following way:

> *I know that right now it's hard for you to imagine ever being ready to not come in for regular counseling sessions. Believe it or not, though, that time will come! I am not going to suggest that we end our sessions before you feel ready, though. It will be a decision we will make together.*

When the timing for termination of the counseling relationship is right, usually both counselor and counselee come to that conclusion within a similar timeframe. When I am sensing that we are almost there, I generally wait for a few weeks to see if the counselee initiates discussion about it. If the client does not do so, I will then broach the subject, often finding that the client had been thinking the same thing but did not know how to bring it up.

Clients often surprise themselves by the spontaneous thoughts that come into their minds in the later stages of Phase III. For example, thinking, "If I didn't have to go to counseling, I could save up to buy x, y, or z." Or, "If I only didn't have my counseling appointment on Thursday, I could get together with my friend for lunch!" These are much different scenarios than what they experienced early on when life revolved around surviving until the next session.

When therapy has been long-term, I do not go from weekly sessions to no sessions. Instead I begin to space sessions out, beginning every other week, with the option to schedule a session in between if necessary. Then we go to every third week, then once a month, and so on. The advantage to clients is that it provides a way to practice increased independence while having the safety net of additional sessions if needed. Clients gather confidence as they realize that they are able to handle difficult challenges without input from the counselor. The end of Phase III is also a time when clients can identify continued growth areas and can discuss how they plan on meeting their growth goals.

The last few months of the counseling process involve looking back at the entire course of therapy in order to summarize the changes that have taken place, celebrate the victories, and grieve the loss of the therapeutic relationship. The grieving process does not only apply to clients, but also to counselors. In fact, counselors need to guard against hanging on to their C-PTSD clients longer than necessary in order to avoid facing the pain of saying goodbye. It is appropriate for counselors to acknowledge to their clients that they, too, are feeling loss as the end comes near, even while they rejoice in the increasing health and wholeness of their clients. In a sense, this is similar to the ambivalence that parents feel as their children grow up and leave home, rejoicing that their job of many years has been accomplished while also adjusting to their children no longer being dependent on them.

I encourage clients to think about how our last session together could be special to them. One of my clients threw a party for just the two of us! With my permission, she brought in a cake and garbage bags full of blown-up balloons, which we attached to the office furniture. Other clients have suggested sharing symbolic gifts (e.g., stickers or bookmarks), or have wanted to read me a poem. As long as what is suggested fits within appropriate boundaries for counseling, I am willing to consider it.

I always leave the door open for further counseling should clients desire it at some point in the future, normalizing it so that they do not feel that they have somehow failed if they want to set up an appointment. Most clients do not take advantage of this offer, but I have had a number of clients come back for even one or two sessions within several years of terminating the original process. Others will send me occasional updates on their lives. Some clients hope that a mutual friendship will be possible after termination of therapy. Ethical codes of conduct in therapy vary on what is considered appropriate contact with former clients. My rule of thumb is, "Once a counselor, always a counselor." In other words, even if ethically permissible, if former clients and counselors develop a more mutual relationship after a period of time, the power differential in a therapeutic relationship makes it very difficult to transform a therapeutic relationship into a truly mutual friendship.

Whether or not there will be any ongoing contact after termination of the formal counseling relationship, the client must clearly understand the boundaries. I remember being shocked at finding out that a client I had transferred to another therapist had communicated to her new therapist how distressed she was about not having heard from me since I moved. I had thought that it was clear that there would be no ongoing contact, but obviously it was not, potentially adding to abandonment issues that were already a struggle for her.

Good endings are crucial. It may very well be the first time that C-PTSD clients have ever experienced the ending of a relationship that did not feel like abandonment. Therefore, although the issues may seem less dramatic than those of Phases I or II, Phase III work requires careful attention.

7

ADDITIONAL TREATMENT CONSIDERATIONS FOR THE CLIENT WITH DISSOCIATIVE IDENTITY DISORDER

DISSOCIATIVE IDENTITY DISORDER (DID), formerly called multiple personality disorder, encompasses a subset of those who suffer from C-PTSD. While DID clients have much in common with other C-PTSD clients, there are some unique challenges in counseling this clinical population.

ADDITIONAL TREATMENT CONSIDERATIONS FOR THE DID CLIENT

- Distinguishing features of DID
- Diagnostic assessment
- Are media portrayals of DID accurate?
- Development of DID
- Modifications to the three-phase model
- Accepting responsibility
- Is full integration the goal?
- The process of integration
- Ritual abuse and mind control
- Organized abuse
- Exceptions to phased treatment
- Take courage

DISTINGUISHING FEATURES OF DID

The key factor distinguishing DID from other dissociative disorders is identity alteration. Identity alteration occurs when dissociated aspects of self actually come out and take over executive functioning of the body. The diagnostic symptom profile for DID involves severe amnesia, severe identity confusion, severe identity alteration, and either severe depersonalization or severe derealization (although both are often present at severe levels). Other specified dissociative disorder (OSDD) can have many of the same features as DID, including a high level of internal fragmentation. However, despite the existence of dissociated identities, only one part of self actually interacts with the outside world. For OSDD, identity alteration would not be rated as severe.

The differences between DID, OSDD, and other C-PTSD clients are illustrated by figures 7.1 and 7.2. As explained in previous chapters containing similar diagrams, each circle represents an individual person whose inner self has been fragmented. The "pie slices" represent distinct parts of the person, and the lines between the slices reflect the degree of communication possible among various parts of the self. The circle's outer line represents the amount of communication that part of self has with other people. The fewer the spaces between segments of a line, the less communication there is between that segment of self and the neighboring segment. Conversely, spaces breaking up a line represent information flow from one part of self to the other, with a greater number of spaces representing increased knowledge of the other.

In figure 7.1, which represents someone with DID, there are variations in the number of spaces in both the lines between sections of the pie as well as

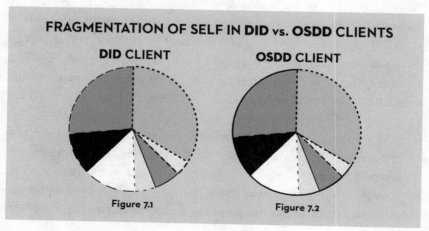

FRAGMENTATION OF SELF IN DID vs. OSDD CLIENTS

DID CLIENT

OSDD CLIENT

Figure 7.1

Figure 7.2

in areas of the outer circle. This illustrates differing amounts of communication that a person with DID has between aspects of self (inner lines) and the outside world. Notice that in figure 7.2, which represents an OSDD client, the inner lines are identical to those in figure 7.1, but the outer circle is a solid line except for one segment. This shows how the internal world of an OSDD client could possibly be identical to the inner world of a DID client. Interactions with the outside world, however, would differ, with only one part of an OSDD client interacting directly with the external environment.

Without identity alteration, individuals with OSDD will not experience many of the challenges that those with DID face. For example, people with OSDD will report memory gaps for periods of time in the past because they have compartmentalized the missing information within one of the dissociated aspects of self. However, such individuals are not likely to have amnesia for current events unless there is ongoing trauma, because only one particular part of self is interacting with the outside world. DID clients, on the other hand, struggle with day-to-day amnesia as various parts of self take executive control of the body (i.e., identity alteration) without other parts of self being co-conscious during those times.

Figure 7.2 could also represent a C-PTSD client who does not have DID or OSDD (see chapter five). The difference between these two types of clients is the decreased sense of separateness and lower degree of complexity of each section of the pie for the C-PTSD client. A DID client, for example, has parts of self whose subjective experience is that of being a totally separate person; it is news to them that they even share the body with other dissociated identities. Such parts of self may have a sense of a separate life history, experience a range of emotion, and present as a multifaceted person.

This is in contrast to parts of self of other C-PTSD clients that may be dissociated but are not as fully developed. For example, a non-DID C-PTSD client may have a part of self that feels as though she is nine years old and who holds a particular trauma memory. However, the memory of a three-hour block of time may be the extent of her life history. In contrast, a DID client may have a part of self that was initially split off to hold a particular trauma memory, but whose presence was then triggered every time she was abused by a particular perpetrator. Her memory of multiple incidents and the necessity of learning to cope with them may have resulted in the formation of a part of self who experiences a number of emotions and who behaves in a variety of ways. The degree of complexity of the dissociated identities will still vary, with some being more like personality fragments than full personalities, but there will be a core of more fully developed dissociated identities in a DID client.

In this chapter I will use the terms *parts of self, dissociated identities,* and *personalities* interchangeably. The term *presenting personality* refers to the dissociated identity that presents for counseling. This is usually the part of self that most often interacts with the outside world.

DIAGNOSTIC ASSESSMENT

In chapter three, various assessment instruments for dissociative disorders were discussed, including both screening measures and diagnostic tools for identifying DID. As mentioned previously, the SCID-D, a semistructured interview based on *DSM* diagnostic criteria for DID, is the gold standard. Informal measures based on clinical observation were also discussed.

One of the big red flags for detecting DID is signs of identity alteration (see chapter three). During sessions, counselors can look for indicators of identity alteration in the form of changes in posture, facial features, mannerisms, affect, and tone of voice. If I think I am observing such changes, I may ask, "How old do you feel right now?" or "Who am I talking to?" or, perhaps, "Do you know who I am?" If I am mistaken and no identity alteration is present, there is no harm done. But if I am accurate, answers to these questions will be revealing. One of the criteria for diagnosing DID in the *DSM-IV* was that the mental health professional had to actually observe identity alteration. According to *DSM-5* criteria, a DID diagnosis can be made based on other indicators of identity alteration without actually observing it.

Intra-interview amnesia is also a clue to DID. While many C-PTSD clients will experience memory gaps for past experiences, it is less likely that they will not remember what happened several minutes earlier in the counseling session. For DID clients, such difficulties with memory are often related to identity alteration. One part of the person may have been present earlier in the session and then switched to another part who was not previously listening in.

Even if formal assessment instruments are not used, familiarity with the types of questions that make up such tools can be very helpful in identifying which dissociative symptoms are being experienced and at what level of severity.

ARE MEDIA PORTRAYALS OF DID ACCURATE?

DID is still a controversial diagnosis. Despite its inclusion in the *DSM* for decades, some mental health professionals deny its legitimacy, contending that clients who present with symptoms of identity alteration are play-acting in a bid for attention, merely mimicking dramatic portrayals in the media.

Certainly, TV shows and movies that depict individuals with DID as having alter personalities who are psychopathic killers, or scenes that show explicit, rapid switching between child, teenaged, and adult states, do not help increase credibility. While such extreme manifestations are possible, in actuality, most people with DID have learned to hide their symptoms so that they can better blend in. This is accomplished by having well-established internal rules around who comes out and when. For example, it is understood that only adult parts of self who have the appropriate educational and training background are allowed out at work. This prevents untenable situations such as the child alters of a surgeon taking executive control of the body in the middle of performing surgery. Similarly, only those who are old enough and competent enough to drive are allowed to get behind the wheel of a car.

High-functioning DID clients are also able to switch states subtly so as to not attract attention to themselves. A social worker with DID could potentially have one part of self who interacts with clients, another part of self who does the paperwork, a different part of self who attends meetings, and yet another part of self who appears in situations where there is interpersonal tension. Coworkers would likely interpret any observable differences between these dissociated identities as related to the differing roles.

Findings from research studies have shown that between 1 and 3.12 percent of the general population in Canada and the United States meet diagnostic criteria for DID (Brand et al., 2016; Dell, 2009). That means that in a medium-sized church congregation of five hundred people, it is probable that five to sixteen individuals have DID. Therefore, you have likely unknowingly interacted with several people with DID in various contexts. Looking back, I am quite sure that what I labeled regression in some of my early trauma clients was actually a child personality of a DID client I had not recognized as such. Not surprisingly, those clients terminated prematurely, probably after figuring out that I wasn't "getting it."

Part of the skepticism associated with the concept of DID is related to a misconception that DID involves having many people share one body.

However, no matter how separate different parts of a person may feel, they are just that: parts of a whole. Also, DID has been viewed as a North American culture-bound phenomenon. However, although there may be some differences in how DID manifests in various cultures, it is clear that DID is found globally, existing in every continent (Rhoades & Sar, 2005). My own research study in the Philippines confirmed the existence of DID in a nonclinical sample of Filipinos, despite the fact that its existence was not acknowledged by mental health professionals in that country (see H. D. Gingrich, 2009).

DEVELOPMENT OF DID

DID is associated with relational trauma that occurs in early childhood, generally before six years of age (Chu, 2011a). Children who are abused later in childhood may still manifest dissociative symptoms in adulthood, perhaps even developing a different dissociative disorder, but they will not exhibit the degree of fragmentation of identity that is the hallmark of those with DID. This is because by middle and late childhood, individuals are far enough along in the normal developmental integrative process that their ability to use dissociation as a defense mechanism has been reduced. Research studies have shown that young children dissociate to a greater extent than adolescents, and that adolescents dissociate more than young adults, with this trend continuing throughout the lifespan (Ogawa et al., 1997).

MODIFICATIONS TO THE THREE-PHASE MODEL

Treatment of DID follows the same three-phase model common to counseling of all C-PTSD clients. There are, however, some adjustments that are necessary when applying the three-phase model to clients with DID. There are additional modifications to be aware of when working with an individual whose abuse involves mind control, which will be discussed in the section on ritual abuse and mind control.

Phase I. Safety can be an even more complicated matter in counselees with DID than with other complex trauma survivors. Similarly, symptom management can also be challenging. The good news is that the dissociative capacities of DID clients can be of great help in containing symptoms.

Safety within the therapeutic relationship. While the same principles apply to developing safety with DID clients as to other C-PTSD clients, the counselor's job is more difficult due to the dissociated identities of DID clients.

For example, instead of working to establish a sense of safety with one client, it is as though the counselor is trying to establish rapport and develop healthy attachments with many individuals. At times the task can seem overwhelming. Good progress may be made with one dissociated identity only to have a new one appear who has not been privy to any of the previous therapeutic work. As a result, counselors feel as though they are starting from scratch. Fortunately, there is some positive spillover in that many parts of the client will be watching or listening in the background as the counselor develops rapport with a specific part of self.

Becoming and remaining a safe person. Becoming a safe person and remaining a safe person can be more problematic for counselors who are working with DID clients. The ability to maintain appropriate, healthy boundaries often is tested when working with this population. The temptation is to make exceptions for DID clients that would not be made for any other client. For example, a terrified child alter may stir up protective, nurturing, positive countertransference reactions in the counselor, resulting in giving permission for the client to sit on the counselor's knee. In an extreme case of broken boundaries, a counselor invited his client to live with him and his family in an effort to protect her, a major ethical violation. In these cases, while well-intentioned, the counselors were not actually safe people for their clients. A good rule of thumb is, "If you would not do it for your other clients, do not make exceptions for a DID client."

Safety from others. Clients with DID are potentially at greater risk of exploitation from other people than are other C-PTSD clients because of the discrete functions parts of self were created to perform. Cindy, for example, is a DID client who is a survivor of multiple forms of extreme child abuse, one of which was forced child prostitution. A part of self named "Sexy One" was formed to deal with the degradation, shame, fear, and physical pain and pleasure associated with prostitution, feelings that were too much for Cindy to cope with. Cindy is a Christian who values sexual purity. However, when a man makes advances, Sexy One appears, believing that it is her role to give a man what he wants. The morning after, Cindy wakes up in a stranger's bed, with no idea how she got there, but with evidence that she has had sex with this man. C-PTSD clients who do not have DID may exhibit promiscuous behavior and not understand the motivation for their actions (i.e., the "B" component of BASK has been dissociated from the other components of their sexual trauma experiences in childhood). However, they are less likely to experience amnesia for their sexual choices in adulthood. For example, when they wake up in the morning after having slept with a man, they will probably remember what happened the night before unless alcohol or drugs are a factor. However, they may not understand why they choose to have casual sex so often.

A subset of DID clients report having been programmed through some sort of ritualistic abuse. These clients are in particular danger from others. This will be discussed in the section below on mind control and ritual abuse.

Safety from self. With DID clients, safety from self takes on entirely new dimensions. The issue is that the dissociated identities believe themselves to be separate people. The recognition that they all share a body and are parts of one whole comes as a result of good therapeutic work. Self-injurious behaviors, therefore, are often the result of one part of self punishing another part of self. Similarly, suicidal behaviors may actually be internally perceived as homicidal tendencies when one dissociated identity wants to kill another dissociated identity, not realizing that if the body dies, they will die too.

In the DID literature, dissociated identities who exhibit these kinds of behaviors are sometimes referred to as "persecutor alters." While the tendency may be to think of such dissociated identities as bad, or perhaps even evil, in reality there is always a good reason for such behavior. It is helpful to view all parts of a person as serving some kind of protective function, including those who seem dangerous. A common scenario is one where a part of self is punishing another part of self for going for counseling or revealing information that has been hidden. The persecutor personality has often been tortured by perpetrators, then threatened that there will be more torture, or that they will be killed, or perhaps family members will be killed, if any word gets out about what has happened to the body.

The contracting for safety with persecutor alters is very similar to negotiating with the parts of self of other C-PTSD clients, with the additional component of having to sometimes work harder to persuade the dissociated identities that they are, in fact, all parts of the same person. In my experience, this is an easier task with clients in their twenties or thirties than it is with those who are middle-aged, perhaps because after many decades of believing that they are separate people, it is harder to change perspectives. The Bible says that "the truth will set you free" (Jn 8:32), and I have certainly seen this at work in these difficult situations. If persecutor alters are able to accept that they are not actually separate people and that life circumstances are now quite different from when they were threatened, DID clients will experience freedom from their self-destructive behavior. Following is a sample dialogue with a persecutor alter.

I would like to talk to the part of Mary that cut up the body so severely this week. (A dissociated identity appears whom the counselor has not met before.)

She needed to be punished! I told her not to talk or she'd be sorry, but she wouldn't shut up! And what's this crap about me being part of Mary?! I'm Cindy!

How old are you, Cindy?

I'm fourteen. She's just so stupid! The cuts were a warning. If she keeps revealing our secrets, I'll cut deeper next time! If she's dead, she won't be able to talk.

I don't know if you're aware of this, but the problem is that you share a body with Mary. So when you cut Mary, you cut yourself, and if she dies, you die too.

Liar! We don't have the same body! We don't look alike at all! She's old and fat and has ugly short brown hair. I'm thin, and I have long blonde hair, and I'm beautiful!

Well, I know that's how you see yourself. But whether I'm looking at Mary or looking at you, I see the same body and same hair color. How about you reach up and touch your hair. (Cindy touches it.) You see, it's short, not long.

I'm confused! I know my hair is long. Who cut it?!

I know it's hard, Cindy, but if you're really honest with yourself, I think you'll realize that you and Mary are parts of the same person.

She just has to shut up!

What are you afraid will happen if she continues to talk to me?

They'll come back and hurt me again.

Cindy, do you know what year it is?

I don't think about stupid things like that.

Well, it's actually 2012. (Cindy looks surprised.) The body is big now, and you all live in Denver, not New York. Did you know that?

No . . . (whispers, uncertainly)

How about you pay more attention this week to what happens to the body and to how things are different from what you remember. I think you'll

find evidence that what I've been telling you is true. The people who threatened you did that a long time ago. Things have changed. Would you be willing to not hurt the body in any way this week until we can talk more about what's really happening now?

Well, I guess I could stop for a week, but I may still have to hurt her later on. She deserves to be punished.

I think you'll find that Mary actually doesn't deserve to be punished. You've believed a lie all these years. Why not give yourself, and Mary, a chance to find out the truth.

I'll see. No promises though.

But you will agree to not hurt the body between now and the next counseling session?

Well . . . Okay, I'll agree for this week, and then we'll see after that.

This is fairly typical of the kinds of negotiations that are necessary in order for the DID client to stay safe. While Cindy may or may not be ready to acknowledge that she is a part of Mary by our next meeting, generally resistance to the idea will have decreased. Notice that the counselor avoids the temptation to find out more about who the perpetrators were or how she was hurt. That is work for Phase II, so unless there is any sense that the client is still at risk from potential perpetrators (which is a possibility), the contracting for safety can happen without knowing such details.

I have found that DID clients perceive their inner worlds, sometimes called the *inscape*, in various symbolic ways. A common metaphor is a house with several stories and numbers of rooms, with dissociated aspects of self having specific locations and/or functions in the house. Another common metaphor is one of an entire kingdom with different regions. Whatever the specific makeup of the inscape, it is perceived by DID clients as at least as real to them as the actual external world.

Just as we can make changes to our external environment, so, too, the inscape of a DID client can be modified. This ability can be helpful with respect to safety. While earlier in the book I talked about how it can be useful for individuals with C-PTSD to visualize an internal safe place, for DID clients the possibilities are endless. So, a safe room can be created for scared child personalities, complete with pillows, blankets, stuffed animals, toys, and anything else that may be comforting. But temporary structures can also be created to contain persecutor personalities and thereby keep them from harming the body or other dissociated identities.

It is important, however, that counselors not mess with the inscape unless there is agreement from the client. Ideally persecutor personalities would themselves agree to be temporarily contained, but if they are unco-operative, and perhaps even dangerous, other parts of the client could make the decision to put them in something like a locked room, or an isolated location in the inscape for a while. Such interventions can be beneficial if used appropriately, but they should be viewed as short-term emergency measures only.

If the presenting personality or other parts of the client are not involved in these types of decisions, or if such interventions are utilized for more than a few days or weeks, the end result can be very destructive. Linda's expe-rience is an example. Linda's therapist placed some personalities she viewed as problematic in an internal cave with bars on it. Others she buried in a mass grave in the inscape because she did not want them to interfere with what she was doing in therapy. Not only did she not obtain Linda's consent for these actions, but she left these parts of Linda in captivity or buried alive permanently. Fifteen years after Linda stopped therapy with that counselor, we discovered these atrocities. The impacted personalities were retrauma-tized because their experiences in the internal world felt real to them. Trusting me was obviously an extremely slow, difficult process for each of these personalities because this previous therapist had abused her power.

Phase II. Trauma processing with DID clients is quite similar to that of other C-PTSD clients with some additional complications. While a par-ticular memory may be contained within a specific dissociated identity, it is also possible that different parts of self may hold particular aspects of a memory, whether that is a particular part of the narrative or various emo-tions associated with the event. So, for example, "Dan" may have taken the physical beating, and then "Janice" appeared once the abuse turned sexual. "Rage" may have taken on the feelings of anger about what was happening, "Little Danny" the fear, and "Naughty Girl" the shame. For all components of the memory to become integrated, all will need to participate in the memory processing of the others. That is, they will need to develop awareness of each other's roles, so that in the end, they will all have a sense of the memory as a whole, resulting in a full trauma narrative.

Similar complications arise with regard to integrating a particular memory into the fabric of the whole self. Dan, Janice, Rage, Little Danny, and Naughty Girl may all have integrated this memory, but what about the other dissociated identities? Ultimately, the information will need to be shared with every part of self. Sometimes all parts of self can be invited to listen in as the memory is processed with the dissociated identities most directly involved. However, there may be vulnerable parts of self who are not yet ready to handle the material. I generally encourage as much shared awareness as possible within the bounds of what the client system as a whole believes to be safe. DID clients are skilled at using dissociation, so they are generally able to create amnestic blocks where necessary. Once a memory is processed, however, the information has a way of filtering through to other parts of self. Counselors need to be aware of this and be prepared to do damage control in the ensuing weeks. Paying continual attention to client safety needs and client self-care is essential as Phase II work progresses.

Phase III. Phase III is both a time of great excitement as well as a time of great loss for DID clients. On the one hand, DID clients are amazed at how much simpler life is when they no longer lose time nor have to constantly vie with different parts of themselves for everything from who will get time out, to who gets to decide what to wear or what to eat for breakfast. Integration of self means integration of not only knowledge of trauma, but also other information, including skills and abilities. For example, where previously only a couple of dissociated identities went to college, everyone now reaps the benefit of that college education. Similarly, artistic talent, athletic ability, and relational skills now become available to all parts of the person. Emotions also are tempered in that they may be more mixed. For example, a dissociated identity that used to be known as Rage contributes the capacity to feel anger to the whole person. However, because others contribute the capacity to feel joy and peace and to resolve conflicts in nonviolent ways, the client will be less likely to express that anger inappropriately.

There are, however, some losses. In the process of full integration, no parts of self are lost, but they are present in a different way than before; they are no longer perceived as separate people and no longer have their own voice. For individuals who have heard voices inside their head for as long as they can remember, the silence can be deafening. Thoughts are subjectively experienced quite differently than voices, which seem to belong to other people. Therefore, some DID clients feel a type of loneliness they have never experienced before. Despite these difficulties, integrated multiples tell me they much prefer being whole to being fragmented.

Just as other C-PTSD clients have to learn coping mechanisms other than dissociation, DID clients must as well. As DID clients have used dissociation to such a great extent, developing other skills can take more time and energy. It can be quite convenient to have another part of self take over when things get tough, but upon integration, the entire person has to face the difficult situation. Clients sometimes bemoan this fact, jokingly remarking that they wish they could dissociate to avoid something they would rather not face.

ACCEPTING RESPONSIBILITY

James was distraught. He had just discovered that a seven-year-old part of him had been left stranded in the middle of an expert ski run. When I asked who could shed some light on what had happened, a cocky fifteen-year-old confessed to having chosen a ski run beyond his ability. Halfway down the slope, he got scared and decided to opt out by disappearing inside, leaving the seven-year-old to deal with the consequences!

Accepting responsibility for one's actions is an important lesson for DID clients to learn. When I contracted with the fifteen-year-old mentioned above to stick around rather than have another dissociated identity bear the brunt of his actions, he was learning increased responsibility.

The issue becomes more complex, however, when looking at responsibility from a systemic perspective. Leaving the seven-year-old in the middle of the ski hill was not the responsibility of the fifteen-year-old only, but of the entire person. Even if the fifteen-year-old refused to stay present, the decision could have been made to switch into an adult state that had some skiing ability rather than traumatize a child part. There are errors of commission and errors of omission. For example, the fifteen-year-old showed irresponsibility in taking off (commission). The rest of James erred by not stepping in to remedy the situation (omission).

Most mental health professionals who work with DID are not in favor of court case outcomes where a dissociated identity commits a crime and the person with DID is found not guilty by reason of insanity. Their concern is that the healing process could be thwarted for not only this individual but also for others with DID if such individuals are not forced to accept responsibility for what the body has done, whether or not all parts of the person were privy to the crime. The intent is not a desire to be punitive, but rather to prevent both this individual and others with DID from committing similar crimes. Other parts of self need to step in and stop a crime from being committed by any one of them.

One of the big advantages to the whole person accepting responsibility for the behavior of any one part is that it results in increased safety. With my DID clients, there have been numerous times when one dissociated identity will be about to attempt suicide but another one comes out and flushes the pills down the toilet or drives to the ER. As clients come to increased acceptance that they are all parts of a whole, the idea of accepting full responsibility becomes easier.

IS FULL INTEGRATION THE GOAL?

Integration is a scary concept for many DID clients. Some dissociated identities feel that integration is akin to murder, for upon integration, they will cease to exist. It is hard for them to grasp that although their experience as an integrated part of the whole person will be somewhat different, their memories, emotions, and abilities will not be lost. Rather, they will gain more.

While I view full integration as a desirable, and perhaps even the best, outcome, it is actually *not* the goal. The main objective is a more functional, coherent person. Therefore, if Phase I work alone helps clients to function better in life, the foremost goal has been met. Other DID clients may choose to go through the memory-processing aspects of Phase II work, sharing the trauma memories among them so that co-consciousness is increased, but decide to retain dissociated identities. In these cases the BASK components of experience will be integrated, but fragmentation of self still remains. However, when communication and negotiation among parts of self become the norm and no time gaps are experienced, the key problems associated with having DID are minimized to the extent that life can run smoothly.

I have occasionally been challenged by other Christian counselors on this point. Their contention is that God wants us to be fully healed and whole, so that anything short of full integration is missing God's best for DID clients. While I can see their point, I do not believe that any of us are fully healed or whole this side of eternity. I also think that it is disrespectful to push our own agendas onto our clients. I have found, however, that decisions to stop short of full integration are often made due to misconceptions about what it would actually be like. Therefore, I do my best to educate clients as to what they could expect if they fully integrated. Ultimately, though, the decision is theirs to make.

THE PROCESS OF INTEGRATION

The process of integration begins as awareness between dissociated identities increases. There are a number of ways to help increase such awareness.

THE PROCESS OF INTEGRATION
- Communication between counselor and parts of self
- Communication among dissociated identities
- Techniques for furthering integration

Communication between counselor and parts of self. Awareness increases as counselors begin to communicate with dissociated identities. This can happen as various ones spontaneously present in session and the counselor summarizes the discussion for the presenting personality, who may have amnesia for that conversation. While the counselor does not want to be in the position of keeping secrets between personalities, it is not always necessary to share all of the details with the presenting personality right away. Trauma content, for example, may be too overwhelming to cope with. At a minimum, I tell the presenting personality the names of any of the other dissociated parts I interacted with during the session, as well as some general information about them, such as age, gender, and at least a broad idea of what we talked about. Ultimately, however, shared knowledge of each dissociated identity's experiences with all parts of self is necessary in order for integration to occur.

As contracts for safety are negotiated between counselors and counselees in Phase I—as all parts of self are invited to "listen in" so that counselors can contract for safety, and as agreements are made—DID clients also gain knowledge about themselves. Each time this happens, it is as though one more brick is removed from the wall between segments of the pie in figure 7.1. When enough bricks are removed, a gap in the wall appears, allowing for a greater degree of co-consciousness.

Communication among dissociated identities. While initially counselors generally mediate negotiations for safety or for resolving other areas of difficulty, over time they should train and encourage their DID clients to use a similar approach when trying to solve day-to-day problems, such as getting to work rather than not showing up because a child part would rather play. The presenting personality can be encouraged to initiate contact with other parts of self in order to have a better idea of how their personality system is formed. Information will be limited because full knowledge of various dissociated identities would involve knowing their trauma histories, work that is relegated to Phase II. However, clients can learn how old various parts of them feel, their genders, and their likes and dislikes. This is analogous to the beginnings of any relationship. We do not generally reveal our innermost secrets to a new friend. It may take months or years for relationships to develop to the point that we trust the other person with deeply personal information. Similarly, DID clients can be encouraged to find out more about themselves as long as all parts are aware of the dangers of revealing too much too soon.

Clients can also be encouraged to find out more about how their system is organized internally. They will discover that there are helper parts who take care of child parts, or aspects of self that can be counted on to pass along helpful information. Often there are various layers of dissociated identities that are exposed over time. The concept of a map can sometimes be helpful in better understanding the inscape. A map offers a visual way for information about dissociated identities and their relationships with each other to become clearer. Most dissociated identities will only be aware of some aspects of the inscape, so the map will continue to develop as various parts pool their knowledge over time. Getting down on paper or on a computer what the inscape looks like can be a way for all parts of self to gain awareness of how their personality system is formed, thereby increasing integration. As healing happens, the inscape changes. Parts, for example, that may have been living in solitary confinement in an internal dungeon can be released, cared for, and invited to live in another internal location. Child parts whose sole experience of the internal world has been the walls of a closet can be taken to an internal nursery where dissociated identities who have developed caregiver functions can nurture them.

Techniques for furthering integration. As mentioned in the previous section, most integration happens spontaneously through the gradual sharing of information and as a result of memory processing. Full integration of dissociated identities can also happen spontaneously. I will never forget my confusion one day as I met with Haley. I had worked with her for many years and knew most of her parts very well. But on this one occasion, I could not figure out which dissociated identity had walked into the session. Finally I said, "You're going to have to help me out here. I thought I was talking to TB (short for "Tough Broad"), but now you seem more like Angry One! Who am I talking to?" The client laughed, replying, "We wondered how long it would take you to figure it out! We're partially integrated now! We already knew each other's memories and shared each other's feelings, so we thought that there wasn't really any more need to stay separate. So here we are!" Never again did I talk to either TB or Angry One separately; from then on they presented as one identity. Gradually others joined them until full integration of all parts occurred.

This kind of spontaneous integration is what I prefer, because when it is client initiated, the timing is clearly right and the process authentic. Some clients prefer an integration ritual, such as visualizing walking toward each other until they blend into one. I will help facilitate something like this, although I do not generally suggest it. It is also possible to have clients experiment with temporary fusions so that they can get a sense of what it feels like without having to fully commit to the process. These types of decisions should be made on a case-by-case basis rather than being viewed as regular protocol.

Sometimes dissociated identities can benefit from the knowledge that integration is even a possibility. In preparation for future integration, for example, I may let child parts know that it is possible for them to grow up, even having several birthdays in a short period of time. One of Haley's parts, named Billy, was initially nine but came into the next session saying that he was now eleven, and a few weeks later informed me that he was now a teenager. When parts of self are of a different gender than the body, I will on occasion suggest that they begin to think of themselves as the same gender as the body. I may also suggest that dissociated identities that are getting ready to integrate begin to visualize themselves as looking similar to the presenting personality so that integration is not so jarring to them. Remember that individuals who dissociate a lot are highly suggestible, increasing the chances that DID clients will actually follow through. These are not necessary tools; they are merely potentially helpful tips for some clients.

If counselors guide their DID clients appropriately through the three phases of counseling, integration will naturally follow.

RITUAL ABUSE AND MIND CONTROL

As mentioned previously, there is a subset of DID clients who are victims of *ritual abuse* (RA) and *mind control* (MC). While DID is controversial, RA and MC are even more contentious. Many mental health professionals deny that victims of RA and MC even exist. There has, however, been mounting evidence that mind-control techniques have been used for decades and that various types of ritualized abuse are practiced, often as part of religious ceremonies (J. R. Noblitt & P. P. Noblitt, 2014). RA was formerly called "satanic ritual abuse" (SRA) in the literature, but after it became clear that it was not only specific satanic cults but other groups that used rituals in which torture was practiced, it became known as "sadistic ritual abuse." More recently it was recognized that MC is a core aspect of all RA and that these MC elements greatly add to the complexities of treatment. Therefore, while some people still refer to SRA, the current literature tends to use the terminology *RA/MC*.

I can barely touch on this complex topic in this book.[1] It is important to recognize its existence, though, because DID treatment becomes much more complicated if RA/MC has been involved. While all C-PTSD clients are at risk of continued abuse by former perpetrators, clients who have been programmed using MC are at unique risk as they are sometimes unknowingly at the mercy of programmed cues. For example, such clients can receive a letter in the mail or a phone call with a specific word or phrase in it that triggers a switch to a specific part of self to obey the programmed command. Often it involves the dissociated identity meeting someone at a specific place and time. Unfortunately, such meetings may result in continued torture as a way to reinforce programming. It is not unusual for the abuse to be perpetrated as a way of dissuading clients from continuing their counseling.

Some of the indicators that clients may have been victims of RA/MC include worsening symptoms during specifically Christian holidays (e.g., Christmas

---

[1]For more information see my coauthored chapter (Miller & Gingrich, 2017) on ritual abuse and mind control in the book *Treating Trauma in Christian Counseling*. For a secular book that gives great, detailed treatment strategies see Miller (2012).

and Easter) as well as occult holidays (e.g., solstice, full moon, Halloween) (Miller, 2012). One of my clients became predictably suicidal every spring until memories were processed of specific satanic rituals that had been performed at that time of year. Not all RA/MC is religious in nature. There is documentation that has recently become declassified of extensive US-government MC experiments.[2] Clients also report having been victims of military MC and RA/MC connected to some secret societies. Triggers will obviously be different for nonreligious RA/MC.

The types of memories that come to light in Phase II can also be a sign of RA/MC. They are sometimes so bizarre and horrific that they seem unbelievable. Some of the incidents that are commonly reported are being buried alive, being impregnated and then forced to give birth only to have the baby killed in a ritual sacrifice, Black Masses involving cannibalism as a mockery of Christian communion, ritualized group rape, marriage to Satan, torture using electric shock—the list goes on and on. Some of these rituals seem to increase the likelihood of demonic involvement in the lives of these clients. This topic will be addressed in chapter eight.

Counselors are unlikely to ever know if events happened as their clients remember them or if drugs or trickery were used to make children believe that something happened that actually did not. For example, did the client actually observe someone being killed in a ritual, or was a fake dagger and fake blood used to make a drugged child believe that they were witnessing a ritualized murder?

For healing to occur, it is not important that counselors or clients know for sure what did or did not happen. Counseling needs to deal with client perceptions. This is one time where counselors may need to proceed as though the reports of their clients are true while recognizing that things may not be as they seem. When clients ask if such horrendous things really happened, I respond that there will likely never be any proof one way or the other, but that there must be some reason that they are so terrified (or whatever emotion is in evidence). If they push the issue, accusing me of not believing them, I will reassure them that I do not think they are lying, but that their healing does not depend on whether or not there is absolute proof that what they remember actually happened in the exact manner they describe.

---

[2]Project MK-Ultra was a CIA experiment on MC. A web search engine will lead you to information on it, including the previously classified documents.

The good news in working with MC is that what is programmed can be deprogrammed. In brief, mind control, or programming, involves torture as a way to force individuals to believe certain things or to behave in specific ways that further the interests of the perpetrator group. Deprogramming takes place as a result of processing the trauma that was used to program the individual.

The bad news is that working with this population is arguably some of the most challenging therapeutic work that exists. There have been good books written on the area of RA/MC, and there are organizations that can offer help.[3] If you think that you have a client who may have experienced RA/MC, it is imperative that you search out these resources and seek supervision from counselors who are experienced in this type of work.

ORGANIZED ABUSE

Organized abuse (OA) is a term that is used when one or more victims are abused by multiple perpetrators working together. RA/MC can be considered a subcategory of OA, as can sex trafficking. But often all of these categories overlap, particularly in cases where the RA/MC perpetrator group is a multigenerational family group. While such groups may identify as religious groups, they inevitably also have connections with other OA groups, so that victims are not only forced to participate in rituals, and tortured as part of MC programming, but are also involved in the commercial sex trade (e.g., used in pornography or forced to participate in pornography). Recently evidence has mounted that victims of familial organized abuse are often abused well into adulthood, sometimes for forty or fifty years (Canadian Centre for Child Protection, 2017). The presenting personality may not even be aware, for example, that other dissociated identities are prostituting themselves in obedience to family members' demands and sending the money to their family members. Or they may think that they are no longer participating in RA rituals, only to find out that some other part of them is responding to a programmed cue to appear at a certain time and place. Recognizing that such abuse is ongoing is, of course, devastating to clients who

---

[3]The International Society for the Study of Trauma and Dissociation sponsors a special interest group for those who work with RA/MC and has resources listed on their webpage (www.isst-d .org), as well as a listserver for therapists working with RA/MC that has been a lifesaver for me. Survivorship (www.survivorship.org) is an organization that exists to support and educate those who have been victims of RA/MC, but their material can be informative to counselors as well. See also Miller's book referenced previously (2012) and her book for RA/MC survivors (2014).

have assumed that they are free from the influence of their abusive families. Even survivors' spouses may have no clue that abuse is ongoing.

EXCEPTIONS TO PHASED TREATMENT

While space does not allow me to say more about RA/MC/OA, I think it is important that counselors are aware of its existence. Otherwise counselees may never actually be safe from their perpetrators. One indication of ongoing abuse—when you are doing everything you are supposed to do as a counselor—is that anytime you begin to see therapeutic gains, your client seems to go backward and get worse, so that no traction is ever made.

It is under these circumstances that an exception to working within a phased treatment approach may be necessary. The goals of Phase I, safety and symptom stabilization, at times may only be accomplished by processing the trauma by which a particular personality was programmed. For example, if the intention of the perpetrator group was to install suicide programming that was to be set off if the individual goes into therapy, there may be no way for the client to be safe without this suicide program being deactivated. The challenge is to continue to work on overall stabilization (Phase I work) even while doing the necessary trauma processing (Phase II work), keeping in mind the necessity of working within the optimal window of tolerance, in order to make safety from others, or safety from self, possible.

TAKE COURAGE

While this chapter has outlined some of the additional things to consider in working with DID, such clients have much in common with other C-PTSD clients. All C-PTSD clients dissociate, but DID clients dissociate to a greater extent. This means that if you have developed some skill at working with C-PTSD clients who do not have a dissociative disorder, you already have most of what you need to work with DID clients. Conversely, if you know how to deal with DID, you will have the necessary tools to work with other C-PTSD clients.

8

SPIRITUAL ISSUES AND RESOURCES IN THE TREATMENT OF COMPLEX PTSD

WHAT KINDS OF SPIRITUAL ISSUES do C-PTSD clients struggle with, and how are these concerns best addressed in counseling? In this chapter I will identify some of the common conflicts C-PTSD clients face in their attempts to relate to God. I will also discuss the pros and cons of using explicit spiritual resources with these clients. While I focus specifically on trauma and Christian spirituality in this chapter, there exists a broader literature that encompasses other religions and differing types of spirituality with respect to trauma. The appendix of *Treating Trauma in Christian Counseling* (H. D. Gingrich & F. C. Gingrich, 2017) includes an extensive summary of

SPIRITUAL ISSUES AND RESOURCES

- Why did God not protect me?
- Confusion between God and perpetrator
- Use of prayer and Scripture within sessions
- Use of spiritual resources outside of sessions
- Inner-healing prayer
- Working with Christian clients who have non-Christian dissociated identities
- Dealing with the demonic
- The counselor as a spiritual resource

these resources. An American Psychological Association Publication, *Spiritually Oriented Psychotherapy for Trauma* edited by Walker, Courtois & Aten (2015) includes both Christianity and other religions among its chapters.

WHY DID GOD NOT PROTECT ME?

The question of why God did not intervene when they were being so terribly hurt is one that clients will inevitably raise at many points in the counseling process. If God is all-powerful, then why did he not stop it? The question is a fair one, but there are no easy answers, and counselors should not attempt to defend God and provide answers. It may be tempting to turn to theology for solutions. However, a theological understanding that focuses, for example, on how God created us with free will and so will not intervene to stop someone who makes a choice that is not in accordance with his will is a good discussion topic for a seminary class, but it is not likely going to reassure C-PTSD clients of God's love for them. Their struggle is not so much with a cognitive question requiring more knowledge but an emotional yearning for certainty that God can be trusted and really does want the best for us. Often, the question comes out of a sense of abandonment and rejection: "If God can do anything, and if he really does love me like the Bible says he does, then why didn't he rescue me?"

I have found that the best-received interventions are empathy and genuineness. For example, an empathic response could be something like, "It sounds as though the abuse was horrendous, but when you cried out to God and he didn't stop it, you felt even worse, like you must be so bad that even God didn't love you." An example of genuineness could be, "I feel so sad thinking about you as a little girl, begging God to get them to stop hurting you. The question you just asked me is one of my top questions for God when I see him face to face." C-PTSD clients are often relieved to hear these responses instead of the easy answers they have, unfortunately, come to expect from Christians.

The good news is that when such clients are given permission to struggle with these types of existential and faith questions, they often can begin to see where God was at work in the situation, even if he did not stop the perpetrators. Haley, for instance, reported being thrown into a cold, damp, rat-infested cellar for several days after having been beaten, tortured, and gang-raped. While the rats were drawn to the smell of the blood seeping from her wounds, she remembers seeing a circle of angels surrounding her, keeping the rats from biting her. Other clients talk about having sensed the presence of the Holy Spirit even while they were being hurt, or of seeing an image of Jesus weeping, both of which communicated a sense of God caring for them. Some C-PTSD counselees have a hard time seeing where God was in the midst of their torture but rejoice that the pain they experienced in the past is enabling them to increasingly reach out to others who are hurting as they themselves progress in their healing journey. Others are able to derive comfort from seeing God at work in their healing process.

Even if it is not often appropriate to discuss a theology of suffering (i.e., theodicy) directly with clients, I believe that it is important for counselors to have worked through the theological issues for themselves. There are some excellent resources available that are particularly helpful for counselors and could be beneficial for some counselees. Diane Langberg's book *Suffering and the Heart of God: How Trauma Destroys and Christ Restores* (2015) is passionately written and particularly powerful. *Between Pain and Grace: A Biblical Theology of Suffering* by Gerald Peterman and Andrew Schmutzer (2016) is written in a more academic style and offers some very interesting perspectives. Most of the chapters in *Treating Trauma in Christian Counseling* (H. D. Gingrich & F. C. Gingrich, 2017) address aspects of suffering in the context of various types of trauma, including one chapter that focuses exclusively on this topic (Langer, McMartin, & Hall, 2017). While not exclusively focusing on suffering, Schmutzer (2011) examines sexuality and sexual abuse in the Bible. He provides a good theological context for a number of issues that are related to how we, as Christians, can think about trauma and abuse. Resources such as these can offer immensely helpful background for counselors working with complex trauma.

CONFUSION BETWEEN GOD AND PERPETRATOR

Particularly problematic are situations where clients have at some level equated God with their perpetrators. Sometimes the link is indirect, such as when an incest survivor was abused by her father, so she assumes that "God the Father" is going to hurt her. There are, however, situations in which perpetrators have explicitly connected God to the suffering of their victims. Sometimes this includes elements of spiritual abuse when Scripture is used to justify inflicting pain. For example, a child who is beaten by his mother as punishment for disobedience while she quotes the verse "Children, obey your parents" (Eph 6:1) will not likely be able to embrace a view of God as loving and compassionate.

In cases of satanic ritual abuse, attempts are sometimes made to discredit Christ by deceiving children into believing that it is Jesus who is abusing them. Children are told that this is Jesus, and a perpetrator may wear a costume that resembles that of storybook pictorial representations of Christ in order to make the lie more believable. Obviously, it will take a lot of work to undo the resulting damage.

USE OF PRAYER AND SCRIPTURE WITHIN SESSIONS

Given the ambivalence C-PTSD clients often experience toward God, great care needs to be taken in the timing of explicit use of spiritual resources. Counselors can err in two directions. At one extreme, counselors might totally avoid this area out of concern for being respectful of their clients' spirituality. That, in effect, conveys the message that God is not a part of the counseling process. At the other extreme are some Christian counselors who believe that making use of the Bible and prayer in counseling is necessary for healing. They might end up being insensitive to the actual needs of their clients. Both extremes can be serious mistakes.

I believe that the best approach is for counselors to take their cues from their clients. If clients bring up a question about God, counselors should be sure to explore it with them. Existential concerns that are raised by clients, such as questions about the purpose of their existence or why they were victimized, can serve as potential openings for more explicit spiritual discussions. Sometimes it may be appropriate to ask, "How does God fit into this?" as long as the counselor does not have a specific agenda. I have always worked in contexts that clearly identified me as a Christian, either because "Christian" was in the name of the counseling agency or because I was teaching at a seminary. Therefore, the topic of God or religion generally comes up in the first session with both Christian and non-Christian clients. This gives me a good sense of where the client is spiritually and whether or not I should explicitly use spiritual resources.

Karen made it very clear within the first fifteen minutes of our initial counseling session that if I quoted Scripture or attempted to pray with her, she would march out of my office and never come back. Karen was a

Christian, but she was struggling with God, both because of the abuse memories that had begun to come back and because some people in her former church community had attempted to use prayer and Bible verses as quick fixes instead of walking with her in her pain. I agreed to let her initiate any discussions about God and to not use prayer and Scripture in our sessions together unless she felt it would be helpful at some point in the future. I did pray regularly for her outside of sessions, and many times, silently, in session, relying on the Holy Spirit to guide our work together.

Three years later (yes, three years!), Karen came into a session and said, "I took my guitar out of the closet this week and played a few worship choruses." This was her way of opening the door to further discussions about spiritual things. Several months later, as she was searching for a church community to connect with, she asked whether we could pray together. Nothing was more exciting for me than seeing Karen heal not only emotionally but also spiritually. If I had tried to force the issue, I believe I may have scared her away and interfered with God's work in her life.

While many C-PTSD clients may be like Karen and shy away from spiritual topics, others may be the exact opposite, asking that Scripture and prayer be an ongoing, explicit part of sessions. This request could possibly indicate a healthy reliance on God as the Great Counselor, with prayer and Scripture verses being used in a constructive way in the counseling process. Spiritual resources, however, can also be used in a conscious or unconscious attempt to circumvent the hard work of Phase II. Therefore, I would suggest that counselors not automatically acquiesce to such a request without doing some further exploration. A counselor could say, for example, "I certainly believe in the power of prayer, but I'm wondering how you are hoping that praying in sessions will help in your counseling process." Sometimes clients will allude to a belief that the counselor's prayers are more powerful than their own prayers. To combat that kind of magical thinking, I tend to either ask C-PTSD clients to lead in prayer while I pray silently with them, or I agree to pray only if they also will pray aloud.

Insight as to the client's motivation for asking for prayer can be gained by inquiring, "What is it you would like me to pray for?" If the response is along the lines of "so that I won't hurt so much," it provides an opportunity to educate the client about the process of healing, a process that requires experiencing pain. The content of the prayer can then be negotiated to fit with the reality of the process. I might say, for example, "What if I pray that God will give you the strength to be able to face your pain, or that you will sense the presence of the Holy Spirit despite the pain?" This is a very different prayer than that originally requested.

The same principles can be used to discern whether use of Scripture is appropriate. For example, a verse such as "And we know that in all things God works for the good of those who love him, who have been called according to his purpose" (Rom 8:28) should be an encouraging reminder to us that God can see the "redemptive possibilities" in anything that comes our way (Benner, 1998b, 137). However, this verse could be prematurely used by counselors with their C-PTSD clients in the hope that it will help them find some purpose in their pain. Rather than encouragement, clients who are in the middle of Phase II, reeling from the horrific memories of their torture, may perceive their counselors as offering quick, unsatisfactory solutions to their questions about God. Worse yet, the interpretation of the verse could be twisted by either counselors or clients to suggest that God wanted them to be hurt so that they would depend on him, or that being abused was somehow a "good" thing.

In contrast, C-PTSD clients who are in Phase III of their healing process, and who have begun to recognize how God is working in their lives, may find comfort in this verse. Thoughtful, well-timed use of Scripture can be of immense help at any phase of the healing process when applied appropriately to specific clients. Many Bible passages include stories and experiences of people who suffered, such as Job and the psalmist. These, along with knowledge of the suffering and death of Jesus, can provide powerful connections to a victim's story. Focusing on Christ and his suffering also allows for the hope of the resurrection to be part of the client's story, whether or not Christ's resurrection is ever explicitly mentioned.

USE OF SPIRITUAL RESOURCES OUTSIDE OF SESSIONS

There are occasions in which counselors can suggest that clients pursue some spiritual activities between sessions. Included can be things such as meditation on a passage of Scripture, encouragement to be aware of God's presence throughout the day, various forms of prayer (e.g., listening prayer, praying the Psalms), finding a church community, practice of silence, participation in worship services, going on a personal retreat, worshiping in various ways (e.g., singing, lighting a candle), communion, baptism, reading Christian literature, and so on. There may be clients who would benefit from use of out-of-session spiritual resources who would not be comfortable with explicit use of such resources in the session itself. For others, such spiritual resources can be used outside of counseling sessions in addition to utilizing in-session prayer and Scripture.

INNER-HEALING PRAYER

I am using the phrase "inner-healing prayer" to encompass a variety of approaches that use prayer to deal with painful memories. While the various approaches differ in terms of the details of their rationale and procedures, they share an emphasis on going back to specific events in the past and then praying for the healing presence of Christ to resolve the pain of those memories by inviting Jesus to come into the memory (Hurding, 1995).

Some of the key proponents of inner-healing prayer are Agnes Sanford, Francis MacNutt, Betty Tapscott, Ruth Carter Stapleton, John and Paula Sandford, David Seamands, Leanne Payne, Siang-Yang Tan, Mike Flynn and Douglas Gregg, Charles Kraft, Karl Lehman (Immanuel prayer), and Ed Smith. Out of this group, Ed Smith's Transformation Prayer Ministry or TPM (formerly Theophostic Prayer Ministry) is a unique and widely used contemporary approach. Training sessions are available on the TPM website free of charge (see www.transformationprayer.org). According to Ed Smith (personal communication, August 23, 2019), TPM can be used effectively with individuals who have been diagnosed with dissociative disorders.

I think that with proper training and careful discernment as to the appropriateness of specific approaches for particular clients, many types of healing prayer can potentially be helpful as part of Phase II work. There are, however, a number of potential pitfalls. Most of these approaches are intended for use by lay counselors who, even with some training, often do not have the necessary background to understand the complexities involved in working with complex trauma survivors. One of the dangers is in opening up painful memories before Phase I work has been solidified, resulting in the client being overwhelmed. Another tendency of some inner-healing approaches is to suggest that praying through one memory will be sufficient as representative of all the other memories. While it may be true that not every traumatic incident needs to be processed separately, particularly in the cases of chronic abuse where there may be incidents that are similar to each other, working through one memory will seldom suffice.

A further caution regarding the use of TPM is the conceptual understanding that at the core of traumatic memory is a "lie," a belief the client held that made them vulnerable to the abuse or the power of the memory over them. While TPM is careful to not "blame the victim," it is not unlikely that the victim may feel responsible for the lies they believed and therefore for the abuse they experienced. There are relatively few even well-trained laypeople who are sensitive and wise enough to make these determinations and adjust the process accordingly.

If clients are both being ministered to by such prayer teams as well as being seen by professional counselors, it may be constructive to obtain informed consent from the client to allow for communication between the leader of the prayer team and the counselor. Constructive input from the counselor could potentially increase the chance that all parties are working toward the same goal. Of course care needs to be taken that any suggestions made by the counselor to a prayer team are offered in a respectful way so that the prayer team is not alienated.

If the counselor and prayer team end up working at cross-purposes despite the counselor's attempts to work cooperatively, the client may need to choose between approaches. Respectfully allowing clients to make their own decisions, and leaving the door open for future counseling if clients choose to pursue inner-healing ministry over counseling, can make it easier for clients to reengage the counseling process if they desire to do so at some point in the future.

While inner-healing prayer approaches have generally been geared for use by church ministry teams or lay counselors, professional counselors could use inner-healing prayer as part of their counseling toolkits. That is, rather than being utilized as an isolated approach that is chosen instead of counseling, inner-healing prayer could be integrated into Phase II memory work as it has been described in chapter five. However, for many C-PTSD clients, inner-healing prayer will not be appropriate, either because they do not identify themselves as Christians, or because they are ambivalent about their relationship with God. Some of the inner-healing approaches are fairly formulaic, making it more difficult for counselors to adapt them to the unique needs of a particular client. A common ingredient of some approaches is that clients are asked to visualize Jesus in the midst of the memory. Being required to visualize Christ in a situation where they did not experience him at the time can be confusing, if not distressful, for clients. Therefore, counselors should carefully assess the suitability of specific inner-healing prayer approaches for particular clients if they wish to use them.

WORKING WITH CHRISTIAN CLIENTS WHO HAVE NON-CHRISTIAN DISSOCIATED IDENTITIES

I once asked a well-known theologian if highly dissociative people would be considered Christians if one or more of their dissociated identities were Christ followers but the rest did not purport to be Christians and were even actively anti-Christian. The question totally floored him, so I was left to wrestle with the issue on my own.

The question of their salvation has been a burning question for a number of my C-PTSD clients who are aware that they have dissociated identities who are not living for God. Those who have been ritually abused may even have dissociated identities that still participate in satanic rituals. "What would happen if I died tonight?" some have asked. That is a question a counselor cannot answer, as only God ultimately knows. However, under these circumstances I remind them of biblical truths that are clear. I tell them that God loves them and deeply desires a relationship with them now and in the future. I then remind them that God knows what has happened to them, understands their current struggles, and that he would not expect of them something that is not currently possible. These truths can be reinforced as clients recognize God's care for them in bringing them into counseling and in the healing that has occurred to that point. In some ways this is only an exaggerated version of the issue that many Christians deal with throughout the Christian life and is reflected in Paul's famous lament, "I do not understand what I do. For what I want to do I do not do, but what I hate I do" (Rom 7:15). We all struggle with parts of ourselves that are not totally committed to Christ—continuing to daily turn over control of our lives to Christ only to sometimes take the control back!

A verse that is particularly meaningful to highly dissociative clients is Psalm 139:13: "For you created my inmost being; you knit me together in my mother's womb." The Living Bible uses the phrase "inner parts" instead of "inmost being," which dissociative clients can particularly relate to. The message I try to convey by pointing them to this verse is that "God created you, and he knows you better than you know yourself. He knows the struggles you are having. He is a merciful God and he loves you, all of you—those who desire to serve him and those who don't." The parable of the lost sheep (Lk 15:3-7) is very applicable in making this point. In this passage the shepherd leaves the rest of his flock to seek out the one sheep that is lost. For someone with dissociated aspects of self, the lost sheep could represent the parts of self who do not know Christ, the Good Shepherd. The image of Jesus searching for parts of self that are lost, and perhaps hurt or scared, is a powerful message of love rather than of abandonment or rejection for these clients.

In my experience, for highly dissociative clients who have even one part of self who would claim to be Christian, all of their other dissociated identities have eventually made a decision for Christ as they learn about him. Some parts of self may have gone to Sunday school and church all their lives, but others will not have heard of Jesus, and still others believe the lies planted by their perpetrators. One of my clients came up with a very creative way to share the gospel with her dissociated identities. She invited all parts of her to attend an internal Bible study led by the Christian parts of her. Included were Bible storybooks for children that her child parts could understand. As various dissociated identities understood who Jesus really was, they gradually made decisions to follow Christ.

DEALING WITH THE DEMONIC

Remember the horror story of Haley and the plate-glass window incident with which I began this book? The well-intentioned people at Haley's church believed that her inner struggles were caused by demons, and they gathered in prayer to try to cast out those spirits. However, they did not realize that Haley's symptoms were not directly caused by demons, and their prayers ended up being harmful rather than helpful to Haley. Unfortunately, it is common in some types of churches to attribute mental health concerns to demonic origins, and many C-PTSD clients are damaged. Even churches that do not generally talk about the demonic or do not even believe that evil spirits are currently active sometimes reassess their theological positions when faced with someone with dissociative symptoms. Their confusion is understandable in that both demonized individuals, as described in Scripture or throughout the history of the church, and people with DID exhibit symptoms of identity alteration such as changes in facial and body expression, different voices, verbal threats, feeling like different people, and self-destructive and other destructive behaviors. When Christians do not understand dissociation, these behaviors are likely to be interpreted in some church circles as evidence of sin in the person's life, or in other church circles as an indication of demonic activity. Both erroneous interpretations can have potentially devastating consequences.

DEALING WITH THE DEMONIC
- Can Christians be demonized?
- Differentiating dissociated identities from evil spirits
- Deliverance prayer
- An expanded view of spiritual warfare

Can Christians be demonized? Among Christians, there are vast differences of opinion as to the role of the demonic, particularly in the lives of individuals who serve Christ. Views range from beliefs that demonic activity is a current reality, to beliefs that Christians can be oppressed (i.e., attacked from the outside) but not possessed, to a view that evil spirits are behind many of our physical, psychological, and day-to-day struggles (Bubeck, 1975). A term I have found helpful is *demonization* because it implies a range of direct and indirect demonic influence (Dickason, 1987). This leaves room for someone to look as though they are possessed but be only partially under the control of demons, total possession not being possible if one is filled by the Holy Spirit (Kraft, 2010).

Differentiating dissociated identities from evil spirits. When is the evil-sounding, threatening voice an evil spirit, and when is it a dissociated identity that has taken on a persecutor role? This is a question fraught with theological landmines with no definitive answers. There have been attempts to make lists of the differences between the two, but ultimately I have found that the distinctions break down. However, one clue that identity alteration is indicative of a dissociated identity rather than a demon is that even a persecutor personality will eventually establish a positive working relationship with the counselor, while demons continue to resist, intent on destroying client and counselor. However, a positive alliance can take a long time, leaving counselors unsure as to what they are dealing with.

The good news is that it is not always necessary to determine what exactly is happening. One of the most helpful pieces of advice I have heard was from a pastor who reminded his audience that if there is demonic involvement, the evil spirits have likely already been around for a long time, so they do not have to be dealt with immediately. This knowledge took a lot of the pressure off.

Deliverance prayer. In Christian circles where individuals believe that demons can have an influence over believers, direct power encounters such as exorcisms or deliverance prayer are often the route chosen to deal with evil spirits. The problem is the potential damage to C-PTSD clients that is inherent in such approaches.

I will never forget the case of Jonathan, a seventeen-year-old male with DID who had been taken in by a caring, Christian family. Both the family and their church community interpreted Jonathan's identity alteration symptoms as evidence of demonic activity, putting pressure on him to acquiesce to a deliverance session. Jonathan realized that he had DID but felt that he had no choice but to go along with what the church people wanted. After all, he was totally dependent on them for his food and shelter. Despite my reservations, Jonathan went ahead with the deliverance ritual, after which he claimed to be fully integrated and no longer in need of therapy. I remember praying, "Lord, if you have truly done a miracle in Jonathan's life, then please forgive my unbelief," because my gut warned me that the change was not authentic. As Jonathan was intent on terminating therapy, I had no option but to let him go in spite of my heavy heart. A year later, Jonathan contacted me, coming in for one more session. He decided to let me in on the truth, that in fact he had not been integrated but had been so traumatized by the deliverance procedure that he had split off another dissociated identity whose role was to appear integrated. In fact, Jonathan informed me that he was more traumatized by the efforts to deal with the demonic than he had been by any other traumatic event.

What he described was not the noisy, out-of-control scenario I was envisioning must have contributed to his sense of trauma. Instead, Jonathan reported that most of the people on the team were praying in one room, with only three individuals quietly praying directly with him in another location. What Jonathan had experienced as so traumatic was the fact that, mistaking dissociated identities for demons, the group had been attempting to cast out dissociated parts of Jonathan. In essence, Jonathan was being inundated with the message that he was evil and needed to die! Unfortunately, Jonathan's reaction is not uncommon.

Despite the dangers, there are times when some Christian counselors believe that deliverance prayer is warranted, for example, in extreme situations such as satanic ritual abuse, in working with those who have a strong tendency toward self-destruction, or with clients who consistently block efforts to apprehend truth. But I question whether the potential benefits outweigh the potential risks, particularly for DID clients prior to full integration. Despite my concerns as a counselor, however, there are occasions in which a client absolutely insists on undergoing such a procedure.

If exorcism-type rituals are entered into, there are ways of maximizing the benefits and minimizing the risks. Research on exorcism has been helpful in identifying the factors that contributed to whether the exorcism procedure was experienced as positive or negative by individuals with DID (Bull, Ellason, & Ross, 1998). Participants consistently gave positive reports of exorcisms that incorporated all of the following factors: permission of the individual, noncoercion, active participation by the individual, understanding of DID dynamics by the exorcist, implementation of the exorcism within the context of psychotherapy, compatibility of the procedure with the individual's spiritual beliefs, incorporation of the individual's belief system, and the willingness to teach the individual how to use the exorcism procedure themselves. Exorcisms that omitted all of these factors were rated very negatively, 100 percent of the time. The same negative finding was true for the absence of all three factors related to the individual's sense of autonomy in the exorcism process (i.e., permission, noncoercion, and participation).

In Jonathan's case, while he gave permission, and even though the family he lived with denied that any coercion was involved, the reality is that Jonathan did not feel that he had any choice but to agree to the deliverance session. Therefore, he did feel coerced. He also experienced no sense of autonomy because the deliverance team set the agenda. If, for example, all parts of Jonathan had identified that there were spirits of hatred that were not dissociated identities, and they all agreed that they wanted them gone, Jonathan would not have felt that parts of him were being annihilated. Those on the team did not believe in the existence of DID and did not understand dissociation. I, his counselor, was not consulted about the process, and the procedure was not performed in conjunction with a counseling process. Finally, Jonathan did not really believe that he was demonized. He was just going along with what the others wanted. Therefore, the procedure was not in accordance with Jonathan's beliefs, nor did it incorporate his spiritual belief system. In other words, very few of the necessary conditions for a positive client outcome were present in Jonathan's case.

In contrast, all of the above conditions were present when Haley approached me about praying for release from spirits of rage. Haley initiated the discussion, and no coercion of any part of her was involved as all of her was in agreement that some of her intense anger was due to demonic influence. Therefore, we were acting on Haley's spiritual beliefs. Haley had completed Phase II work and had worked extensively on anger issues, so this was not an attempt to circumvent difficult emotional processing. She merely felt that it was time to deal with the last vestiges of this issue in her life. While I was present in the room and silently agreeing with her in prayer, it was Haley who demanded in Jesus' name that the spirits leave, after which she felt a spiritual and emotional release.

I was living in Canada when I met with Haley, and Canadian licensing laws and ethical codes did not preclude such procedures at that time. If I had been licensed in the United States, I would have had substantial limitations in doing this kind of work. If Haley had given written, informed consent, I may have been protected to some degree, but if she had decided to grieve me to a licensing board, my license still could have been in jeopardy. Unlicensed counselors, lay counselors, or pastors may not have this additional factor to consider, but they certainly need to make sure that all of the conditions are met as outlined in the study described above.

An expanded view of spiritual warfare. Fortunately, there are alternatives to deliverance prayer or exorcism rituals. This is good news for Christian counselors who do not want to risk doing further damage to their C-PTSD clients or who are concerned about the ethics of counselors being involved in these kinds of activities. Deliverance prayer or exorcism rituals are not synonymous with spiritual warfare. While there are examples of power encounters in Scripture, spiritual warfare is a much broader concept (Powlison, 1995).

In Ephesians 6:10-17, we are exhorted to

> be strong in the Lord and in his mighty power. Put on the full armor of God, so that you can take your stand against the devil's schemes. For our struggle is not against flesh and blood, but against the rulers, against the authorities, against the powers of this dark world and against the spiritual forces of evil in the heavenly realms. Therefore put on the full armor of God, so that when the day of evil comes, you may be able to stand your ground, and after you have done everything, to stand. Stand firm then, with the belt of truth buckled around your waist, with the breastplate of righteousness in place, and with your feet fitted with the readiness that comes from the gospel of peace. In addition to all this, take up the shield of faith, with which you can extinguish all the flaming arrows of the evil one. Take the helmet of salvation and the sword of the Spirit, which is the word of God.

This passage of Scripture is clearly addressing spiritual warfare, but the focus is "withstanding assault." The focus is on resistance by focusing on truth, "developing character," focusing on the message of the gospel, using faith in God and the knowledge of our salvation in order to defend against attacks, while relying on the Word of God and prayer.[1] Practicing regular spiritual disciplines is the best way of doing this (Bufford, 1988). Christian clients who meditate on God's Word and pray regularly are strengthening their spiritual armor, and thus interfering with Satan's attempts to control them (Powlison, 1995). Similarly, focusing on issues of identity in Christ is using truth to combat the enemy (Anderson, 1991).

Truth is also at the core of the counseling process. Although most people have not likely thought of counseling as spiritual warfare, I believe that counselors are helping clients battle Satan's lies, which, in effect, is spiritual warfare, whether or not counselors or their clients are aware of it (Kraft, 2010). As C-PTSD clients engage in Phase II trauma-processing work, I believe this to be especially true. For example, as rage and hatred are resolved through counseling, any spirits of rage or spirits of anger that may have had control of the client may no longer have grounds to do so. Similarly, in Phase III, as clients work on establishing healthy relationships and making behavioral choices that are honoring to God, Satan has to flee. This is why it is not necessarily important to know for sure if a specific client is demonized or

---

[1] Notes to Ephesians 6:10-17. From *NIV Study Bible*, 1985, Grand Rapids: Zondervan.

not. Even if there is demonic control, good Christian counseling will result in freedom for the client. I find that incredibly exciting!

THE COUNSELOR AS A SPIRITUAL RESOURCE

Up to this point I have been discussing the appropriateness of explicitly using spiritual resources in the counseling process with C-PTSD clients. In the counseling literature it is recognized that the person of the counselor is the most powerful change agent in any counseling relationship.[2] The Christian counselor's spirituality—as a core part of who they are—is, in effect, an important spiritual resource, whether used explicitly or implicitly.

Explicitly, there may be times when it is appropriate for counselors to share aspects of their own faith, although great care must be taken in deciding which clients may benefit, how much to share, and the best timing for the intervention. Self-disclosure of any kind on the part of the counselor is an ethical consideration that has been much discussed in the therapeutic literature. The power differential between counselor and client means that self-disclosure could have unintentional coercive elements. This can be all the more true with spirituality. Nevertheless, with appropriate discernment, spiritual self-disclosure can potentially be helpful. Possible ways of doing this are to use self-disclosure to communicate: personal spiritual data (e.g., denominational affiliation, theological training), personal feelings about God (based on one's own experience), professional opinions (e.g., book recommendations on spirituality or religion), spiritual metaphors (e.g., an image of how the counselor sees the client in relation to God), spiritual experiences (e.g., a special time of connection to God), and spiritual mistakes (e.g., how a confession ritual helped a counselor deal with the responsibility he felt for a broken relationship) (Denney, Aten, & Gingrich, 2008).

Even if explicit spiritual self-disclosure is not deemed helpful with specific clients, the implicit faith of the counselor will undoubtedly permeate the counseling session by informing therapeutic decisions, impacting how the client is responded to, and providing hope.

It is not enough to be a Christian who counsels. In order to be an effective Christian counselor for C-PTSD clients, Christ must be central to the healing process, whether that fact is explicitly acknowledged by the counselee or not.

---

[2]See Sbanotto, H. D. Gingrich, and F. C. Gingrich (2016) for a summary of that literature.

The Holy Spirit, after all, is the greatest counselor (Jn 14:16-17). He knows us and our clients, inside and out. The best counselor training in the world cannot compete with the guidance of the Holy Spirit in bringing healing to clients.

I am not saying that good training is not necessary. If that were the case, I would not be a full-time counselor educator and I would not be writing this book. My point is merely that the more tools we have, the greater the chance that the Holy Spirit can make use of our skills. In the midst of numerous counseling sessions, as I have been silently pleading with God to show me what the client needs, I have suddenly had a flash of insight. Was this the result of intuition, of my training, of my years of counseling experience, or was it a direct message from the Holy Spirit in response to my prayer? I think it may have been all of the above.

Listening well takes practice. Identifying the Holy Spirit's voice takes practice. If I do not foster my relationship with God in the rest of my life, how can I possibly expect to hear his voice in the midst of a counseling session? This is, fortunately, not a hard-and-fast rule, as God in his care for our clients can work despite our limitations. However, when counselors are more attuned to the Holy Spirit, I believe that everyone benefits.

9

VICARIOUS TRAUMATIZATION AND BUILDING COUNSELOR RESILIENCE

WHILE SELF-CARE IS ESSENTIAL for all Christian counselors, this issue is even more vital for those who see C-PTSD clients because the work can be so emotionally and spiritually exhausting. Week after week, month after month, and year after year, I listened as Haley described how she had been physically, emotionally, and spiritually tortured. She described oral, anal, and vaginal rape with objects and by many men, gang rapes, child prostitution, beatings, surgery performed without anesthetic, teeth pulled to make room for oral sex, bestiality, forced torture of others, cannibalism, and ritualistic abuse. A client load of several like Haley is bound to take its toll on the counselor.

VICARIOUS TRAUMATIZATION AND BUILDING COUNSELOR RESILIENCE

- Vicarious traumatization
- Building resilience
- Walking wounded
- Preparing for the long haul

In this chapter, the focus shifts from what happens inside of a counseling session with the client to what counselors can do both inside and outside of the sessions to take care of themselves. Although focusing on one's own reactions and on what it takes to keep oneself whole is important for all counselors, the intensity of working with C-PTSD clients can easily overwhelm even the most experienced of counselors. Vicarious traumatization is a very real danger, particularly if counselors do not take active measures to protect and sustain themselves. I will discuss vicarious traumatization, then offer suggestions on how counselors can stay physically, emotionally, and spiritually healthy so that they can continue to be helpful to their C-PTSD clients.[1]

VICARIOUS TRAUMATIZATION

Burnout, compassion fatigue, secondary traumatic stress, and *vicarious traumatization* are terms that have some overlapping symptoms but are not synonymous. Burnout is the broadest of the four in that anyone can experience physical, emotional, and spiritual exhaustion related to their work or ministry, whether or not the stress is related to people-helping. Compassion fatigue could be viewed as a subcategory of burnout that is reserved for individuals who are depleted as a result of being in a helping role.

Secondary traumatic stress and vicarious traumatization, however, while related to burnout and compassion fatigue, are specifically tied to indirect exposure to traumatic events. As a result of the 9/11 terrorist attacks, for example, there were people who developed PTSD symptoms from merely watching images on TV of the Twin Towers collapsing. Similarly, children of some Holocaust survivors have exhibited posttraumatic symptoms despite not even being alive during World War II. Families of war veterans can also experience vicarious traumatization simply by living with the veteran who may be exhibiting PTSD symptoms. Counselors, too, can be so negatively impacted by the trauma narratives they are exposed to through the stories of their clients that they can experience symptoms of vicarious traumatization.

Table 9.1 contains a list of questions, organized according to the *DSM-5* posttraumatic symptoms areas of intrusion, avoidance/numbing, and changes in arousal and reactivity. If you answer affirmatively to any of these questions, it could be an indication that you are experiencing some vicarious traumatization.

---

[1]Eriksson, Wilkins, and Frederick (2017) give an excellent overview of this topic, including distinguishing among terms, and citing the authors who originated these terms. For example, Figley (1995) is credited with first using the term *secondary traumatic stress*, while Pearlman (1995) and her associates originated the label *vicarious traumatization*.

Symptoms with a sexual or spiritual content may be more problematic for Christian counselors than they are for their nonreligious counterparts. It can be very disconcerting, for example, for Christian counselors to admit to themselves that they are being sexually excited by narratives involving sexual trauma, let alone admit it to someone else. This is exactly the type of countertransference reaction that should be discussed with one's own therapist, a supervisor, or a colleague, but because of the shame involved, it is often ignored.

Table 9.1. Symptoms of vicarious traumatization

CATEGORY OF SYMPTOM	SPECIFIC SYMPTOMS
Intrusive	• Do you have more nightmares than usual? • Is dream content related to the content of counseling sessions? • Do you have intrusive thoughts, images, or feelings about something your clients have shared with you? • Do emotions pop up out of nowhere or do you have more intense emotional reactions than situations warrant? • Are you sometimes sexually aroused by the sexually explicit content of your clients' trauma narratives?
Avoidance	• Do you dread meeting with particular clients? • Do you feel shut-down emotionally? • Do you find yourself avoiding certain people or situations that remind you of your clients or their trauma narratives? • Are you isolating yourself? • Are you avoiding sexual intimacy? • Are you finding excuses to stay away from church or from spending time alone with God? • Do you catch yourself daydreaming, or do you feel as though you are in a daze? • Do you feel as though you are just going through the motions of life? Are you more forgetful than usual?
Negative alterations in cognitions and mood	• Are you feeling depressed or anxious? • Have you lost your sense of joy? • Are you increasingly jaded or sarcastic? • Are you frequently experiencing a sense of hopelessness and helplessness? • Does it seem as though there is nothing but pain and suffering in the world? • Do you wonder if God cares about your counselees? About you? • When the pace of your counselees' progress is slow or seems absent, do you feel guilty? • Have you lost your sense of confidence in your counseling abilities?
Marked alterations in arousal and reactivity	• Are you more irritable than usual? • Do you lose your temper easily? • Do you startle easily? • Do your nerves feel on edge? • Does the world feel like a dangerous place? • Do you experience surges of adrenaline without obvious cause?

Similarly, as Christian counselors listen to C-PTSD clients telling their stories, they might find themselves wrestling with spiritual questions that can shake the very foundations of their faith. They may struggle with the same questions that their clients are asking, such as how a good God can allow such evil things to be done to vulnerable children. If counselors are not willing to face their questions and doubts, they may end up consciously or unconsciously avoiding contact with other Christians, attendance at church services, Bible reading, or other religious activities because of the discomfort that is triggered.

Such vicarious trauma symptoms do not generally disappear with the passing of time. If you notice such symptoms in yourself, do what you would recommend to your clients: deal with the situation rather than hope that it will just go away.

BUILDING RESILIENCE

Building physical, emotional, spiritual, and professional resilience is essential to preventing compassion fatigue and vicarious traumatization. Just as regular exercise, sleep, attention to good nutrition, and immunizations can help build resistance in the fight against physical disease, there are also ways in which counselors can bolster their psychological and spiritual immune systems.

BUILDING RESILIENCE

- Physical
- Emotional
- Spiritual
- Professional

Physical resilience. Scripture makes it clear that we are to take care of our bodies because they are "temples of the Holy Spirit" (1 Cor 6:19). Research findings increasingly point to the interconnectedness of the physical, psychological, and spiritual aspects of self (Benner, 1998a; Sbanotto, H. D. Gingrich & F. C. Gingrich, 2016). Therefore, as counselors pay attention to building their resilience physically, there is positive spillover into the emotional and spiritual realms. As mentioned earlier, I know that when I am physically tired or ill, I have a tendency to feel more down emotionally. If I am sleep-deprived, getting more rest will be the most helpful. Of greatest benefit would be getting an adequate amount of sleep on a regular basis.

A health care provider told me once that I am the "most athletic nonathletic" person he knows! I stopped signing up for physical education classes in high school as soon as I was allowed to because it brought down my grade point average so much! I also was tired of the humiliation that came from being picked last for a team. As a young adult, however, I discovered that I enjoyed physical activities that were noncompetitive, and I began incorporating them into my lifestyle. I enjoy walking, biking, swimming, hiking, and skiing, but only if I feel no pressure to keep up with anyone else. As I love being outdoors and enjoy nature, outdoor activities are much more inspiring to me than indoor ones. Though I am still too self-conscious to join an aerobics class, I have made aerobic exercise a backyard activity for over thirty years—much to the chagrin of our two oldest sons when they were easily embarrassed teenagers.

While the freedom to go at my own pace is what has allowed me to get regular exercise, other people are motivated more by competition. Playing a team sport or training for a race is what keeps them active. Some find it easier to exercise if they are doing it with someone else. The key is to experiment with various activities in order to find the conditions that will enable you to get regular exercise over the long term.

I am one of many individuals who holds stress in their back and shoulders. Regular visits to my chiropractor and massage therapist not only serve to alleviate symptoms, but also help prevent more serious back problems. If I use a hot tub to help relax my muscles, I can decrease the number of visits to my massage therapist. Developing an awareness of where stress hits you physically and taking steps to circumvent the problem is of utmost importance. Diet and food supplements to strengthen the body where it is potentially vulnerable may also enhance physical resilience.

Emotional resilience. In order to deal with the overwhelming emotions of C-PTSD clients, it is particularly important for counselors to build emotional resilience.

Dealing with unresolved personal issues. While counselors do not have to embody the epitome of mental health in order to be helpful to their counselees, it is important to be far enough along in our own healing process that we do not serve as a barrier to the healing of others. For example, it is

EMOTIONAL RESILIENCE

- Dealing with unresolved personal issues
- Supportive relationships
  - Colleagues
  - Friends
  - Family
- Setting appropriate boundaries
- Finances
- Ethical and legal matters

not helpful to "leak" our unresolved issues or emotions onto our clients in response to their issues. I believe that we can only walk with our counselees as far as we have been able to go ourselves. If, for example, counselors have not dealt with their own trauma, they will, even unconsciously, veer away from topics or emotions that could potentially trigger posttraumatic responses in themselves. It is also possible for counselors who have not been victims of trauma to hold some deep-seated pain related to other events or relationships. Such counselors may unconsciously tend to avoid doing deep affective work with clients, because at some level they fear that their own pain will surface. Bringing recordings of sessions with C-PTSD clients into supervision can be extremely helpful in detecting where counselors have inadvertently kept clients from fully engaging their emotions or traumatic experiences.

God may also use spouses, friends, sermons, prayer, or his Word to point out such tendencies. Sometimes awareness alone is adequate for taking care of the problem, but it may also be necessary for counselors to seek help from their own therapists in order to work through any issues that surface as a result of seeing C-PTSD clients. Even seasoned therapists may be caught off-guard by this type of countertransference. These unexpected emotional or behavioral reactions to clients or session content are part of what makes working with C-PTSD so challenging.

We may be surprised at our responses, but God is not. Jeremiah 17:9 states, "The heart is deceitful above all things and beyond cure. Who can understand it?" We will not always be aware of the reasons behind our reactions to our clients, as we too have deceitful hearts that distort our perceptions. This side of eternity, we will always be in the process of growth and healing.

Asking God to show us where there are still hidden, damaged places in our hearts, particularly those that could interfere with helping our counselees experience freedom, should be an ongoing invitation.

Supportive relationships. It is not unusual for compassionate, empathic counselors to find that the majority of their relationships, even outside the office, are ones where they are doing most of the giving. Without also benefiting from relationships where they can reveal weakness and allow others to be in a listening, helping role for them, compassion fatigue is inevitable. Therefore, mutual relationships or relationships where counselors are able to receive more often than they give—with colleagues, friends, and family—should be fostered.

Counselors of C-PTSD clients need colleagues who understand the unique challenges of working with this population. While supervisory or mentoring relationships are possibilities, peers can also be important. For a period of several years, I met monthly with two other counselors who were also doing a lot of C-PTSD work. Our times together were a combination of peer supervision, emotional support, and spiritual strengthening. We empathized with each other, offered suggestions with regard to clinical interventions, used gentle confrontation when we noticed countertransference, and prayed together. This group was literally a lifeline for me as I struggled with some extremely difficult cases.

Private practice can be lonely. Counselors might want to consider a group practice, agency setting, or shared office space where there is natural contact with other people. Even a brief social interaction between heavy sessions can help counselors keep some perspective and increase joy.

If counselors live in areas where they are isolated from knowledgeable colleagues, online video calls, chatrooms, or other web-based aids to communication are alternatives to gathering in person. Supervision or consultation can also be conducted via secure internet connections if no one is available locally.

Of course, care has to be taken to protect client confidentiality, either through obtaining written, informed consent from clients or by disguising client information well enough that their identities are protected. This can be done, for example, by using a pseudonym, changing gender or age, modifying family constellation and geographic location, as well as altering specific events.

Just as colleagues are important to counselors in the maintenance of emotional health, counselors who do such agonizing work would be wise to surround themselves with friends who are psychologically and spiritually healthy. While it may be a good idea to have a few relationships with individuals who can understand what it is like to be a counselor of C-PTSD clients, not all friendships necessarily have to consist of a lot of intense emotional involvement. Shared interests or activities that have nothing to do with counseling or direct people-helping can be refreshing. I enjoy, for example, relationships with fellow members of the chamber choir I sing in. My fellow musicians know that I am a counselor and professor, and while I have developed a couple of good friendships, conversations with other choir members are primarily focused on our shared love of music. Other friendships are based on fun and laughter through game nights or recreational activities. They serve as a good counterbalance to the seriousness of C-PTSD work. Laughter is good medicine.

Family is another group that can support counselors in their emotional health. When we are struggling personally, those closest to us cannot help but be directly or indirectly impacted. It is challenging for spouses of counselors or other loved ones to know how to best support those they care for when client confidentiality prevents full disclosure of what is so upsetting to them. Counselors are free, however, to talk about their own emotional responses. Session content can also be judiciously discussed as long as material is carefully camouflaged using the means discussed previously. A rule of thumb is to modify identifying information in such a way that a specific client could not be identified by someone else, even in a face-to-face, random encounter.

I have been fortunate in that my husband is also a therapist, and we have always worked for the same agencies. This has allowed me to talk freely to him because he has been covered by the informed consent agreed to by my counselees. However, I have had to be careful to not overload him emotionally as he has had his own difficult clients and teaching responsibilities to deal with. One person cannot be expected to take on such a large emotional burden without experiencing compassion fatigue themselves! The idea is not to merely transfer the burden from one set of shoulders to another. That is why it is important for counselors to intentionally create a broad network of support around them, including colleagues and supervisors as well as friends.

While our children indirectly suffer when we are not at our best emotionally, time with them can also be restorative. Their spontaneity can pull us back into the realm of the living, reminding us that there is more than pain and death in this world. Nothing helped to shake off the remnant of a tough counseling day as when my little one excitedly ran to greet me, arms outstretched, yelling, "Mama! Mama!" While the days of such unbridled enthusiasm at my arrival ended for my older boys with the advent of their adolescence, their teasing derision of all things emotional, and skepticism regarding counseling, while sometimes frustrating, has also kept me from taking myself and my work too seriously. C-PTSD is not to be taken lightly, but counseling is only one aspect of what God has called me to do. Parenting is a good reminder of that fact.

Extended family, if the family system is relatively healthy, can serve a similar function. Parents and siblings may not understand what is involved in counseling ministry, let alone the emotional toll that working with trauma survivors entails. However, knowing that there are people who are on your side, no matter what, who love you for who you are and not what you do, is a wonderful gift.

Setting appropriate boundaries. I discussed setting appropriate relational boundaries in chapter four, using the case of Simon. I cared about Simon and was concerned that the intensity of his memory work was contributing to his suicidal feelings. So I gave him my home phone number and encouraged him to phone me if he was really having trouble. He started calling me every night, and by the time I realized my mistake we were already in a destructive relational pattern. However, once I finally got the courage to acknowledge my error and to set long-overdue boundaries, Simon's healing took a leap forward. My main point in that chapter was that boundaries need to be created in order to protect clients. Setting boundaries, however, is also an important safeguard against compassion fatigue. Counselors cannot take regular crisis phone calls in the middle of the night, for example, and expect to be able to maintain physical resilience. Instead, they will find themselves depleted. Allowing Simon to call me at home on a daily basis became so emotionally and physically exhausting that it almost ended my counseling ministry.

Counselor-client boundaries are not the only ones to consider. Equally important are setting other types of interpersonal boundaries. Hurting people are drawn to those with good listening skills. If counselors are not careful, they will find their emotional reserves drained by church attendees, neighbors, family members, and even casual acquaintances who may be desperate to be heard. Experienced counselors may be sought out by pastors or church leaders for their relational problem-solving skills or be asked to teach Sunday school classes or lead retreats related to areas in their expertise. Counselor-professors may be sought after to teach adjunct courses overseas or in their home countries or to present at professional conferences. Trauma experts may be invited to work on crisis response teams.

The needs are great, particularly in a world where trauma is so rampant. No one person can do it all, however, so it is essential for counselors to prayerfully determine where they should give their time and attention and when they should say no. If God, spouse, children, and friends are neglected, then something is out of balance.

Finances. C-PTSD clients often are not functioning well enough to earn a decent living or even to be self-supporting. This can have a spillover effect onto counselors, particularly those in private practice, as these clients may not be able to afford the regular counseling fee. Insurance coverage does not necessarily solve the dilemma, as companies will often only pay for a limited number of sessions per year. Such difficulties with payment are problematic because if counselors are under their own financial stress, or simply want to maintain a certain standard of living, it is hard for them to build emotional resilience.

One of the ways to deal with this issue is for counselors to take on only a specific percentage of clients who cannot pay the full fee. Some counselors I know "tithe" their practice—that is, they will see 10 percent of their clients for a minimal fee and may have a waiting list for these slots. Others use a sliding fee scale but set a clear lower limit. This may mean limiting the number of C-PTSD clients that counselors have on their caseloads.

When clients are highly motivated, I have found that they are able to come up with creative ways of paying for counseling. Some take on additional work, while others are able to ask for partial subsidies from friends, family members, or their churches.

Sometimes the counselor's income can be subsidized through other means. Establishing a nonprofit organization can provide a platform for fundraising. Counselors working in developing countries can sometimes raise ministry support. I know some Filipino counselors, for example, who are able to offer counseling services because some wealthier Filipinos invest in them financially.

There was a period of years when my husband's teaching position and small counseling practice, composed mainly of professional couples, subsidized my full-time counseling practice that was primarily made up of C-PTSD clients. We did not have a large family income, and we lived frugally, but we made enough money to not be overly anxious about finances.

Often financial stress is related to counselors' expectations with regard to standard of living. If counselors live beyond their financial means, it will take an emotional toll—so will living within their means but desiring a higher standard of living. If God is leading you to work with C-PTSD clients, you may have to wrestle with what that will mean financially. This may involve either adjusting your expectations or finding ways to supplement your income so that financial issues will not interfere with your emotional well-being.

Ethical and legal matters. In order to prevent potential ethical or legal difficulties from emerging at some point in the future, counselors need to familiarize themselves with the ethical codes and laws that govern their counseling work. Such regulations can involve matters such as child-abuse reporting laws, confidentiality, privacy, required content of client progress notes, client file storage, court subpoenas, informed consent for treatment, dual relationships, and so on. The requirements of ethical practice may differ for licensed counselors, pastoral counselors, and lay counselors. Sometimes membership in a professional counseling association can provide a member benefit of free legal consultation that C-PTSD counselors may need to take advantage of. Knowing what is required of you within your jurisdiction in your work with all clients, including those with C-PTSD, is essential for emotional resilience.

Spiritual resilience. When counselors work with C-PTSD clients, they are confronted by human depravity at its worst and exposed to Satan's lies and deceit. I sometimes feel as though I am standing in a dumpster, attempting to sort through my clients' emotional and spiritual garbage in order to salvage what is good and can be built upon. I also find that it is easy to become confused about basic spiritual realities such as the difference between truth and lies. While this is a common consequence of doing complex trauma work, we can choose to not live in the garbage or in the confusion. When we spend time in God's presence and focus on who he is, we are cleansed spiritually and emotionally, much like taking a shower cleanses us physically. Being with God washes the emotional and spiritual dirt down the drain. As we are cleansed, our minds become renewed and we are more easily able to discern the difference between truth and lies. We remember whom God created us and our clients to be, and we are more able to reject what Satan hopes we and our clients will believe about ourselves.

If we try to work through the spiritual and emotional garbage on our own we will surely fail. The good news is that we do not have to because God invites us to come to him with our burdens. For example, 1 Peter 5:7 reminds us to "cast all your anxiety on him because he cares for you." As we come before God in our neediness and emptiness, waiting for him to fill us, we will be strengthened and restored.

SPIRITUAL RESILIENCE

- Prayer
- Meditating on God's word
- Spending time in solitude
- Reading devotional materials
- Gathering with other believers
- Creative activities (e.g., fine arts, dance, music)
- Regular rhythms of rest and renewal
- Any activity that results in greater intimacy with God

Spiritually resilient people make it a life habit to come before God in emptiness, waiting to be filled. Of course, different people will come to God in diverse ways. Even as every marriage relationship is unique, each person's relationship with God will be distinctive. Therefore, I am not going to suggest formulas, but instead will provide some food for thought that can help counselors become aware of what may be beneficial in nurturing their personal relationship with God.

Prayer. David Benner, in his book *Opening to God* (2010), discusses prayer as both conversation and communion, a distinction I have found helpful in that it has parallels to intimacy in human relationships. While it would be difficult to have a close relationship with anyone without some times of deeply sharing desires, wants, and needs, basking in the loved one's presence is also an aspect of intimacy. If several days go by, for example, where my husband and I do not engage in some significant conversation, our relationship inevitably suffers. Enjoying a sunset together, watching TV side by side, or exchanging glances across a room can also increase a sense of intimacy.

Similarly, an important aspect of prayer is explicitly conversing with God, bringing ourselves and our requests before him and listening for his answers. However, prayer as communion, an awareness and acknowledgment of God's presence, is also essential. I love the outdoors, spending as much time as I can outside, preferably surrounded by nature. In fact, most of this book has been written in my backyard, where I can look up from my computer and enjoy the flowers and trees that God has created. In these brief moments, I am communing with God. When I camp, hike, or ski, I also choose to make these activities a part of my prayer times in the form of communion with God.

Honesty is an important part of any relationship, and God invites us to be honest with him. I believe that God is big enough to handle our doubts and questions. Giving ourselves permission to come before God as we truly are, in both our weakness and our strength, can help build resiliency. It is not as though we can hide ourselves from God, even if we want to! As Jeremiah 23:24 states, "'Who can hide in secret places so that I cannot see them?' declares the LORD."

Other spiritual activities. Spiritual activities such as meditating on God's Word, spending time in solitude, reading devotional books, and gathering with other believers are all well-established ways of increasing spiritual resilience. In addition, many people find that creative activities help them connect with God, who is the source of all creativity.

Singing, for example, is an important aspect of my spiritual health. I enjoy both contemporary Christian music and sacred classical music, so I have found ways of honoring both parts of me by singing on my church worship team and/or by participating in sacred music choirs at particular points in my life. I also spend time singing to God when I am alone. Music is the most natural way of expressing my praise and worship to God, as well as the medium through which I can most clearly discern God's voice. It is important for Christian counselors to discover what is life-producing for them.

There is definite overlap between building spiritual resiliency and building physical and emotional resiliency. Meeting with a mentor or prayer partner could be categorized under both supportive relationships and developing spiritual intimacy in that both emotional and spiritual needs are being met. Some runners tell me that there is a spiritual element to what they do. The list could be endless. Ultimately, if the activity draws us closer to God and helps us to become more like the people he created us to be, spiritual resiliency is being strengthened.

Regular rhythms of rest and renewal are indispensable for maintaining spiritual resiliency. The biblical term for this is "keeping sabbath." While Jesus stripped away some of the legalistic rules regarding how people observed sabbath, he regularly set aside time to be alone with God and with his disciples. We, too, need to develop the rhythm of regularly resting from our normal routines in order to have space and time for focusing on God. We can also benefit from setting aside occasional larger chunks of time to complement our regular practices. Ruth Haley Barton expands on these ideas in her book *Sacred Rhythms: Arranging Our Lives for Spiritual Transformation* (2006).

Professional resilience. Steps can also be taken to hone resilience professionally. If counselors are ill-equipped to work with C-PTSD clients, the toll on them will be greater. Therefore, obtaining supervision, reading applicable books, attending relevant conferences or webinars, joining special interest groups (either in person or online), and taking specialized courses are all ways in which counselors can better prepare themselves to work effectively with complex trauma.

I know few professionals who work exclusively with C-PTSD clients. A full caseload of trauma survivors is heavier than most counselors can handle well. I recommend that counselors see a variety of clients, interspersing C-PTSD clients with those presenting with other difficulties. I remember recognizing that I had a pattern of feeling totally drained of energy every Tuesday. As I sought to understand why, I realized that I had scheduled two difficult C-PTSD clients on the same day. The problem was readily solved by simply switching one appointment to a different day.

Professional resilience can also be built by varying professional tasks. After a number of years of doing full-time therapy, I reduced my client load slightly and became involved in some teaching and student-life activities. I was able to use my office at the college for both counseling and academic purposes, which enabled me to go back and forth between various activities throughout the day. For example, I would see a couple of clients in the morning, then take a forty-five-minute break by attending the chapel service. I would then see another client, after which I would go over to the dining hall to eat and laugh with students or fellow faculty members. In this way, I had constant, built-in reminders that there was more to life and the world than severe trauma and pain. While the amount of time I spent working each day increased, my sense of emotional and spiritual well-being was actually enhanced by the variety and scheduling of tasks. Counselors should experiment with what works the best for them.

WALKING WOUNDED

Sometimes, despite our best attempts to build resilience, counselors find themselves unable to cope with the demands of seeing C-PTSD clients. Stressors in other areas of our lives and circumstances beyond our control can greatly impact the ability to counsel effectively. Although I would not have met *DSM-5* criteria for a depressive disorder, I went through a two-year period of time where I experienced some significant depression related to a long and painful infertility process, the disintegration of a valued friendship, and some draining C-PTSD counselees. I continued to meet with my clients and was able to compartmentalize well enough to be of continued help to them. However, I was not at my best because my own pain was at times distracting. I did things that I knew should help, such as journaling, emotionally processing with my husband and some close friends, praying, reading psalms of lament, singing, and listening to music, but it did little to lift my depression. Eventually I swallowed my pride and went for counseling myself—a move that, in retrospect, I should have made earlier.

There may be times in which counselors' personal problems are severe enough that they need to take a break from doing counseling for a period of time. This is, of course, not ideal for C-PTSD clients, for whom counseling is generally long-term and where developing safety is such a huge issue. The goal is for counselors to do as little damage to clients as possible, while giving adequate attention to their own needs. Ideally, transitioning a C-PTSD client to a new counselor should happen over a number of weeks or months, but this may not be possible if the counselor is in crisis. In such cases, the new counselor will have to handle the brunt of working through the client's abandonment issues.

Sometimes it is possible for counselors to continue to see their C-PTSD clients while referring on other clients who are not as likely to be negatively impacted by transitioning to another therapist. This is the option I took when we adopted our first child with only a couple of weeks' notice that he was moving in. I knew that I could not continue working full time during this huge adjustment period. My preference would have been to take a total break from seeing clients, but I felt that the potential negative impact on my C-PTSD clients was much greater than my desire to totally put my practice aside. Therefore, I chose to refer my other clients to new counselors while continuing to see several C-PTSD clients. Other counselors might have chosen differently. Consultation with trusted others can be helpful in making such difficult decisions. Ultimately, however, counselors have to take care of themselves if they are to avoid the deep burnout that could cause them to leave their counseling ministries permanently.

PREPARING FOR THE LONG HAUL

Several years after completing my master's degree, I discovered that a number of my former classmates were no longer working in the counseling field. While some may not have been well-suited for counseling ministry in the first place, others had the potential to become skilled counselors but instead burned out from compassion fatigue or vicarious traumatization.

Because the needs of C-PTSD clients are often so great, it is tempting for counselors to invest more time and energy with these clients than they typically would with their other counselees. Doing this for one client may not result in obvious negative effects on the counselor. As the number of C-PTSD clients in any particular caseload grows, however, the demands on the counselor will grow, increasing the risk of negative effects on the counselor's health.

It is advisable for counselors to regularly assess our stress levels, perhaps with the aid of feedback from others who know us well and can see past our own blind spots. Inevitably there will be times in life that are more stressful than others, both in terms of our personal lives and our ministry lives. If high stress levels are temporary and we are healthy to begin with, it is easier to bounce back. However, ongoing moderate or high levels of stress will take their toll. A helpful question to ask is, "If my stress level remains at its current level, what do I predict might happen down the road?" If you do not like the conclusion you come to, it might be a good time to reevaluate how you spend your time and energy. This could mean cutting back in some ways, such as in the total number of C-PTSD clients that you see, or the number that you counsel in a given day. It also could mean increasing beneficial activities. For example, you may need to add activities that refuel you or that increase your sense of joy. Occasionally rereading this chapter could be one way of reminding yourself of possible ways of appropriately caring for yourself so that you can continue to provide helpful ministry to C-PTSD clients for years to come.

10

HOW THE CHURCH CAN HELP

Church congregations tend either to provide environments conducive to healing or to be toxic faith communities for individuals suffering from C-PTSD. As the needs of such individuals are so great, appropriately ministering to them is a challenge, but not impossible. In this chapter I will discuss the role that counselors can play in helping congregations to become better trauma-informed, particularly with respect to C-PTSD and dissociation. I will also offer information about resources that counselors can make churches aware of, or that pastors and lay leaders can take advantage of as they attempt to be helpful to this population.

HOW THE CHURCH CAN HELP
- Educating about C-PTSD
- Providing emotional and spiritual support
- Churches and Christian counselors in partnership

EDUCATING ABOUT C-PTSD

Perhaps the biggest stumbling block for churches is a lack of understanding about C-PTSD and dissociation. Highly dissociative individuals are at increased risk of being misunderstood by other Christians, particularly as fears about possible demonic involvement often arise. This is where educating pastors, lay leaders, lay counselors, life coaches, spiritual directors, and other members of church congregations can be of immense help.

The role of counselors. In my position as a professional counselor I have availed of opportunities to educate church people about trauma and dissociation. I have, for example, made numerous presentations to laypeople on how to help adult survivors of abuse, recognizing that there will likely be those in the audience who are trauma survivors themselves. I have also been invited to help church congregations better understand dissociation and DID. At other times I have accepted invitations to discuss the role of the demonic in survivors of complex trauma.

EDUCATING ABOUT C-PTSD
- The role of counselors
- The role of pastors
- Resources

In addition to group-oriented instructional activities, education about complex trauma can also be given on a one-to-one basis with the pastor or support person of a particular C-PTSD client. I have found that the best way to do this is to have the counselee initially invite the support person to be a part of a counseling session so that there is no sense of keeping secrets. After an initial face-to-face meeting, any necessary follow-up can be done using the telephone or email. Of course, written, informed consent needs to be obtained from a client if another person is attending a session or if information is shared. I have found that the extra time and energy that is spent educating key support people is worth the investment, as they can then pass on the information to appropriate others, again with client consent. What counselors need to avoid is receiving emails, phone calls, or text messages from a number of support people connected to any one client, as the time involved can easily become unmanageable. Instead, having a key contact person within a church congregation can be helpful, whether that is a pastor, friend, or other support person.

While C-PTSD clients should be encouraged to take responsibility to access their own support systems when needed, there are times, particularly in crisis situations, when it can be useful for counselors to communicate with the key church contact person. For example, if the client is too distressed to drive herself home, needs the immediate company or prayer support of others, or has just been hospitalized, having an emergency number can be important. If counselors can facilitate the process of their clients making such calls, it helps to empower them rather than encourage increased dependency on the counselor. However, it may take some time to get low-functioning counselees to the point where they are able to reach out in this fashion. Whether the contact is counselor or client initiated, the key person should be adequately prepared ahead of time to meet such challenges so that the response can be helpful rather than harmful.

The role of pastors. Pastors can be encouraged to preach on topics that address the issues that those with C-PTSD face. For example, sermons that address the evils of abuse, acknowledge the reality of suffering, and encourage individuals to seek answers to hard questions can give trauma survivors permission to be more open about their struggles. Once the survivor is identified in the church, leaders can help them access the help they need, whether that involves resources within the church or referral to counselors or others (e.g., social workers, medical doctors, or lawyers).

Since they are in positions of influence, pastors can potentially initiate discussions among church leaders about beginning programs or training people who can minister to those with C-PTSD. They can also be involved in helping to develop policies and procedures geared to the prevention of child abuse or spiritual abuse within the church setting.

Once they learn to identify the potential dangers of emotional over-involvement and to recognize the importance of boundaries with regard to time and energy with complex trauma survivors, pastors can pass on that knowledge to other church leaders and support people. For a C-PTSD individual, having a pastoral person understand them will greatly increase the potential for healing.

Resources. There are a number of educational resources available to both complex trauma survivors and those who wish to be of help to them. The International Society for the Study of Trauma and Dissociation (ISSTD) is a secular professional organization that has a lot to offer to counselors, but also has resources for survivors and lay helpers, including referral lists to counselors who work with C-PTSD throughout the world.[1] The Sidran Foundation

---

[1]See the ISSTD website at www.isst-d.org.

is another secular organization with excellent resources for survivors of complex trauma and those who are attempting to be helpful to those with C-PTSD.[2] There are also local organizations in various cities that focus on specific subcategories of complex trauma, such as adult survivors of sexual abuse.

The American Association of Christian Counselors and the Christian Association for Psychological Studies offer conferences that often have education tracks and resources available on trauma, including complex trauma. They can also serve a networking function.

Lydia Discipleship Ministries (LDM) focuses specifically on offering resources for counselors, family members, and support people of individuals with C-PTSD, including those with DID. One of the unique aspects of LDM is that its resources include material not merely on how to emotionally support complex trauma survivors but also on how to nurture their spiritual growth. One of the key resources it offers is a manual that provides all of the information necessary to set up a yearlong discipleship group specifically designed for severely wounded people. The manual includes: how to make a proposal to your church to offer such a group, the ideal composition of a group ministry team, how to choose and train members of the team, and a detailed curriculum for each week. LDM also serves an important networking function for Christian organizations that are involved with complex trauma survivors.[3] A biannual DID symposium serves both a networking and informational function.

Life Model works with churches and other communities to offer training and resources to help those with complex trauma backgrounds, including those with DID, in their midst. They have recently expanded their resources to include other categories of hurting people.[4]

THRIVEtoday is an organization that offers resources and trainings for church congregations that are intended to help individuals learn basic relational skills.[5] While they are not specifically geared toward survivors of complex trauma, as we discussed in chapter two, those with C-PTSD often have significant developmental gaps that impact relational functioning.

---

[2]See the Sidran Foundation website at www.sidran.org.
[3]See the LDM website at www.lydiadm.org.
[4]See the Life Model website, www.lifemodelworks.org, which includes links to the THRIVE website as well as information about Shepherd's House.
[5]See the THRIVEtoday website at www.thrivetoday.org

THRIVEtoday can help C-PTSD survivors develop the relational skills that they may have missed out on.

While not specifically directed toward a Christian audience, the book *Coping with Trauma-Related Dissociation* is an excellent resource for highly dissociative individuals and those attempting to help them (Boon, Steele, & van der Hart, 2011). It is a practical skills training manual that includes discussions and explanations about common challenges faced as well as exercises that can aid in developing new coping skills.

PROVIDING EMOTIONAL AND SPIRITUAL SUPPORT

Individuals with C-PTSD can make emotional demands that can easily overload their support systems. Recognizing this upfront can help churches find ways for their members to share the load so that no one person or family is as likely to burn out. It is also important to determine who has the gifts and abilities to be helpful to this population and in what ways. The analogy of the church as the body of Christ (Eph 4:11-13) is fitting because everyone has a role to play but we all have specific functions.

PROVIDING EMOTIONAL AND SPIRITUAL SUPPORT
- Formal care
- Informal care

Formal care. Support of survivors can be built into church programming. In this section we will look at some specific examples of such formal care.

Groups. Groups such as Celebrate Recovery have become popular in some Christian circles. These programs can be helpful to some trauma survivors, particularly if they are struggling in a specific area such as addictions. While Celebrate Recovery has the advantage of incorporating Scripture into a twelve-step program (Alcoholics Anonymous–based), it does not go into as much depth in its questions and exercises as some of the other more focused twelve-step programs. One church I know uses Adult Children of Alcoholics (ACA) material as leaders have found it more helpful for individuals who are really struggling emotionally. While intended for use with those who grew up in alcoholic families, the principles can be applied to anyone who has grown up in a dysfunctional family. As this is generally the case for those with C-PTSD, the ACA workbook could be helpful to groups wanting to include this population.

FORMAL CARE

- Groups
- Lay counseling
- Mentoring, spiritual direction, and life coaching
- Assigned helpers

The yearlong group curriculum designed by LDM (see "Resources" section above) is unique in that its focus is on how to help severely hurting individuals develop stronger, healthier relationships with God by realistically confronting the barriers to such growth. The first few weeks, for example, examine common distortions individuals can have about God due to relational hurts in their past. After participating in the group for a year, members are much better prepared to benefit from regular church programming and more general small groups. Training for group leaders includes an understanding of the effects of trauma and information about specific subgroups of potential group members (e.g., those with DID).

Any type of group could be offered either as a midweekly group or as a Sunday adult education class for people who are experiencing severe emotional pain. Attendees could include complex trauma survivors along with those overwhelmed by other life circumstances. If churches are large enough, they could potentially offer a group specifically for abuse survivors. The advantage of having a more homogenous group is that specific issues relevant to that population can be addressed. A disadvantage to a group containing all complex trauma survivors is that group members could potentially trigger each other in ways that could make the group chaotic. This might be a particular concern for a group of people with DID. However, integrating a few individuals with DID into a broader group of hurting people can minimize some of the potential dangers.

Such groups should not be viewed as therapy groups; that is beyond the scope of what most churches are equipped to handle. The group could be identified as more of a psychoeducational group or a support group (Greggo, 2008). This would allow some deeper issues to be addressed without the expectations that therapy is being done. Such groups could also help individuals develop a healthy view of God, as their perceptions are so often distorted. Those leading such groups need to have thought through a theology of suffering so that they are not caught off-guard by questions that may arise in the group. The goal is not to provide simplistic answers that will only be frustrating, if not damaging, to group members, but rather to allow them to wrestle with the reality of their own suffering, alongside the apparent contradiction that God is good and loving. Some of the organizations referred to above can be helpful in providing resources for such groups.

Lay counseling. Lay counselors can be helpful to those with C-PTSD as long as they are under supervision and do not attempt to go beyond their level of expertise. The safest model would be one in which the counselee is also seeing a professional counselor and has given consent for there to be some level of ongoing communication between the professional counselor and the lay counselor. This would obviously only work if there is mutual respect between the counselors and they are not working at cross-purposes.

I believe that the greatest potential risk of doing unintentional damage comes from lay counselors who attempt to do trauma processing. In Christian circles this may take the form of utilizing some type of inner-healing prayer to deal with trauma memories. As I mentioned in previous chapters, the danger lies in uncovering traumatic material without adequate training or knowledge in how to contain the intrusive symptoms or properly pace the work. While I realize that many lay counselors can effectively be used by God in amazing ways with this population, I have had to pick up the pieces of healing prayer gone awry too many times to not issue a strong caution. Inner-healing prayer used as a technique by mental health professionals within a broader conceptual framework of trauma treatment is infinitely safer in my opinion.

Often what happens when individuals with C-PTSD have had bad experiences with lay counselors is that they will separate themselves from that particular church body due to fear that they will be blamed for not trusting God enough or that they will be further harmed by individuals who mean well but are not adequately prepared to minister to people at such a deep level of woundedness. Unfortunately the lay counselors and church leaders may never know why the individual disappeared, with the result that the same mistakes can be repeated with other individuals. One way to prevent such a pattern is by following up with all counselees who have been in relationship with lay counselors in order to get some feedback about the ministry so that adaptations can be made as needed.

Lay counselors can certainly be helpful in a supportive role, either as an adjunct to professional counseling as mentioned above, or as a way of helping individuals with a complex trauma background cope with the challenges of day-to-day life. The key to success is to ensure that appropriate boundaries are in place. While this is difficult enough for professional counselors, lay counselors may struggle even more because they likely have less of an understanding of countertransference issues. Those who are in helping roles out of a desire to rescue hurting people may be at particular risk of taking on more responsibility for the counselee than is helpful or warranted. In my experience, this inevitably ends in the lay person cutting off the relationship with the survivor when they feel overwhelmed or taken advantage of, resulting in one more experience of abandonment and perhaps even a sense of emotional retraumatization for the C-PTSD survivor.

Mentoring, spiritual direction, and life coaching. Complex trauma survivors with spiritual concerns and questions can benefit from spiritual guidance provided by mentors or spiritual directors. The key to ministering effectively to this population is to focus on the specific needs of individuals rather than to stick to a predetermined mentoring or spiritual direction agenda. On the one hand, an ability to listen empathically while gently challenging perceptual errors is a definite asset. On the other hand, black-and-white thinking or the need for quick resolution will be liabilities.

If individuals have been ritually abused by religious cults, mentors and spiritual directors will need to educate themselves about how such groups twist Scripture and about the meaning of their religious practices in order to understand the intense negative reactions their mentees or directees may show toward certain concepts or activities. For example, a practice that many ritual abuse survivors report is the eating of human flesh and the drinking of human blood as a perversion of eating the body of Christ and drinking his blood in Christian communion. Without understanding that the sacrament of communion may be triggering for such individuals, mentors or spiritual directors may be at a loss. Conversely, if they are able to figure out why the C-PTSD individual is reacting negatively, mentors or spiritual directors may either be able to help the individual reclaim the sacrament for Christ or encourage them to process the issue with a professional counselor.

Life does not go on hold while those with C-PTSD are in the process of healing. Bills need to be paid, jobs managed, and decisions made. Christian life coaches can be helpful in providing direction for individuals with regard to the present and future, even while counselors may be working with them on past trauma. If an individual is receiving counseling as well as life coaching, it is important to ensure that they are supplementing each other and not working at cross-purposes.

Assigned helpers. While well-intentioned and sometimes necessary, matching an individual with C-PTSD to a volunteer helper has its pitfalls. People do not generally appreciate being someone's "project," and while volunteers may not consciously be aware of having such an attitude, there can nevertheless be a danger of one person attempting to "fix" another.

Complex trauma survivors need a variety of types of people in their lives. They require those with listening ears and shoulders to cry on. However, they can sometimes benefit the most from just being around healthy individuals and families. If sharing a meal or engaging in a mutually enjoyable activity is all that is required of some support people, the number of people who can be of help is greatly expanded. Increasing times of fun and laughter without minimizing the presence of pain can be a great gift to a complex trauma survivor.

Informal care. Ideally, complex trauma survivors should be encouraged to develop their own support networks, as such relationships will tend to develop more naturally than ones where a church leader brings two people together. Church leadership can help encourage such relationships by offering resources and information as needed. A church culture that encourages members of the church body to reach out to each other is most conducive to people being open to involvement in others' lives.

One characteristic of informal care is that church leaders have less control over the parameters of such relationships. This is both a positive and a negative—positive in that there is potentially fertile ground for greater spontaneity and mutuality in these relationships, but negative in that without awareness of C-PTSD dynamics, the relationships can get messy and spill over into the general life of the church.

The reality, though, is that because we are all imperfect (Rom 3:23), anything involving people will get messy; it is unavoidable! Even the disciples had conflicts about how ministry should be done (e.g., Mk 10:13-14) and who was the greatest leader among them (Lk 9:46). These difficulties were not used as justification for avoiding the messiness of ongoing relationships, but rather guidance was given for how to deal with such conflicts (e.g., Mt 18:15-17).

CHURCHES AND CHRISTIAN COUNSELORS IN PARTNERSHIP

We desperately need each other! C-PTSD clients need help and support far beyond what any one counselor can offer. Conversely, Christian counselors will be greatly hindered in their work with C-PTSD clients if we do not see church communities as allies in the healing process. The primary focus of this chapter has been on how churches can offer help and support to individuals with C-PTSD. However, churches can also serve as desperately needed places of sanctuary and restoration for Christian counselors. Although toxic churches exist, we can all be involved in making churches healthy, healing places for everyone.

The following poem, written by an individual with C-PTSD, communicates well her longing for a healing church community.

A Search for Better Things

What you have to understand is that we're scared
Terrified
even if we do not show it
Life has been a little . . . harsh
We need community
people to teach us what it is to be human
and not just a thing to be used or discarded at whim
We need kindness and patience
not just a scripture plastered across the head
Sometimes, even what you think are good words,
were bad words to us instead
We need a safe place to stay
Consider that what might be normal to you
might seem just as foreign to us
Sometimes we just need a place to be
time to breathe

and see what "normal" really is
Some of us are hollow inside
little pockets of emptiness
Our need could suck the planet dry, but we still need you
Know where you stand
so we can know where to stand too
Sometimes we need you to help keep things clear for us
Live what you say
Trust is a fragile thing
don't abuse it
Listen to what we say, not what you want to hear
the story might not be nice, but it is ours
Sometimes it would help if you would hear it
and not try to fix it
The past will always be broken, but the future has a way to mend
help us hold on to that hope
and to know that good can exist
That maybe God hasn't left us yet
Tell about the God you know
share your stories with us
Help us see the Light in things
without forcing us to believe
Walk with us
one step at a time
as we search for better things

I began this book with the account of Haley, who in terror ran through a plate-glass window when a group of well-intentioned Christian women, who did not understand dissociation, attempted to cast demons out of her. Despite her distrust of Christians after this incident, Haley continued in counseling with me. Her memories of abuse and torture were horrendous, making the years of Phase II work hard on us both. But Haley's story has a hopeful ending! Haley's "search for better things" has brought her integration of self and experience, a job she loves, a vibrant relationship with Christ, good friends, and reconnection with some family members. Everything is not perfect. Her childhood abuse has left physical injuries that have become more problematic as she ages. Although she feels comfortable with individual Christians and has found a type of Christian community with them, she has not found a church home where she feels accepted. However, despite continued struggles, she is full of joy and thankfulness to God. It is my prayer that this book will play a part in the healing of many more "Haleys."

DISSOCIATIVE EXPERIENCES SCALE (DES-II)

Various versions and scoring systems for this scale are available on different websites. It was developed by E. B. Carlson, & F. W. Putnam, (1993).

This questionnaire consists of twenty-eight questions about experiences that you may have in your daily life. We are interested in how often you have these experiences. It is important, however, that your answers show how often these experiences happen to you when you are *not* under the influence of alcohol or drugs.

To answer the questions, please determine to what degree the experience described in the question applies to you, and circle the number to show what percentage of the time you have the experience.

Example:

0%	10	20	30	40	50	60	70	80	90	100%
(never)										(always)

1. Some people have the experience of driving or riding in a car or bus or subway and suddenly realizing that they don't remember what has happened during all or part of the trip.

0%	10	20	30	40	50	60	70	80	90	100%

2. Some people find that sometimes they are listening to someone talk and they suddenly realize that they did not hear part or all of what was said.

0%	10	20	30	40	50	60	70	80	90	100%

3. Some people have the experience of finding themselves in a place and having no idea how they got there.

0%	10	20	30	40	50	60	70	80	90	100%

4. Some people have the experience of finding themselves dressed in clothes that they don't remember putting on.

0%   10   20   30   40   50   60   70   80   90   100%

5. Some people have the experience of finding new things among their belongings that they do not remember buying.

0%   10   20   30   40   50   60   70   80   90   100%

6. Some people sometimes find that they are approached by people that they do not know who call them by another name or insist that they have met them before.

0%   10   20   30   40   50   60   70   80   90   100%

7. Some people sometimes have the experience of feeling as though they are standing next to themselves or watching themselves do something and they actually see themselves as if they were looking at another person.

0%   10   20   30   40   50   60   70   80   90   100%

8. Some people are told that they sometimes do not recognize friends or family members.

0%   10   20   30   40   50   60   70   80   90   100%

9. Some people find that they have no memory for some important events in their lives (for example, a wedding or graduation).

0%   10   20   30   40   50   60   70   80   90   100%

10. Some people have the experience of being accused of lying when they do not think that they have lied.

0%   10   20   30   40   50   60   70   80   90   100%

11. Some people have the experience of looking in a mirror and not recognizing themselves.

0%   10   20   30   40   50   60   70   80   90   100%

12. Some people have the experience of feeling that other people, objects, and the world around them are not real.

0%   10   20   30   40   50   60   70   80   90   100%

13. Some people have the experience of feeling that their body does not seem to belong to them.

0%   10   20   30   40   50   60   70   80   90   100%

14. Some people have the experience of sometimes remembering a past event so vividly that they feel as if they were reliving that event.

0%   10   20   30   40   50   60   70   80   90   100%

15. Some people have the experience of not being sure whether things that they remember happening really did happen or whether they just dreamed them.

0%   10   20   30   40   50   60   70   80   90   100%

16. Some people have the experience of being in a familiar place but finding it strange and unfamiliar.

0%   10   20   30   40   50   60   70   80   90   100%

17. Some people find that when they are watching television or a movie they become so absorbed in the story that they are unaware of other events happening around them.

0%   10   20   30   40   50   60   70   80   90   100%

18. Some people find that they become so involved in a fantasy or daydream that it feels as though it were really happening to them.

0%   10   20   30   40   50   60   70   80   90   100%

19. Some people find that they sometimes are able to ignore pain.

0%   10   20   30   40   50   60   70   80   90   100%

20. Some people find that they sometimes sit staring off into space, thinking of nothing, and are not aware of the passage of time.

0%   10   20   30   40   50   60   70   80   90   100%

21. Some people sometimes find that when they are alone they talk out loud to themselves.

0%   10   20   30   40   50   60   70   80   90   100%

22. Some people find that in one situation they may act so differently compared with another situation that they feel almost as if they were two different people.

0%   10   20   30   40   50   60   70   80   90   100%

23. Some people sometimes find that in certain situations they are able to do things with amazing ease and spontaneity that would usually be difficult for them (for example, sports, work, social situations, etc.).

0%   10   20   30   40   50   60   70   80   90   100%

24. Some people sometimes find that they cannot remember whether they have done something or have just thought about doing it (for example, not knowing whether they have just mailed a letter or have just thought about mailing it).

   0%   10   20   30   40   50   60   70   80   90   100%

25. Some people find evidence that they have done things that they do not remember doing.

   0%   10   20   30   40   50   60   70   80   90   100%

26. Some people sometimes find writings, drawings, or notes among their belongings that they must have done but cannot remember doing.

   0%   10   20   30   40   50   60   70   80   90   100%

27. Some people sometimes find that they hear voices inside their head that tell them to do things or comment on things that they are doing.

   0%   10   20   30   40   50   60   70   80   90   100%

28. Some people sometimes feel as if they are looking at the world through a fog so that people and objects appear far away or unclear.

   0%   10   20   30   40   50   60   70   80   90   100%

SCORING THE DES-II (DES)

Add up the percentages and divide by 28 (the number of questions). Total scores can range from 0 to 100.

DES SCORES EXPLAINED[1]

Scores of 30 or more indicate a high degree of dissociation; scores that are under 30 indicate low levels of dissociation.

DID AND THE DES

Only 1% of people with dissociative identity disorder have been found to have a DES score below 30. A very high number of people who score above 30 have been shown to have posttraumatic stress disorder or a dissociative disorder other than DID.

---

[1]The rest of this appendix is either taken directly from or adapted from Dissociative Experiences Scale - II, traumadissociation.com. Retrieved Feb. 23, 2019, from www.traumadissociation.com/des. Permission to copy or use is granted on this website.

CLINICAL USES OF THE DES

If a person scores in the high range (above 30), then the DES questions can be used as the basis for a clinical interview, with the clinician asking the client to describe examples of the experiences they have had for any questions about experiences which occur 20% of the time or more. Alternatively, the Dissociative Disorders Interview Schedule (DDIS) or Structured Clinical Interview for Dissociative Disorders (SCID-D) can be used to reach a diagnosis.

AVERAGE DES SCORES IN RESEARCH	
General Adult Population	5.4
Anxiety Disorders	7.0
Affective Disorders	9.35
Eating Disorders	15.8
Late Adolescence	16.6
Schizophrenia	15.4
Borderline Personality Disorder	19.2
Posttraumatic Stress Disorder	31
Dissociative Disorder Not Otherwise Specified (now Other Specified Dissociative Disorder)	36
Dissociative Identity Disorder	48

Appendix B

COPING MECHANISMS

ALTERNATIVES FOR WHEN YOU'RE FEELING ANGRY OR RESTLESS

- Scribble on photos of people in magazines
- Viciously stab an orange
- Throw an apple/pair of socks against the wall
- Have a pillow fight with the wall
- Scream very loudly
- Tear apart newspapers, photos, or magazines
- Go to the gym, dance, exercise
- Listen to music and sing along loudly
- Draw a picture of what is making you angry
- Beat up a stuffed bear
- Pop bubble wrap
- Pop balloons
- Splatter paint
- Scribble on a piece of paper until the whole page is black
- Fill a piece of paper with drawing crosshatches
- Throw darts at a dartboard
- Go for a run
- Write your feelings on paper then rip it up
- Use stress relievers (e.g., squeeze a ball, use a fidget toy, etc.)
- Build a fort of pillows and then destroy it
- Throw ice cubes at the bathtub wall, at a tree, etc.
- Get out a fine-tooth comb and vigorously brush the fur of a stuffed animal (but use gentle vigor)
- Slash an empty plastic soda bottle or a piece of heavy cardboard or an old shirt or sock

- Make a soft cloth doll to represent the things you are angry at; cut and tear it instead of yourself
- Flatten aluminum cans for recycling, seeing how fast you can go
- On a sketch or photo of yourself, mark in red ink what you want to do, cut and tear the picture
- Break sticks
- Cut up fruit
- Make yourself as comfortable as possible
- Stomp around in heavy shoes
- Play handball or tennis
- Yell at what you are breaking and tell it why you are angry, hurt, upset, etc.
- Buy a cheap plate and decorate it with markers, stickers, cutouts from magazines, words, images (whatever expresses your pain and sadness), and when you're done, smash it (Please be careful when doing this.)

ALTERNATIVES THAT WILL GIVE YOU A SENSATION (OTHER THAN PAIN) WITHOUT HARMING YOURSELF

- Hold ice in your hands, against your arm, or in your mouth
- Run your hands under freezing cold water
- Snap a rubber band or hair band against your wrist
- Clap your hands until it stings
- Wax your legs
- Drink freezing cold water
- Splash your face with cold water
- Put PVA/Elmer's glue on your hands then peel it off
- Massage where you want to hurt yourself
- Take a hot shower/bath
- Jump up and down to get some sensation in your feet
- Write or paint on yourself
- Arm wrestle with a member of your family
- Take a cold bath
- Bite into a hot pepper or chew a piece of ginger root
- Rub liniment under your nose
- Put tiger balm on the places you want to cut (Tiger balm is a muscle relaxant cream that induces a tingly sensation. You can find it in most health food stores and vitamin stores.)

ALTERNATIVES THAT WILL DISTRACT YOU OR TAKE UP TIME

- Say "I'll self-harm in fifteen minutes if I still want to" and keep going for periods of fifteen minutes until the urge fades
- Color your hair
- Count to ten, getting louder until you are screaming
- Sing on the karaoke machine
- Complete something you've been putting off
- Take up a new hobby
- Make a cup of tea
- Tell jokes and laugh at jokes
- Play solitaire
- Count to five hundred or one thousand
- Surf the net
- Make as many words out of your full name as possible
- Count ceiling tiles or lights
- Search ridiculous things on the web
- Color coordinate your wardrobe
- Play with toys, such as a slinky
- Go to the park and play on the swings
- Call up an old friend
- Go "people watching"
- Carry safe, rather than sharp, things in your pockets
- Do school work
- Play a musical instrument
- Watch TV or a movie
- Paint your nails
- Alphabetize your CDs or books
- Cook
- Make origami to occupy your hands
- Doodle on sheets of paper
- Dress up or try on old clothes
- Play computer games or painting programs, such as Photoshop
- Write out lyrics to your favorite song
- Play a sport
- Read a book/magazine

- Do a crossword
- Draw a comic strip
- Make a chain link out of paper counting the hours or days you've been self-harm free using pretty colored paper
- Knit, sew, or make a necklace
- Make "scoobies": braid pieces of plastic or lace, to keep your hands busy
- Buy a plant and take care of it
- Hunt for things on eBay or Amazon
- Browse the forums
- Go shopping
- Memorize a poem with meaning
- Learn to swear in another language
- Look up words in a dictionary
- Play hide-and-seek with your siblings
- Go outside and watch the clouds roll by
- Plan a party
- Find out if any concerts will be in your area
- Make your own dance routine
- Trace your hand on a piece of paper; on your thumb, write something you like to look at; on your index finger, write something you like to touch; on your middle finger, write your favorite scent; on your ring finger, write something you like the taste of; on your pinky finger, write something you like to listen to; on your palm, write something you like about yourself
- Plan regular activities for your most difficult time of day
- Finish homework before it's due
- Take a break from mental processing
- Notice black-and-white thinking
- Get out on your own, get away from the stress
- Go on YouTube
- Make a scrapbook
- Color in a picture or coloring book
- Make a phone list of people you can call for support and allow yourself to use it
- Pay attention to your breathing (breath slowly, in through your nose and out through your mouth)
- Pay attention to the rhythmic motions of your body (walking, stretching, etc.)
- Learn HALT signals (hungry, angry, lonely, tired)

- Choose a random object, like a paper clip, and try to list thirty different uses for it
- Pick a subject and research it on the web; alternatively, pick something to research and then keep clicking on links, trying to get as far away from the original topic as you can
- Take a small step toward a goal you have

ALTERNATIVES THAT ARE COMPLETELY BIZARRE. AT THE LEAST, YOU'LL HAVE A LAUGH

- Crawl on all fours and bark like a dog or another animal
- Run around outside screaming
- Laugh for no reason whatsoever
- Make funny faces in a mirror
- Without turning orange, self-tan
- Pluck your eyebrows
- Put faces on apples, oranges, or other sorts of food
- Go to the zoo and name all of the animals
- Color on the walls
- Blow bubbles
- Pull weeds in the garden

ALTERNATIVES FOR WHEN YOU'RE FEELING GUILTY, SAD, OR LONELY

- Congratulate yourself on each minute you go without self-harming
- Draw or paint
- Look at the sky
- Instead of punishing yourself by self-harming, punish yourself by not self-harming
- Call a friend and ask for company
- Buy a cuddly toy
- Give someone a hug with a smile
- Put a face mask on
- Watch a favorite TV show or movie
- Eat something ridiculously sweet
- Remember a happy moment and relive it for a while in your head
- Treat yourself to some chocolate
- Try to imagine the future and plan things you want to do
- Look at things that are special to you

- Compliment someone else
- Make sculptures
- Watch fish
- Play with a pet
- Have or give a massage
- Imagine yourself living in a perfect home and describe it in your mind
- If you're religious, read the Bible or pray
- Light a candle and watch the flame (but please be careful)
- Go chat in a chat room
- Allow yourself to cry; crying is a healthy release of emotion
- Accept a gift from a friend
- Carry tokens to remind you of peaceful, comforting things/people
- Take a hot bath with bath oil or bubbles
- Curl up under a comforter with hot cocoa and a good book
- Make affirmation tapes inside you that are good, kind, gentle (sometimes you can do this by writing down the negative thoughts and then physically re-writing them into positive messages)
- Make a tray of special treats and tuck yourself into bed with it and watch TV or read

ALTERNATIVES FOR WHEN YOU'RE FEELING PANICKY OR SCARED

- "See, hear, and feel" five things, then four, then three and count down to one which will make you focus on your surroundings and will calm you down
- Listen to soothing music; have a CD with motivational songs that you can listen to
- Meditate or do yoga
- Name all of your soft toys
- Hug a pillow or soft toy
- Hyperfocus on something
- Do a "reality checklist"—write down all the things you can list about where you are now (e.g., "It is the 9th of November, 2020, I'm in a room, and everything is going to be alright")
- With permission, give someone a hug
- Drink herbal tea
- Crunch ice
- Hug a tree
- Go for a walk if it's safe to do so

- Feel your pulse to prove you're alive
- Go outside and attempt to catch butterflies or lizards
- Put your feet firmly on the floor
- Accept where you are in the process; beating yourself up only makes it worse
- Touch something familiar/safe
- Leave the room
- Lay on your back in bed comfortably (eyes closed), and breathe in for four seconds, hold for two, out for four, hold for two. Make sure to fill your belly up with air, not your chest. If your shoulders are going up, keep working on it. When you're comfortable breathing, put your hand on your belly and rub up and down in time with your breathing. If your mind wanders to other things, move it back to focusing only on the synchronized movement of your hand and breathing.
- Give yourself permission to . . . (keep it safe)

ALTERNATIVES THAT WILL HOPEFULLY MAKE YOU THINK TWICE ABOUT HARMING YOURSELF

- Think about how you don't want scars
- Treat yourself nicely
- Remember that you don't have to hurt yourself just because you're thinking about self-harm
- Create a safe place to go
- Acknowledge that self-harm is harmful behavior: say "I want to hurt myself" rather than "I want to cut"
- Repeat to yourself "I don't deserve to be hurt" even if you don't believe it
- Remember that you always have the choice not to cut: it's up to you what you do
- Think about how you may feel guilty after self-harming
- Remind yourself that the urge to self-harm is impulsive; you will only feel like cutting for short bursts of time
- Avoid temptation
- Get your friends to make you friendship bracelets; wear them around your wrists to remind you of them when you want to cut
- Be with other people
- Make your own list of things to do instead of self-harm
- Make a list of your positive character traits
- Be nice to your family, who in return, will hopefully be nice to you
- Put a Band-Aid on the area where you'd like to self-harm

- Recognize and acknowledge the choices you have NOW
- Pay attention to the changes needed to make you feel safe
- Notice "choices" versus "dilemmas"
- Lose the "should/could/have to" words. Try "What if . . ."
- Kiss the places you want to self-harm or kiss the places you have healing wounds. It can be a reminder that you care about yourself and that you don't want this.
- Choose your way of thinking, try to resist following old thinking patterns
- The butterfly project: draw a butterfly on the place(s) that you would self-harm. If the butterfly fades without self-harming, it means it has lived and flown away, giving a sense of achievement. Whereas if you do self-harm with the butterfly there, you will have to wash it off. If that does happen, you can start again by drawing a new one on. You can name the butterfly after someone you love.
- Write the name of a loved one (a friend, family member, or anyone else who cares about you) where you want to self-harm. When you go to self-harm remember how much they care and that they wouldn't want you to harm yourself.
- Think about what you would say to a friend who was struggling with the same things you are and try to be a good friend to yourself
- Make a bracelet out of duct tape and put a line on it every day (or any period of time) you go without self-harm. When it's full of lines, take it off, make a chain out of all the bracelets, and hang it up somewhere where you can be reminded of your great progress.

ALTERNATIVES THAT GIVE THE ILLUSION OF SEEING SOMETHING SIMILAR TO BLOOD

- Cover yourself with plasters where you want to cut
- Give yourself a henna or fake tattoo
- Make "wounds" with makeup, like lipstick
- Take a small bottle of liquid, red food coloring and warm it slightly by dropping it into a cup of hot water for a few minutes. Uncap the bottle and press its tip against the place you want to cut. Draw the bottle in a cutting motion while squeezing it slightly to let the food color trickle out.
- Draw on the areas you want to cut using ice that you've made by dropping six or seven drops of red food color into each of the ice-cube tray wells.
- Paint yourself with red tempera paint.
- "Cut" your skin with nail polish (it feels cold, but it's hard to get off)

ALTERNATIVES TO HELP YOU SORT THROUGH YOUR FEELINGS

- Phone a friend and talk to them
- Make a collage of how you feel
- Negotiate with yourself
- Identify what is hurting so bad that you need to express it in this way
- Write your feelings in a diary
- Free write (write down whatever you're thinking at that moment, even if it doesn't make sense)
- Make lists of everything, such as blessings in your life
- Make a notebook of song lyrics that you relate to
- Call a hotline
- Write a letter to someone telling them how you feel (but you don't have to send it if you decide not to)
- Start a grateful journal where every day you write down three good things that happened: things that you accomplished/are grateful for/made you smile. Make sure the journal is strictly for positive things. Then when you feel down you can go back and look at it

Thank you to Junie B and her friends who compiled this list over a couple of decades. Used with permission.

REFERENCES

BOOKS AND ARTICLES

Adamson, L. B., & Frick, J. E. (2003). The still face: A history of a shared experimental paradigm. *Infancy*, 4(4), 451-73. doi:10.1207/S15327078IN0404_01

Ainsworth, M. D. S., Blehar, M., Waters, E., & Wall, S. (1978). *Patterns of attachment: A psychological study of the Strange Situation*. Hillsdale, NJ: Erlbaum.

American Psychiatric Association. (2000). *Diagnostic and statistical manual of mental disorders* (4th ed., text rev.). Washington, DC: Author.

American Psychiatric Association (2013). *Diagnostic and statistical manual of mental disorders* (5th ed.). Washington, DC: Author.

Anderson, N. T. (1991). *The bondage breaker*. Eugene, OR: Harvest House.

Anton, J., & Fortune, M. M. (Producers), & Gargiulo, M. (Director). (1992). *Hear their cries* [Video]. Seattle: FaithTrust Institute.

Arnold, C., & Fisch, R. (2011). *The impact of complex trauma on development*. Lanham, MD: Jason Aronson.

Barton, R. H. (2006). *Sacred rhythms: Arranging our lives for spiritual transformation*. Downers Grove, IL: InterVarsity Press.

Bass, E., & Davis, L. (1988). *The courage to heal: A guide for women survivors of child sexual abuse*. New York: HarperCollins.

Bateman, A. W., & Fonagy, P. (Eds.). (2012). *Handbook of mentalizing in mental health practice*. Arlington, VA: American Psychiatric Publishing.

Benner, D. G. (1998a). *Free at last! Breaking the bondage of guilt and emotional wounds*. Belleville, ON: Essence Publishing.

Benner, D. G. (1998b). *Care of souls: Revisioning Christian nurture and counsel*. Grand Rapids: Baker Books.

Benner, D. G. (2010). *Opening to God: Lectio divina and life as prayer*. Downers Grove, IL: InterVarsity Press.

Berlin, L., Cassidy, J., & Appleyard, K. (2008). The influence of early attachments on other relationships. In J. Cassidy & P. R. Shaver (Eds.), 333-47. *Handbook of attachment: Theory, research, and clinical applications* (2nd ed.). New York: Guilford Press.

Berne, E. (1964). *Games people play: The basic handbook of transactional analysis*. New York: Random House.

Blizard, R., & Shaw, M. (2019). Lost-in-the-mall: False memory or false defense? *Journal of Child Custody*, 16, 20-41. doi:10.1080/15379418.2019.1590285

Boon, S., Steele, K., & van der Hart, O. (2011). *Coping with trauma-related dissociation: Skills training for patients and therapists*. New York: W. W. Norton & Company.

Bowlby, J. (1988). *A secure base: Parent-child attachment and healthy human development*. London: Routledge.

Bradley, S. J. (2000). *Affect regulation and the development of psychopathology*. New York: Guilford Press.

Bradshaw, J. (1990). *Homecoming: Reclaiming and championing your inner child*. New York: Bantam Books.

Brand, B. L., Sar, V., Stavropoulos, P., Kruger, C., Korzekwa, M., Martinez-Taboas, A., & Middleton, W. (2016). Separating fact from fiction: An empirical examination of six myths about dissociative identity disorder. *Harvard Review of Psychiatry*, 24(4), 257-70.

Braun, B. G. (1988). The BASK model of dissociation: Clinical applications. *Dissociation*, 1(2), 16-23.

Bubeck, M. I. (1975). *The adversary: The Christian versus demon activity*. Chicago: Moody Press.

Bufford, R. K. (1988). *Counseling and the demonic*. Dallas: Word Books Pub.

Bull, D., Ellason, J., & Ross, C. (1998). Exorcism revisited: Some positive outcomes with dissociative identity disorder. *Journal of Psychology and Theology*, 26, 188-96.

Canadian Centre for Child Protection. (2017). *Survivors' Survey Executive Summary 2017*. Winnipeg, Manitoba: Author. Retrieved from www.protectchildren.ca/pdfs/C3P_SurvivorsSurveyExecutiveSummary2017_en.pdf.

Carlson, E. B., & Putnam, F. W. (1993). An update on the Dissociative Experiences Scale. *Dissociation, 6*, 16-27.

Cassidy, J., & Shaver, P. R. (Eds.). (2016). *Handbook of attachment: Theory, research, and clinical applications* (3rd ed.). New York: Guilford Press.

Centers for Disease Control and Prevention. (2019). Adverse Childhood Experiences (ACEs). Retrieved from www.cdc.gov/violenceprevention/childabuseandneglect/acestudy/index.html.

Chu, J. A. (2011a). *Rebuilding shattered lives: Treating complex PTSD and dissociative disorders* (2nd ed.). Hoboken, NJ: John Wiley & Sons.

Chu, J. A. (2011b, November). *Update on the memory wars*. Plenary address delivered at the International Society for the Study of Trauma and Dissociation Annual Meeting, Montreal, Canada.

Corrigan, F. M. (2014a). Threat and safety: The neurobiology of active and passive defense responses. In U. F. Lanius, S. L. Paulsen, & F. M. Corrigan (Eds.). *Neurobiology and treatment of traumatic dissociation: Toward an embodied self* (pp. 29-50). New York: Springer.

Corrigan, F. M. (2014b). Defense responses: Frozen, suppressed, truncated, obstructed, and malfunctioning. In U. F. Lanius, S. L. Paulsen, & F. M. Corrigan (Eds.). *Neurobiology and treatment of traumatic dissociation: Toward an embodied self* (pp. 131-52). New York: Springer.

Courtois, C. A., & Ford, J. D. (Eds.). (2009). *Treating complex traumatic stress disorders: An evidenced-based guide*. New York: Guilford Press.

De Joung, A., Resick, P. A., Zoellner, L. A., van Minnen, A., Lee, C. W., Monson, C. M., . . . Bicanic, I. A. E. (2016). Critical analysis of the current treatment guidelines for complex PTSD in adults. *Depression and Anxiety (33)*, 359-69.

Dell, P. F. (2006). The Multidimensional Inventory of Dissociation (MID): A comprehensive measure of pathological dissociation. *Journal of Trauma & Dissociation, 7*(2), 77-106.

Dell, P. F. (2009). The long struggle to diagnose multiple personality disorder (MPD): Partial MPD. In P. F. Dell & J. A. O'Neil (Eds.), *Dissociation and the dissociative disorders: DSM-V and beyond*. New York: Routledge, 403-28.

Dell, P. F., & O'Neil, J. A. (2009). *Dissociation and the dissociative disorders: DSM-IV and beyond*. New York: Routledge.

Denney, R. M., Aten, J. D., & Gingrich, F. (2008). Using spiritual self-disclosure in counseling and psychotherapy. *Journal of Psychology & Theology, 36*(4), 294-302.

Dickason, C. F. (1987). *Demon possession and the Christian: A new perspective*. Chicago: Moody Press.

Eriksson, C. B., Wilkins, A. M., & Frederick, N. (2017). Trauma, faith, and care for the counselor. In H. D. Gingrich & F. C. Gingrich (Eds.), *Treating trauma in Christian counseling* (pp. 78-96). Downers Grove, IL: IVP Academic.

Escobar, J. I. (1995). Transcultural aspects of dissociative and somatoform disorders. *Psychiatric Clinics of North America: Cultural Psychiatry, 18*(3), 555-69.

Figley, C. R. (1995). Compassion fatigue as secondary traumatic stress disorder: An overview. In C. R. Figley (Ed.), *Compassion fatigue: Coping with secondary traumatic stress disorder in those who treat the traumatized* (pp. 1-20). New York: Brunner/Mazel.

Foa, E. B., Zandberg, L. J., McLean, C. P., Rosenfield, D., Fitzgerald, H., Tuerk, P. W., . . . Peterson, A. L. (2018). The efficacy of 90-minute versus 60-minute sessions of prolonged exposure for posttraumatic stress disorder: Design of a randomized controlled trial in active duty military personnel. *Psychological Trauma, 11*, pp. 307-18.

Follette, V. M., Iverson, K. M., & Ford, J. D. (2009). Contextual behavior trauma therapy. In C. A. Courtois & J. D. Ford, *Treating complex traumatic stress disorders: An evidenced-based guide*. New York: Guilford Press, 264-85.

Gibson, M. (Producer & Director). (2004). *The passion of the Christ* [Motion Picture]. Beverly Hills, CA: New Market Films.

Gingrich, H. D. (2002). Stalked by death: Cross-cultural trauma work with a tribal missionary. *Journal of Psychology and Christianity, 21*, 262-65.

Gingrich, H. D. (2009). Assessing dissociative symptoms and dissociative disorders in college students in the Philippines. *Journal of Aggression, Maltreatment, & Trauma, 18*, 403-18.

Gingrich, H. D. (2013). *Restoring the shattered self: A Christian counselor's guide to complex trauma* (1st ed). Downers Grove, IL: IVP Academic.

Gingrich, H. D. (2018). Cross-cultural trauma work with a tribal missionary: A case study. *Frontiers in the Psychotherapy of Trauma and Dissociation, 1*(2), 174-91.

Gingrich, H. D., & Gingrich, F. C. (Eds.). (2017). *Treating trauma in Christian counseling.* Downers Grove, IL: IVP Academic.

Greggo, S. P. (2008). *Trekking toward wholeness: A resource for care group leaders.* Downers Grove, IL: InterVarsity Press.

Herman, J. (2015). *Trauma and recovery: The aftermath of violence—from domestic abuse to political terror* (2015 ed.). New York: Basic Books.

Hopper, E., Grossman, F., Spinazzola, J., & Zucker, M. (2018). *Reaching across the abyss: Treatment of adult survivors of childhood emotional abuse and neglect.* New York: Guilford Press.

Howell, E. F. (2005). *The dissociative mind.* Hillsdale, NJ: The Analytic Press.

Hurding, R. (1995). Pathways to wholeness: Christian journeying in a postmodern age. *Journal of Psychology and Christianity, 14*, 293-305.

Hyman, I. E., & Loftus, E. F. (1997). Some people recover memories of childhood trauma that never really happened. In P. S. Appelbaum, L. A. Uyehara & M. R. Elin (Eds.), *Trauma and memory: Clinical and legal controversies.* New York: Oxford University Press, 102.

Jackson, C., Nissenson, K., & Cloitre, M. (2009). Cognitive-behavioral therapy. In C. A. Courtois & J. D. Ford, *Treating complex traumatic stress disorders: An evidenced-based guide* (pp. 243-263). New York: Guilford Press.

Koerner, K. (2012). *Doing Dialectical Behavior Therapy: A practical guide.* New York: Guilford Press.

Kraft, C. H. (2010). *Deep wounds, deep healing: An introduction to deep-level healing* (Rev. ed.). Ventura, CA: Regal Books.

Langberg, D. (2015). *Suffering and the heart of God: How trauma destroys and Christ restores.* Greensboro, NC: New Growth Press.

Langer, R., McMartin, J., & Hall, M. E. L. (2017). Theological perspectives on trauma: Human flourishing after the Fall. In H. D. Gingrich & F. C. Gingrich (Eds.), *Treating trauma in Christian counseling* (pp. 39-54). Downers Grove, IL: IVP Academic.

Lanius, U. F., Paulsen, S. L., & Corrigan, F. M. (Eds.). (2014). *Neurobiology and treatment of traumatic dissociation: Toward an embodied self.* New York: Springer.

Levine, P. (2015). *Trauma and memory: Brain and body in a search for the living past.* Berkeley, CA: North Atlantic Books.

Levitt, J. T., & Cloitre, M. (2005). A clinician's guide to STAIR/MPE: Treatment for PTSD related to childhood abuse. *Cognitive and Behavioral Practice, 12*, 40-52.

Lyons-Ruth, K., Dutra, L., Schuder, M., & Bianchi, I. (2006). From infant attachment disorganization to adult dissociation: Relational adaptations or traumatic experiences? *Psychiatric Clinics of North America, 29*, 63-86.

Maier, S. F., & Seligman, M. E. P. (1976). Learned helplessness theory and evidence. *Journal of Experimental Psychology General, 105*, 3-46. doi:10.1037/0096-3445.105.1.3

Main, M., Hesse, E. & Kaplan, N. (2005). Predictability of attachment behavior and representational processes at 1, 6, and 19 years of age: The Berkeley Longitudinal Study. In K. E. Grossmann, K. Grossmann, & E. Waters (Eds.). *Attachment from Infancy to Adulthood: The Major Longitudinal Studies.* New York: Guilford Press, 245-304.

Mara, T. (2005). *Dialectical behavior therapy in private practice: A practical & comprehensive guide.* Oakland, CA: New Harbinger Publications.

Martin, S. H. (1990). *Shame on you! Help for adults from alcoholic and other shame-bound families.* Nashville: Broadman Press.

Mierendorf, M. (Director & Producer). (1993). *Multiple personalities: The search for deadly memories* [television program]. New York: Time Warner Entertainment.

Miller, A. (2012). *Healing the unimaginable: Treating ritual abuse and mind control.* London: Karnac Books.

Miller, A. (2014). *Becoming yourself: Overcoming mind control and ritual abuse.* London: Karnac Books.

Miller, A., & Gingrich, H. D. (2017). The treatment of ritual abuse and mind control. In H. D. Gingrich & F. C. Gingrich (Eds.), *Treating trauma in Christian counseling* (pp. 257-77). Downers Grove, IL: IVP Academic.

Muller, R. (2018). *Trauma and the struggle to open up: From avoidance to recovery and growth.* New York: W.W. Norton & Company.

Nijenhuis, E. R. S. (2009). Somatoform dissociation and somatoform dissociative disorders. In P. F. Dell & J. A. O'Neil (Eds.), *Dissociation and the dissociative disorders: DSM-V and beyond.* New York: Routledge.

Nijenhuis, E. R. S., Spinhoven, P., Van Dyke, R., van der Hart, O., & Vanderlinden, J. (1997). The development of the Somatoform Dissociation Questionnaire (SDQ-5) as a screening instrument for dissociative disorders. *Acta Psychiatrica Scandinavica, 96,* 311-18.

Noblitt, J. R., & Noblitt, P. P. (2014). *Cult and ritual abuse: Narratives, evidence, and healing approaches* (3rd ed.). Santa Barbara, CA: Praeger.

Noricks, J. (2011). *Parts psychology: A trauma-based, self-state therapy for emotional healing.* Los Angeles: New University Press.

Ogawa, J. R., Sroufe, L. A., Weinfield, N. S., Carlson, E. A., & Egeland, B. (1997). Development and the fragmented self: Longitudinal study of dissociative symptomatology in a nonclinical sample. *Development and Psychopathology, 9,* 855-79.

Pearlman, L. A. (1995). Self-care for trauma therapists: Ameliorating vicarious traumatization. In B. H. Stamm (Ed.), *Secondary traumatic stress: Self-care issues for clinicians, researchers, and educators* (pp. 51-64). Lutherville, MD: Sidran Press.

Peterman, G., & Schmutzer, A. (2016). *Between pain and grace: A biblical theology of suffering.* Chicago: Moody Publishers.

Powlison, D. (1995). *Power encounters: Reclaiming spiritual warfare.* Grand Rapids: Baker Books.

Pressley, J., & Spinazzola, J. (2017). Beyond survival: Application of a complex trauma treatment model in the Christian context. In H. D. Gingrich & F. C. Gingrich (Eds.), *Treating trauma in Christian counseling.* Downers Grove, IL: IVP Academic, 211-31.

Putnam, F. W. (1989). *Diagnosis and treatment of multiple personality disorder.* New York: Guilford Press.

Putnam, F. W. (1997). *Dissociation in children and adolescents: A developmental perspective.* New York: Guilford Press.

Resick, P. A., Monson, C. M., & Chard, K. M. (2017). *Cognitive processing therapy for PTSD: A comprehensive manual.* New York: Guilford Press.

Rhoades, G. F., Jr., & Sar, V. (2005). *Trauma and dissociation in a cross-cultural perspective: Not just a North American phenomenon.* New York: Haworth.

Rogers, C. (1957). The necessary and sufficient conditions of therapeutic personality change. *Journal of Consulting Psychology, 21*(2), 95-103.

Ross, C. A. (1997). *Dissociative identity disorder: Diagnosis, clinical features, and treatment of multiple personality* (2nd ed.). New York: John Wiley & Sons.

Ross, C. A. (2000). *The trauma model: A solution to the problem of comorbidity in psychiatry.* Richardson, TX: Manitou Communications.

Rothschild, B. (2000). *The body remembers: The psychophysiology of trauma and trauma treatment.* New York: W. W. Norton & Company.

Rothschild, B. (2017). *The body remembers: Revolutionizing trauma treatment* (Vol. 2). New York: W. W. Norton & Company.

Sbanotto, E. A. N., Gingrich, H. D., & Gingrich, F. C. (2016). *Skills for effective counseling: A faith-based integration.* Downers Grove, IL: IVP Academic.

Schmutzer, A. J. (2011). A theology of sexuality and its abuse: Creation, evil, and the relational ecosystem. In A. J. Schmutzer (Ed.), *The long journey home: Understanding and ministering to the sexually abused.* Eugene, OR: Wipf & Stock, 105-35.

Schore, A. N. (2003). Early relational trauma, disorganized attachment, and the development of a predisposition to violence. In M. F. Solomon & D. J. Siegel (Eds.), *Healing trauma* (pp. 107-67). New York: W. W. Norton & Company.

Schore, A. N. (2009). Right-brain affect regulation: An essential mechanism of development, trauma, dissociation, and psychotherapy. In D. Fosha, D. J. Siegel, & M. Solomon (Eds.), *The healing power of emotion: Affective neuroscience, development, and clinical practice* (pp. 112-44). New York: W. W. Norton & Company.

Schwartz, R. C. (1997). *Internal family systems therapy.* New York: Guilford Press.

Segal, Z. V., Williams, J. M. G., & Teasdale, J. D. (2013). *Mindfulness-based cognitive therapy for depression* (2nd ed.). New York: Guilford, 97.

Seligman, M. E. P. (1972). Learned helplessness. *Annual Review of Medicine, 23*(1), 407-12.

Sells, J., & Hervey, E. G. (2011). Forgiveness in sexual abuse: Defining our identity in the journey toward wholeness. In A. J. Schmutzer (Ed.), *The long journey home: Understanding and ministering to the sexually abused* (pp. 169-85). Eugene, OR: Wipf & Stock.

Selye, H. (1974). *Stress without distress: How to use stress as a positive force to achieve a rewarding lifestyle.* New York: New American Library.

Shapiro, R. (2016). *Easy ego state interventions: Strategies for working with parts.* New York: W.W. Norton & Company.

Siegel, D. J. (2003). An interpersonal neurobiology of psychotherapy: The developing mind and the resolution of trauma. In M. F. Solomon & D. J. Siegel (Eds.), *Healing trauma: Attachment, mind, body, and brain* (pp. 1-56). New York: W. W. Norton & Company.

Siegel, D. J. (2009). Emotion as integration: A possible answer to the question, What is emotion? In D. Fosha, D. J. Siegel, & M. Solomon (Eds.), *The healing power of emotion: Affective neuroscience, development, and clinical practice* (pp. 145-71). New York: W. W. Norton & Company.

Siegel, D. J., & Bryson, T. P. (2011). *The whole-brain child: 12 revolutionary strategies to nurture your child's developing mind.* New York: Delacorte Press.

Smith, E. (2002). *Theophostic Ministry: Advanced training series, level two: Dissociation and trauma based mind control.* Campbellsville, KY: New Creation Publishing.

Stavropoulos, P. A., & Kezelman, C. A. (2018). *The truth of memory and the memory of truth: Different types of memory and the significance for trauma.* Milsons Point, NSW, Australia: Blue Knot Foundation. Retrieved from www.blueknot.org.au.

Steele, K., Boon, S., & van der Hart, O. (2017). *Treating trauma-related dissociation: A practical, integrative approach.* New York: W. W. Norton & Company.

Steinberg, M. (1993). *Structured Clinical Interview for DSM-IV Dissociative Disorders (SCID-D).* Washington, DC: American Psychiatric Press.

Struthers, W. M., Ansell, K., & Wilson, A. (2017). The neurobiology of stress and trauma. In H. D. Gingrich & F. C. Gingrich (Eds.), *Treating trauma in Christian counseling.* Downers Grove, IL: IVP Academic.

Tan, S. Y. (2011). Mindfulness and acceptance-based cognitive therapies: Empirical evidence and clinical applications from a Christian perspective. *Journal of Psychology and Christianity, 30,* 243-49.

Taylor, D. (2017). Treating sexual trauma through couples therapy. In H. D. Gingrich & F. C. Gingrich (Eds.), *Treating trauma in Christian counseling* (pp.119-40). Downers Grove, IL: IVP Academic.

Tracy, S. R. (2005). *Mending the soul: Understanding and healing abuse.* Grand Rapids: Zondervan.

Tronick, E. (2007). *Still Face Experiment* [Video]. Retrieved from www.youtube.com/watch?v=apzXGEbZht0.

Van der Kolk, B. (1997). Traumatic memories. In P. S. Appelbaum, L. A. Uyehara & M. R. Elin (Eds.), *Trauma and memory: Clinical and legal controversies.* New York: Oxford University Press.

Van der Kolk, B. (2014). *The body keeps the score: Brain, mind, and body in the healing of trauma.* New York: Viking.

Walker, D. F., Courtois, C. A., & Aten, J. D. (Eds.). (2015). *Spiritually oriented psychotherapy for trauma.* Washington, DC: American Psychological Association. doi:10.1037/14500-002, 15-28

Watkins, J. G., & Watkins, H. H. (1997). *Ego states: Theory and therapy.* New York: W. W. Norton & Company.

Weinfield, N. S., Sroufe, L. A., Egeland, B., & Carlson, E. (2008). Individual differences in infant-caregiver attachment: Conceptual and empirical aspects of security. In J. Cassidy & P. R. Shaver (Eds.), *Handbook of attachment: Theory, research, and clinical application.* New York: Guilford Press.

Welburn, K. R., Fraser, G., Jordan, S. A., Cameron, C., Webb, L. M., & Raine, D. (2003). Discriminating dissociative identity disorder from schizophrenia and feigned dissociation on psychological tests and structured interviews. *Journal of Trauma & Dissociation, 4*(2), 109-30.

WEBSITES

Adult Children of Alcoholics World Service Organization: www.adultchildren.org
American Association of Christian Counselors: www.aacc.net
Celebrate Recovery: www.celebraterecovery.com
Christian Association for Psychological Studies: www.caps.net
Diagnostic and Statistical Manual of Mental Disorders (DSM-5): www.DSM5.org
Ellert R. S. Nijenhuis, Ph.D., Psychotraumatologist: www.enijenhuis.nl
EMDR Network: https://emdrresearchfoundation.org
Eye Movement Desensitization and Reprocessing International Association: www.emdria.org
False Memory Syndrome Foundation: www.fmsfonline.org
International Society for the Study of Trauma and Dissociation: www.isst-d.org
Life Model: www.lifemodel.org
Lydia Discipleship Ministries: www.lydiadm.org
Sidran Institute: Traumatic Stress Education and Advocacy: www.sidran.org
Trauma Center (Justice Resource Institute): www.traumacenter.org.

AUTHOR INDEX

SUBJECT INDEX

An Association for Christian Psychologists,
Therapists, Counselors and Academicians

CAPS is a vibrant Christian organization with a rich tradition. Founded in 1956 by a small group of Christian mental health professionals, chaplains and pastors, CAPS has grown to more than 2,100 members in the U.S., Canada and more than 25 other countries.

CAPS encourages in-depth consideration of therapeutic, research, theoretical and theological issues. The association is a forum for creative new ideas. In fact, their publications and conferences are the birthplace for many of the formative concepts in our field today.

CAPS members represent a variety of denominations, professional groups and theoretical orientations; yet all are united in their commitment to Christ and to professional excellence.

CAPS is a non-profit, member-supported organization. It is led by a fully functioning board of directors, and the membership has a voice in the direction of CAPS.

CAPS is more than a professional association. It is a fellowship, and in addition to national and international activities, the organization strongly encourages regional, local and area activities which provide networking and fellowship opportunities as well as professional enrichment.

To learn more about CAPS, visit www.caps.net.

The joint publishing venture between IVP Academic and CAPS aims to promote the understanding of the relationship between Christianity and the behavioral sciences at both the clinical/counseling and the theoretical/research levels. These books will be of particular value for students and practitioners, teachers and researchers.

For more information about CAPS Books, visit InterVarsity Press's website at www.ivpress.com/christian-association-for-psychological-studies-books-set.